The Frankfurt School and the Challenge of Fascism

Fascism is a well-defined historical phenomenon, but its political-ideological offshoots have extended into today's democracies. How should we understand the mimetic and dissimulating capacity of fascism? Starting from the analyses of the exponents of the first Frankfurt School in their rethinking of the Marxian relationship of structure and superstructure, this study considers how fascism may be defined as a specific organization of power together with a form of economic planning accompanied by a masochistic propensity to power. Drawing on archival research at the Horkheimer and Marcuse *Archiv* in Frankfurt, the author guides us through unpublished documents of the Institute of Social Research in the years 1938–1939 concerning the plan to formulate "a theory" on fascism. This was never produced as a single work, allowing space instead to the flourishing of different contributions. The objective of this book is to provide an internal systemic reading of fascism, finding points of mutual integration among critical theorists whenever possible while revealing irreconcilable divergencies when necessary. This topical book will be of interest to academics and researchers working in the areas of philosophy, the history of ideas, legal philosophy, critical theory, economics and political science.

Claudio Corradetti is Professor of Political Philosophy at the University of Rome Tor Vergata, Italy.

The Frankfurt School and the Challenge of Fascism

An Intellectual and Philosophical Reconstruction

Claudio Corradetti

Routledge
Taylor & Francis Group
LONDON AND NEW YORK

First published 2026
by Routledge
4 Park Square, Milton Park, Abingdon, Oxon OX14 4RN

and by Routledge
605 Third Avenue, New York, NY 10158

Routledge is an imprint of the Taylor & Francis Group, an informa business

British Library Cataloguing-in-Publication Data
A catalogue record for this book is available from the British Library

ISBN: 978-1-041-04865-7 (hbk)
ISBN: 978-1-041-04866-4 (pbk)
ISBN: 978-1-003-63034-0 (ebk)

DOI: 10.4324/9781003630340

Typeset in Galliard
by Apex CoVantage, LLC

This book is dedicated to the memory of Mario Corradetti, an Italian military internee (IMI) in the concentration camps of Sandbostel and Wietzendorf (1943–45), to my father for his initiatives to recover the historical memory of the concentration camps, and to all the Italian military internees who refused to take up arms after September 8, 1943. The rejection of fascism in Italy has taken on, and continues to take on, many forms, each of which is worthy of our gratitude.

Contents

Acknowledgements

There are many colleagues to whom I owe a heartfelt thank you for the insights and encouragement that accompanied the writing of this text. First of all, I am indebted to William Scheuermann, a friend and colleague with whom I have long been engaged in dialogue on Frankfurt School issues and beyond. Martin Jay, a pioneer in studies on the early Frankfurt School, provided invaluable advice and bibliographic suggestions during my research stay in the United States. I would also like to thank my Italian colleagues Paolo Quintili and Giorgio Cesarale for their interest in and support for this research. The staff of the library of Goethe University made themselves available to provide me with digitized material from some unpublished typescripts of the Horkheimer and Marcuse *Archiv*. My appreciation also goes to the participants in the seminar on Critical Theory and Fascism which I organized in March 2023 at the Austrian Historical Institute. Special thanks go to Federico Rampinini and Ludovica Marciano for their youthful enthusiasm and their always-ready collaboration, as well as to Andreas Gottsmann, the director of the Institute, for allowing its realization. The booksellers of Serendipity in Rome lived up to the name of their bookstore by helping me find books I would never have thought of. A heartfelt thank you goes to my family: to my wife, Valentina; my son, Carlo; and the newest arrival, Linda. Their joy and complicity allowed me to engage with topics so close to and yet so distant from them.

These chapters are reformulated reprints from the following journals:

Chapter 2, *State, law, capital*, expands on a previously published article: C. Corradetti, "Coercion or Privatization? Crisis and Planned Economies in the Debates of the Early Frankfurt School", *Jus Cogens* 6(1), 2024, pp. 7–28.

Appendix. *The Frankfurt School of Critical Theory* is a revised version of C. Corradetti, "The Frankfurt School and Critical Theory", *Internet Encyclopedia of Philosophy*, 2012: https://iep.utm.edu/critical-theory-frankfurt school/.

*Translations of non-English texts are all mine.

Introduction[1]

Why write a book today on the Frankfurt School's critique of fascism? There seem to be three main reasons. First, there is a personal conviction that current times reflect darkly some of the historical traits of the political and economic instability of the 1930s. Just as today's ultra-liberal capitalism has cast off the values and structures of liberal democracy, fascism emerged through the authoritarian reorganization of early 20th-century liberalism. Authoritarianism and capitalism may share a common fate. Second, there is the somewhat surprising observation of a scarcity of studies directly analyzing this issue. Therefore, it seems useful to reconstruct the bibliographic and interpretative trajectory of the Frankfurt School studies on fascism. Finally, there is a third reason related to a mystery: a book announced in the 1938–1939 reports of the Institut für Sozialforschung (IfS) that never appeared. This report mentions the intention to develop a "theory of fascism".[2] However, no trace of this text has been found, nor has any relevant documentation emerged from various archival searches. None of the subsequent publications or typescripts intended to formulate a comprehensive theory of fascism or to address even one of the points mentioned in the 1938–1939 document.

The proposed program involved examining authoritarian social tendencies related to "contradictions within the national economy and . . . increasing contradictions on the world market, . . . the existence of a permanent army of unemployed and . . . growing working class organization".[3] The underlying hypothesis was that although the rise of fascism opposed workers' needs, the

1 "Whoever wants to explain antisemitism must speak of National Socialism. . . . Whoever does not want to speak of capitalism must also remain silent about fascism". In M. Horkheimer, *Die Juden und Europa*, 1939, p. 115. Translation is mine. The original German edition will be followed. To this, Poulantzas objected that "it is he who does not wish to discuss *imperialism* who should stay silent on the subject of fascism", in N. Poulantzas, *Fascism and Dictatorship. The Third International and the Problem of Fascism*, [1970] 2018, p. 17.

2 Cfr. M. Horkheimer, "[*Idee, Aktivität und Programm des Instituts für Sozialforschung*]", [1938] 1985, p. 162; IfS, *International Institute of Social Research. A Report on Its History, Aims and Activities 1933–1938*, 1939, p. 36.

3 Ibid.

DOI: 10.4324/9781003630340-1

capitalist class used fascism instrumentally, aiming to stifle the possibility of a socialist transformation of society. This theory was to include a "compar[ison] between German and Italian ideologies and institutions", concluding with a thesis on the "merely superficial"[4] differences between the two countries. In both cases, fascism sought to dismantle any potential democratic openness in political life by using economic planning in a "caricatured and reactionary form"[5] and for warlike purposes. The inability to trace this work or subsequent writings reflecting the original intentions suggests at least one hypothesis: the Frankfurt School scholars realized the impossibility of condensing the complexity of fascism's analysis into a single study, both as a historical-political phenomenon and as a psycho-social phenomenon. Hence, the current attempt to retrospectively synthesize, in a collective framework, the various themes and viewpoints expressed. A detailed plan with corresponding activities can be found in the Institute's report for the decade 1934–1944, titled *Ten Years on Morningside Heights* [1944].[6] This report includes a specific section on the investigation of National Socialism, listing relevant research areas along with corresponding publication and teaching activities. It clearly outlines the fascism research areas that the IfS would expand upon in the following years. The analysis of authority, a key concept of the time, is associated with issues related to the authoritarian transformation of the German family and society—without excluding specific investigations into the hierarchical structure of Chinese society studied by Wittfogel or Argentine society analyzed by Weil.[7]

It is thus understood how the Frankfurt School scholars followed the evolution of the concept of authority through the transition from a liberal economy to a war economy: i.e., the totalitarian reorganization of the Nazi state and the restriction of private property, as well as the development of themes related to the psychological conditions of German workers, cultural product transformations and a research program on anti-Semitism.[8] Reconstructing the Frankfurt School's critique of fascism means also piecing together a fragmented analytical framework that does not always conform to unified positions—an underlying context that likely contributed to the de facto abandonment of the announced school project on fascism analysis.

The aim of the proposed research is therefore to start from the diversity of voices involved, attempting to construct a kind of meta-text, a meta-narrative

4 Ibid.

5 Ibid.

6 IfS, "Ten Years on Morningside Heights: A Report on the Institute's History, 1934 to 1944", 1944, online.

7 K. A. Wittfogel, "The Foundations and Stages of Chinese Economic History", 1935; K. A. Wittfogel, "Die Theorie der orientalischen Gesellschaft", 1938; F. Weil, *Argentine Riddle*, 1944.

8 A detailed list of books, articles, reports and unpublished typescripts related to the analysis of National Socialism from 1934 to 1944 is found in IfS, *Ten Years on Morningside Heights: A Report on the Institute's History, 1934 to 1944*, L. Löwenthal collection and F. Pollock collection, 1944, pp. 30–31.

reworking of the Frankfurt School's reflection on fascism based on studies, lectures and seminars organized over the first three decades of the IfS's activities. In other words, it will propose a hypothesis of a meta-framework of a fascism theory that the Frankfurt School never developed as a comprehensive vision or in a unified form but which seems at least broadly reconstructable. This is not intended as a mere external synthesis of sometimes manifestly irreconcilable theses. On the contrary, it aims to develop an internal and coherent-as-possible perspective capable of uniting and separating subjects and positions within a shared philosophical-conceptual structure. To this end, the essential theoretical foundations from which subsequent Frankfurt School elaborations will begin have been identified. In seeking shared reasons among IfS members regarding the need to overcome a deterministic view of the base-superstructure relationship typical of vulgar Marxism, Fromm's perspective on the suppression of libidinal drive in the structural organization of labour is considered fundamental. This cognitive acquisition served as a common catalyst for what would become the IfS's subsequent critiques of capitalism and ideology. Methodologically, the use of primary sources and unpublished archival material aims to introduce historical-documentary elements, highlighting fundamental theoretical assumptions and their possible social updates. Theoretical elaborations have been treated as conceptual grafts onto a historical base. Both levels were then merged to form a meta-evaluative thesis. It is certainly within a collective characterized by shared philosophical-political assumptions that significant points of disagreement regarding the interpretation of the Marx-Weber-Freud triad should be understood. These disagreements have not precluded the possibility of proceeding with an organic reconstruction of analytical methods or the opportunity for the interpreter to advance a comprehensive hermeneutic thesis. The issues addressed here are today more than ever pressing scientific-methodological challenges that benefit from a historical background enriched by past experience. This is not intended to prophesy a theory of historical cycles and recurrences, but rather to draw a parallel between recurring events, such as the cyclical crises of capitalism and its superstructural transformations unfolding both in the reorganization of state powers and in the realm of psychic-cultural production. Just as the financial crisis of 1929 marked the hallmark of an era, so too did the crisis of liberal democracy in the 20th century accompany the verticalization of the centres of capitalist economic power, the growing disparity between rich and poor and the colonization of the political sphere by the economic-productive regime. It is not only a question of considering the post-1989 East-West balance of power (i.e., NATO) on one side and Russia and its allies on the other. It is also necessary to ask what consequences would arise if the production of goods no longer found a market, if the market became saturated or if purchasing power was no longer sufficient to meet the costs of goods.

These are the questions that have led to a reconsideration of the stages of critical reflection on fascism, with the belief that for the Frankfurt School's inner circle, fascism was something far broader than a phenomenon historically circumscribed to the experience of the Third Reich and its closest authoritarian regimes. Traces of fascism were considered by the Frankfurt School to be present even in democratic American society. Jay, however, argued that the view of American society held by some IfS members was rather a distorted consequence of a socially self-segregated experience as exiles in the new continent. For Jay, the resulting sense of resentment is the true reason for the critique of mass society authoritarianism and the fetishism of commodities in American liberalism.[9] The themes involved in the dynamics and stratification of long-term fascism mobilize, however, more than the hypothesis of discomfort resulting from certain social isolation. The critique of authoritarianism in American society would, in principle, be compatible with the idea that fascism originated from a fundamentally psychic matrix accompanied by forms of material production organization yet not reducible to them—leaving open the possibility of its entrenchment even within democratic power structures. It should not be underestimated that the identification of authoritarian tendencies within American society was based on the hypothesis of a reorganization of state capitalism that, according to Pollock's view, also included Roosevelt's New Deal model. Thus, the identification of long-term development trajectories was considered part of a shared research program among the inner circle members. They recognized a developmental trend toward totalizing forms of administration, where even the possibility of immanent criticism would be lost. For the Frankfurt School, "critique" was Hegelianly equivalent to a "comparing the thing with its own concept" not reducible to a solipsistic rejection of the existing.[10]

This work intends to advance first of all a historiographical-conceptual thesis according to a unified direction of the Marxian distinction of base and superstructure. In the early sections of the text (Chapters 1 and 2), the IfS's critique of Nazism has been examined, starting from the reorganization of the capitalist economy for war purposes. The debates generated during IfS seminars contributed not only to the drafting of important essays that appeared in the *Zeitschrift für Sozialforschung* (ZfS), the official publication of the IfS, but also to the development of that theoretical-conceptual apparatus later used for intelligence reports for the United States. These reports, primarily commissioned to Neumann, Marcuse and Kirchheimer between 1943 and 1945 by the Research and Analysis branch (R&A) of the Office of Strategic Services (OSS) of the US Department of State, were only recently declassified. The phases of theoretical elaboration and activism will be reconstructed, defining them in terms of "thought and action" against fascism—suggesting also an interpretative hypothesis of the overall philosophical reflection program of the early Frankfurt School.

9 M. Jay, *The Dialectical Imagination: A History of the Frankfurt School and the Institute of Social Research 1923–1950*, 1973.

10 M. Horkheimer, T. W. Adorno (eds.), Institut für Sozialforschung, *Soziologische Exkurse*, [1956] 2013 p. 169 ff.

Chapter 3, on the other hand, deals with superstructural aspects of the psyche and the formation of ideas and ideologies. Here, Frankfurt School theses are examined starting from the extension of Freudian psychoanalysis of the ego and mass theory to German society. The emergence of a new authoritarian anthropological subject guided the analysis of the role of the family, particularly the role of the paternal figure.[11] The chapters in this section address the study of the psyche in its function as the matrix of social organization and cultural production. Specific attention is given to post-Freudian reworkings of the psyche in its relationship to social institutions, as well as the link between the psyche, cultural critique and fascist tendencies in post-war liberal societies. Culture is seen as the product of a totalizing ideology while utopia provides the Marcusean ideal for a renewed society capable of fulfilling the political-economic transformation expectations of Horkheimer and Adorno. As will be explained, the Frankfurt School's reworkings of the base-superstructure relationship considered that a possible separation of the two concepts makes sense only analytically and not when applied to real societal phenomena. Thus, the examination of productive aspects of the economy cannot avoid also addressing psychic or ideological-superstructural issues and vice versa. It was deemed useful to include an Appendix offering a comprehensive presentation of the key moments and central ideas that accompany the developments of the Frankfurt School up to the present day. This choice was motivated by the desire to make the text as accessible as possible, even to those approaching an understanding of the Frankfurt School's concerns for the first time. Critical theory has been—and continues to be—a worldview capable of producing illuminating theses on politics and social change. However, its representatives have too often been seen as totemic figures of the past, rather than as intellectuals still capable of guiding contemporary research on society. The redefinition of the concept of praxis and social emancipation will thus become a crucial element in neutralizing today's fascist tendencies. This concept will encompass both the objective-constitutive aspect of labor, which brings about a transformation of the existing order, and the critical-political activity of the subject. The discomfort that, according to Freud, civilization has unleashed throughout history does not allow us to maintain an attitude of easy optimism.[12] The Frankfurt School scholars were well aware of this, and today we cannot ignore the evidence. In light of this, we can, however, continue to utilize the Frankfurt School's investigative categories while upholding Horkheimer's incitement: "This was our principle: pessimists in theory and optimists in practice".[13]

This hope is thus given credence in the present work.

11 On the rethinking of the concept of authority in the Frankfurt critical tradition, starting from the studies of '36 on the family, see A. Söllner, *Geschichte und Herrschaft. Studien zur materialistischen Sozialwissenschaft 1929–1942*, 1979.

12 Note that in German, the term "*Kultur*" means both "culture" and "civilization".

13 M. Horkheimer, "Kritische Theorie gestern und heute", [1969] 1970, p. 353.

1 The Frankfurt School facing fascism

A historiographical-conceptual framework

Should we consider fascism an ever-present danger in modern societies? Should we view fascism as a persistent threat within modern societies, akin to a virus that, once introduced into an ecosystem, becomes irreversibly ingrained? In 1995, during a lecture at Columbia University, Umberto Eco introduced the concept of "eternal fascism"[1] or "Ur-fascism".[2] Eco aimed to regard fascism as both an enduring and a multifaceted phenomenon. While Franco and Salazar were not inspired by imperialism and Balkan fascism was not driven by colonial promotion, these all represented variants of the same phenomenon: fascism in its broadest sense.[3] The cases of Romanian, Spanish, Hungarian and Austrian fascism—the latter absorbed into National Socialism only after the *Anschluss* of 1938—proved more controversial. Expanding beyond European borders, some countries exhibited tendencies toward right-wing radicalism and authoritarianism and were thus labelled as fascist. For example, Peronism in Argentina, Gaullism in France and even Nixon's presidency in the United States were considered by some as forms of fascism. Moreover, the concept of fascism has been invoked to describe Saddam Hussein's Iraqi regime as "Middle Eastern fascism". The term "red fascism" has also been used to refer not only to the terrorist turn of brigades communism but also to the Chinese response to the Tiananmen student protests in 1989.[4] Today, finally, with the intent of "denazification", there is even an attempt to justify the Russian military invasion of Ukraine.[5] This issue is not new; as early as 1929, the Soviet Komintern

1 With the generic expression "fascism" (in lowercase letter), I refer to a meta-category primarily encompassing Italian Fascism and German National Socialism. By extension, this category will also be applied to other historically definable forms of fascism.

2 U. Eco, "Ur-Fascism", [1995] 2020.

3 Ibid., pp. 15–16.

4 E. Gentile, *Fascismo. Storia e interpretazione*, 2002, p. 35. For an analysis of the Italian, European and epochal character of fascism, as well as its various dimensions—psychological, philosophical, political etc.—see the collection of texts edited by R. De Felice, *Il fascismo. Interpretazioni dei contemporanei e degli storici*, 1970.

5 For a useful, albeit historically dated, critical examination of the term "fascism", see R. Griffin, *The Nature of Fascism*, [1991] 2006.

DOI: 10.4324/9781003630340-2

had delegitimized Western social democracy by labelling it "social-fascism" due to its alleged complicity in "strengthening of capitalism and bourgeois dictatorship".[6] Togliatti considered this stance a grave mistake, accompanied by a general underestimation of the growing threat of true fascism in Europe.[7] More broadly, the tendency to interpret historical events through an economic-mechanistic lens led the Third International to anticipate the imminent collapse of monopolistic capitalism, which had taken on an imperialist character.[8] However, Lenin's definition of imperialism encompassed not only the strictly economic transformation of production modes but also the political sphere of relations. The Comintern thus became responsible for an erroneous historical forecast because it was based on a reductionist interpretation of Lenin's thought. This prevented them from grasping the explosive rise of fascism, which did not merely represent a transitory phase preceding the collapse of capitalism.[9]

Often, behind the various faces of fascism lies the authoritarian intent to purify customs that no longer align with state orthodoxy. The ongoing challenge remains understanding where fascism truly resides: in what is deemed fascist for not conforming to official dictates or within the judging subject: i.e., the ideological premises used.

It could be argued, as Croce (and also Meinecke) did,[10] that fascism was an "intellectual and moral disease",[11] not simply "an Italian disease, but a contemporary disease"[12] treated, however, in 1944. This historiographical interpretation differed from that of the Rosselli brothers and the radical democrats, who saw fascism as a form of revelation of the crisis of Italian parliamentarism dating back to Crispi. It also distinguished itself from the Marxist perspective, which posited that fascism and Nazism were a continuation of bourgeois capitalism. Löwith also referred to Croce in his text *My Life in Germany Before and After 1933: A Report* [1940].[13] Here, the author analyzed the philosophical positions, particularly those of Heidegger, which had provided theoretical support for the political dissolution of the European spirit. Having established the need to develop guiding criteria capable of capturing the specifically historical-ideological phenomenology of fascism, the idea maintains the merit of capturing its constant and similarly dissimulative essence: the ability to persist in appearance and change according to socio-historical contexts. Implicit

6 F. Gaeta, *Democrazie e totalitarismi dalla prima alla seconda guerra mondiale. Profili di storia contemporanea 1918–1945*, 1989, p. 395.
7 P. Togliatti, "Alcuni problemi dell'Internazionale Comunista", 1962, pp. 299–333.
8 N. Poulantzas, *Fascism and Dictatorship. The Third International and the Problem of Fascism*, [1970] 2018, pp. 36–52.
9 Ibid.
10 F. Meinecke, *The German Catastrophe. Reflections and Recollections*, 1963.
11 B. Croce, "Chi è 'fascista'?", vol. 2, 1973, p. 48.
12 B. Croce, "Il fascismo come pericolo mondiale", vol. 1, 1973, p. 16.
13 K. Löwith, *My Life in Germany Before and After 1933: A Report*, [1940] 1994.

in this is the idea that fascism did not end after World War II, and the current resurgence of neo-fascisms compels us to reflect on the protean nature of this phenomenon. In other words, today we face the task of explaining why "fascism was an integral part of the history of European culture".[14] Thus, while it is legitimate to question the validity of some uses of the term, it is equally essential to consider whether fascism should be viewed as an immanent category rather than a meta-historical and eternal one. This will be the definition reconstructed from the Frankfurt School's reflections spanning the 1930s to the 1960s.

The Frankfurt School intended fascism as a concept definable based on a certain propensity for the use of power, where a specific psychic inclination is accompanied by a centralization of economic (capitalist) production. Typologically differentiated forms of production organization, such as the distinction between monopoly capitalism and state capitalism, should be traced back to this premise.

The immanent use of the concept preserves the theoretical status of fascism as well as the understanding of its phenomenological possibility. It would be dangerous and ultimately counterproductive to allow a historically definable socio-political phenomenon like fascism to merge with a purely psycho-anthropological inclination, an abstract and atavistic propensity for radical evil tied to humanity since its origins. Such a view would undermine the relevance of the phenomenon itself: that is, that mass fascism primarily emerged in reaction to the economic, political, military and ideological crises resulting from World War I.[15] Certainly, identifying the broader historical roots of fascism in the Jacobinism of the French Revolution remains a viable historiographical avenue. However, these broader frameworks can at most illustrate the long-term genesis of fascism without providing contextual specificity. Hence, it appears that both a definition that is too narrow and one that is too loose would fail to do justice to the theoretical and historical-political character of the concept, ultimately causing the term to lose its critical or historical poignancy. Thus, only a historically nuanced analysis of both the proximate causes and more distant roots would stand as the most adequate means to account for the emergence and transformations of historical fascisms.[16]

1.1 Prototypical fascisms: Italian Fascism and German National Socialism

To further articulate the aforementioned theoretical-empirical thesis, it would be appropriate to present the historiographical position adopted for defining

14 Z. Sternhell, *The Birth of Fascist Ideology. From Cultural Rebellion to Political Revolution*, [1989] 1994, p. 3.

15 M. Mann, *Fascists*, 2004, p. 5.

16 For a useful theoretical guide aimed at identifying the various explanatory dimensions of historical fascisms, see R. Kühnl, *Fascismus Theorien: Ein Leitfaden. Aktualisierte Neuauflage*, 1990.

the phenomenological-empirical scope of fascism. It will be argued that Italian Fascism and German National Socialism represent prototypical forms of fascism, against which subsequent historical forms have adopted some, but not all, their defining traits. Both fascisms expressed two revolutionary ideological forms that emerged without civil war, though through class struggle quickly transformed into nationalist movements.[17] They shared a rejection of parliamentary democracy and a vision of a direct union between the people and political leadership, mediated by a totalitarian ideology.[18] The first occurrence of the term "totalitarian system" can be attributed to Amendola in a 1923 article published in *Il Mondo* [*The World*]. However, "totalitarianism" was also used by Basso in *La rivoluzione liberale* [*The Liberal Revolution*] of 1925, while the positive use of the term appeared shortly after in Gentile and Mussolini. Another connotation of the term was given at the end of the 1930s by Pope Pius XI, who saw in the Church a "totalitarian" regime of human belonging to God.[19] A strictly political definition of the new totalitarian paradigm replacing the liberal-democratic model is to be traced back to the theorization proposed by Voegelin in 1933 with *Rasse und Staat*, as well as by Florinsky, who, in *Fascism and National Socialism* of 1936, postulated a methodological analogy between Soviet communism and fascism. This research was followed in 1940 by Borkenau's study *The Totalitarian Enemy*.[20] Italian Fascism and German National Socialism shared many common ideological points such as syndicalism, corporatism, nationalism, militarism, imperialism, authoritarianism and, more generally, the idea of a rebirth and palingenesis of the myth of racial superiority.[21] They also dialectically expressed the relationship between the revolutionary movement and the totalitarian bureaucratic apparatus. According to Nolte, there would be a fundamental difference between these two. While for Italian Fascism, praxis—as organization and impetus for action—would precede thought, for National Socialism, the opposite would be true. However, this characterization seems problematic when analyzed in the light of the Schmittian decisionism of the 1930s as an exemplification of German fascist thought. The situation appears to be much more complex and contradictory than conceptualized by Nolte.

17 For a different view that instead considers three revolutionary acts of National Socialism as central, see H. Rauschning, *The Revolution of Nihilism: Warning to the West*, 1939. On the idea of a political rupture as opposed to the continuity thesis of historical-economic progression, see N. Poulantzas, *Fascism and Dictatorship: The Third International and the Problem of Fascism*, [1970] 2018, p. 25.

18 See G. Mosse, *The Crisis of German Ideology: Intellectual Origins of the Third Reich*, 1981, p. 4.

19 On this matter, see D. Fisichella, *Totalitarismo: Un regime del nostro tempo*, 1987.

20 Respectively E. Voegelin, *Rasse und Staat*, 1933; M. T. Florinsky, *Fascism and National Socialism: A Study of the Economic and Social Policies of the Totalitarian State*, 1936; F. Borkenau, *The Totalitarian Enemy*, 1940.

21 Cfr. S. Payne, *Fascism: Comparison and Definition*, 1980.

In historical fascisms, society was supposed to conform only to a vision based on the elitism and heroism of a group of privileged individuals, characterized by masculinity, dynamism and disregard for death, but also freedom.[22] Fascism thus defined an era, that of the years between the two world wars, in which a series of political-economic and (pseudo) theoretical convictions matured.[23] German and Italian Fascism formed from a young political class in power in which physical prowess and beauty were sealed by the aesthetic taste of official art—it is no coincidence that the percentage of members of the NSDAP, the National Socialist German Workers' Party, under 30 was 40%. From the perspective of expectations for the younger generations, prototypical fascisms thus offered prospects for emancipation from the family and social realization. This was achieved in exchange for direct commitment to the state through sports practice, military, civilian careers and so on. Critique of society, informed opposition and diversity of viewpoints and lifestyles were forms of individual freedom and self-determination intolerable to historical fascisms. Some central factors underlying the rise of fascism in Europe concerned the following transformations:[24]

- The crisis of European society in the transition from liberal capitalism to monopoly capitalism
- The centralization of the economy and politics, as well as the rise of repressive and racist ideology
- The mutual support alliance between capital, the military and state officials and the dismantling of the rule of law in society
- The deeply anti-communist view of politics and society (even though using similar means such as propaganda)

In the view of the historiographical hypothesis suggested here, Italian Fascism and German National Socialism constituted prototypical phenomena to which other forms of authoritarianism were connected through similarities and differences. Political authoritarianism, ideologies and ways of life that, although not leading to a historical socio-political system, nevertheless retained some essential traits, should also be considered as broadly fascist. In this regard, the hypothesis of prototypical fascisms is accompanied by a categorical abstraction sensitive to the articulations of historical fascisms. An implicit element of this thesis is that by the early 1930s, the Frankfurt School considered the difference

22 On the "denying and despising character of freedom" in fascist ideology, see B. Croce, *Il fascismo come pericolo mondiale*, vol. 1, 1973, p. 8.

23 Among the most enlightening texts analyzing the economic structure of National Socialism is M. Y. Sweezy, *The Structure of the Nazi Economy*, 1941, p. 7 and following. It is stated at the outset that the economy of the Nazi totalitarian state, even in peace time, was aimed at preparing for a total war economy.

24 H. Dubiel e A. Söllner, *Wirtschaft, Recht und Staat im Nationalsozialismus: Analysen des IfSs für Sozialforschung 1939–1942*, 1992, p. 29.

between Italian and German Fascism as part of the same genre of fascism. In its paradigmatic versions, fascism ideologically presented itself as the failed legacy of the early 20th-century crisis of liberalism and Marxism, the crisis of capitalism and, more generally, that of the social class from which it emerged: the bourgeoisie. From the ashes of the latter, fascism was able to gain traction as a transversal mass movement among diverse social groups: workers, the unemployed, white-collar workers and the lumpenproletariat. But perhaps even more so, Italian Fascism and German National Socialism provided a collective expression of the crisis of bourgeois individualism stemming from the free market of the early 20th century, the property-owning self and the loss of its social and identity status following the First World War.[25] They produced "states of exception"[26] that were distinct from forms of regime and state, even if authoritarian, but based on a more or less catastrophic equilibrium, such as the Bonapartist or Caesarist model, respectively. If prototypical historical fascisms were partly the result of the economic and political devastation of the Great War, then the link to psychological subordination that emerged was that of a political-economic humiliation of the defeated countries and the parallel economic recovery of the victorious countries. In relation to this point, one might find the reason Europe of those years was divided between a democratic West (with the exception of Portugal and Spain) and an authoritarian East. The war booty was the partition of the old colonial empires where Italy, despite being among the winning countries, received a "mutilated victory" in the 1919 Treaty of Versailles.[27] Fascist ideology thus provided a common reactionary cloak under which impoverished masses found spiritual comfort in the name of a mythologization of the past and a spontaneous renewal of the present.

During the early movement formations, the combat squads chose the symbol of classical Romanity *par excellence*—the fasces, represented by a bundle of sticks. In the fasces, there is no structure holding the parts together: not a party but a spontaneous group. This is exactly what happened at the origin of fascism when, at the rally in Piazza San Sepolcro on March 23, 1919, in Milan, around a hundred people of various political backgrounds and social origins gathered under a single banner. Originating as an ideologically heterogeneous movement, early Italian Fascism united former republicans, disillusioned

25 Gaeta's observation seems entirely agreeable: "The defeat of the European workers' movement in the 1920s was not identified with the failure of the Leninist hypothesis, but was consummated in the destruction of democracy". In F. Gaeta, *Democrazie e totalitarismi dalla prima alla seconda guerra mondiale: Profili di storia contemporanea 1918–1945*, 1989, p. 114.

26 N. Poulantzas, *Fascism and Dictatorship: The Third International and the Problem of Fascism*, [1970] 2018, pp. 57–64.

27 The reasons for this historical judgment must be attributed to the failure to implement the 1915 Treaty of London, which Italy had signed with the Entente. On this topic, see F. Gaeta, *Democrazie e totalitarismi dalla prima alla seconda guerra mondiale: Profili di storia contemporanea 1918–1945*, 1989, pp. 28–31.

liberals, socialists, syndicalists and even futurists who all gathered under the aegis of a nationalist and interventionist spirit. Regarding the many interpretations offered, Croce observed that fascism emerged as an interclass phenomenon, born from a loss of "faith . . . not only in rational liberalism but also in Marxism".[28] While the idea that fascism expressed a true rational theory and was thus far from being an anti-intellectual movement is more recently supported by historian James Gregor in his view of fascism as a variant of Marxism,[29] others, like Sternhell, have argued that fascist ideology emerged from the confluence of Sorelian revolutionary revisionism and French nationalism. This ideological syncretism would then have crossed the Alps during the Great War due to the actions of the Italian interventionist movements of '14 and their post-war ideological legacy. The revolutionary nationalism of 1848 and 19th-century Romanticism seemed to be the basis of the concept of "*völkisch*" (the ethical, the popular) which reached National Socialism after a series of internal transformations. It is from this *côté* that the anti-Semitism of the 1930s, in its macabre theoretical and political implementations, would have been formed. Indeed, theories on nationalism considered that the identity of a people depended on geographic residence. Being a desert people with no roots, Jews were "viewed as shallow, arid, 'dry' people".[30] Thus, Hitler's ideological contribution to Aryan racial superiority had only a partial antecedent in the theory of racial biological determinism (elements already present in *Mein Kampf* [1925–1926],[31] with references to Gobineau, H. S. Chamberlain, Günther or Spengler.

Another common matrix for the two prototypical fascisms was the political mysticism that spontaneously linked to the romantic inspiration of the fascist

28 B. Croce, "Chi è 'fascista'?", vol. 2, 1973, p. 48. On the composite nature of the social base of fascism, predominantly formed by the small and medium bourgeoisie, see R. De Felice (ed.), "Introduzione", in *Il fascismo: Interpretazioni dei contemporanei e degli storici*, 1970, p. XI and following. The author also notes that Mussolini, between 1926 and 1928, while initiating a radical purge of the more extreme and petty-bourgeois factions of the PNF in order to come to terms with pre-fascist political elites and moderate fascists, maintained a solid bourgeois base as long as it remained functional to the support of what became "a regime" (p. XIX and following). According to De Felice, there is a difference between the revolutionary movement and the conservative regime of fascism.

29 A. James Gregor, *The Faces of Janus: Marxism and Fascism in the Twentieth Century*, 2000; A. James Gregor, *Mussolini's Intellectuals: Fascist Social and Political Thought*, 2005. Others, such as Nolte, have argued the much more controversial thesis that Nazism was an ideological reaction to the atrocities of Soviet communism, as discussed in E. Nolte, "Vergangenheit, die nicht vergehen will", *Frankfurter Allgemeine Zeitung*, June 6, 1986.

30 G. Mosse, *The Crisis of German Ideology: Intellectual Origins of the Third Reich*, 1981, p. 4.

31 A. Hitler, *Mein Kampf*, [1925–6] 2006.

hero. In the *Dottrina del fascismo* [*The Doctrine of Fascism*] [1932], Mussolini wrote that

> The proud squadrist motto "*me ne frego*", [I don't care] written on the bandages of a wound, is an act of philosophy that is not merely Stoic; it is the essence of a doctrine that is not only political: it is an education in combat.[32]

This heroic-nihilistic outcome rested on a long-term tradition with intellectual origins both in Nietzsche and in the 19th-century Russian literature and philosophy of Turgenev, Chernyshevsky, Bakunin, Dostoevsky and others. The advent of National Socialism in Germany brought this philosophical-literary process to political completion. In Rauschning's text *The Revolution of Nihilism* [1938], we find the first examination of the link between nihilism and Nazism. The latter was defined as a revolutionary movement lacking true ideology but oriented toward a vacuous decisiveness.[33] Before being seen as a result of the economic crisis of the 1920s and 1930s, the origin of fascism should be traced back to the formulation of a new doctrinal corpus in response to the ideological crisis of liberalism and socialism and the subsequent creation of an autonomous synthesis paradigm expressed in the form of "national socialism".[34] Fascist ideology achieved a union between revolutionary syndicalism and radical nationalism, the latter inspired, at least in the Italian case, by Corradini's theorization presented in *Il nazionalismo italiano* [*The Italian Nationalism*] [1914].[35] Thus, through the paradoxical process of including the proletariat within the nation-state, which was followed by a parallel process of centralization of political power, the strange creature—the fascist state of Behemoth, as Neumann defined the Third Reich—was generated.[36]

According to the current historiographical orientation, despite their common roots, there would be an insurmountable distance between fascism and National Socialism: that is, the issue of anti-Semitism and the biological determinism of races. For Sternhell and Mosse, this component was specifically

32 B. Mussolini, "Dottrina del Fascismo", [1932] 1934, p. 13.

33 H. Rauschning, *The Revolution of Nihilism*, 1939, p. 59 e seq. For an examination of the historiographical trends in the interpretation of Nazism, see M. Mustè e C. Scognamiglio, *Il giudizio sul nazismo: Le interpretazioni dal 1933 ad oggi*, 2005.

34 Given that the difficulty with which the idea that fascism was built upon a true set of doctrines has only recently emerged in historiography, it is worth quoting a passage from a letter by Mussolini to Bianchi dated August 26, 1921, in which he argues that "Italian fascism, under penalty of death or, worse, suicide, must give itself 'a body' of doctrines". In B. Mussolini, *Opera Omnia*, vol. 17, p. 414 ff.

35 E. Corradini, *Il nazionalismo italiano*, [1914] 2020.

36 F. Neumann, *Behemoth: The Structure and Practice of National Socialism 1933–1944*, [1942] 2009.

Germanic and not comparable to the original ideological matrix of fascism.[37] It only entered Italian Fascism from 1938 with the enactment of racial laws. For Mussolini and his followers, up to that point, it was the myth of race, rather than anti-Semitism in a programmatic sense, that represented the most authentic basis of Italian superiority. It should be noted, however, that discriminatory positions were already present from the origins of the fascist movement, as the prohibition of membership in the PNF (National Fascist Party) for Jewish citizens was already included in Article 8 of the 1921 statute. Regarding the regime's structures, a separate consideration is warranted for the distinction between the aspiration and realization of totalitarianism left behind by prototypical fascisms. In the case of Italian Fascism, a separation was maintained, at least during the first decade, between the party (PNF), the state and political leadership (with these components only being hierarchized from the conquest of Ethiopia in 1936), whereas in German National Socialism, the *Führer* figure completely absorbed the functions of the state, thus enabling the construction of a direct relationship between the people, administration and political leadership, facilitating a rapid transition from authoritarianism to totalitarianism.[38] The point was that the process of reclaiming an individualistic-identity dimension characteristic of prototypical fascisms was accompanied by a naturalistic and conformist conception of society. The hierarchical-social verticalization that resulted reproduced a condition of state nature internal to the fascist state itself. From the paradoxical alliance of authoritarianism, mass society and naturalism arose the well-known aberrations manifested in both the form of purges of the enemy (Jews, political dissidents etc.) and the pursuit of a domain space (colonization, total war). Adorno and Horkheimer did not fail to highlight these elements. According to the two scholars, National Socialism originated from a process of reducing the tension between life and education in favour of resolving the social in the natural.[39] The loss of the dialectical contrast between a sociality made up of guarantees for humanity and institutions transformed the social critique of Romanticism into the mythologization of primitive elements of life: race, heroism and an "absolutization of the naked institution, of pure and simple domination".[40] Both Italian Fascism and National Socialism were

37 Z. Sternhell, *The Birth of Fascist Ideology*, [1989] 1994. For example, Mosse argues that "Racism and antisemitism were not a necessary component of fascism, and certainly not of those parts of the movement that looked for their model to Italy, where until 1936, racism was not part of official doctrine". In G. Mosse, *The Fascist Revolution: Towards a General Theory of Fascism*, 1999, p. 31.

38 E. Nolte, *Three Faces of Fascism*, [1963] 1965, p. 27. Nolte emphasizes the need to specify the notion of fascism in order to avoid creating overly broad categories that would lump fascism together with Bolshevism. See also, ibid., p. 36 ff.

39 Cfr. M. Horkheimer, T.W. Adorno and Institut für Sozialforschung (eds.), *Soziologische Exkurse*, [1956] 2013, p. 22 ff.

40 Ibid.

characterized by a continuous attempt to politicize both public and private life, encompassing every aspect of society, including art and aesthetic sense.

At the same time, however, the Fascist state freed itself from national economic apparatuses, entrusting private capital with an increasingly extensive control of the market. Behind Mussolini's political rise, starting with the March on Rome, were the great industrial barons who soon became convinced that fascism was a lucrative business, the best investment for war profits.[41] As Mussolini himself stated on November 7, 1921, during the founding congress of the Fascist Party in Rome: "In economic matters, we are liberals because we believe that the national economy cannot be entrusted to collective and bureaucratic entities. . . . We are against the economic state".[42] It will be shown how the development of an ideological legitimization system became the functional means for the construction of the Fascist platform in its (not fully successful) attempt to create a new type of man.[43] However, while for Italian Fascism, the new man was meant to reflect the aesthetic ideals of futurism, including fascination with technical innovation, speed etc., for National Socialism, the need for productive modernization was accompanied by the idea of a *Volk* (people) oriented toward the search for pre-industrial purity and integrity. Paradoxically, then, the *Volk* were to be protected from Western civilization.[44]

Overall, both Italian and German fascist ideologies aimed to level the masses culturally and politically. The single party propaganda related to a new man and a social order echoing ancient mythological splendour presented itself as a tool of a political theology that, in the case of Italian Fascism, saw in the figure of the citizen-soldier the implementation of Mussolini's motto: "Believe, obey, fight". Cloaked in symbols exalting the Romanity of the people, the political aestheticization was realized, as in the case of the *Decennale della Rivoluzione fascista* [Tenth Anniversary of the Fascist Revolution] with the *Mostra della rivoluzione fascista* [*Exhibition of the Fascist Revolution*] held at the Palazzo delle Esposizioni in Rome in 1932. Similarly, the regime, in sublimating the eternity of the myth of the Duce and the renewal of tradition, initiated the construction of neighbourhoods like EUR, erecting monuments such as the Palazzo della Civiltà Italiana, renamed "Square Colosseum" for its quadrangular plan and modern reinterpretation of Roman architecture. In the case of National Socialism's cultural matrices, right-wing intellectuals and ideologists such as Jünger, Sombart and Schmitt (not to forget Heidegger)—even when not explicitly aligned with the Nazi party—were witnesses to a deep connection with the tradition of German Romanticism, through the thought

41 On this matter, see E. Rossi, *Padroni del vapore e fascismo*, 1966, p. 31 ff.

42 Cited in E. Rossi, *Padroni del vapore e fascismo*, 1966, p. 38.

43 E. Nolte, *Three Faces of Fascism*, 1965, p. 25 and p. 57.

44 J. Herf, *Reactionary Modernism: Technology, Culture and Politics in Weimar and the Third Reich*, 1985, p. 6.

(interpolated) of Nietzsche and a form of irrationalism and ambivalent openness toward technique. This was complemented by the anti-Semitic image of the subversive Jew theorized by Feder: either as a communist or as affiliated with a financial elite. In both cases, it was a vision aimed at exalting the mythical character of the spiritual renewal of society, the total subordination of the individual to the state and a totalitarian conception of politics. The Frankfurt School approached the understanding of fascism in an original manner, as introduced in the overall reconstruction of the definition of fascism delineable retrospectively from their writings. For Horkheimer, the reasons leading to the Second World War were to be found not so much in the measures taken at Versailles against Germany, but in "the shortsightedness"[45] with which the Germans approached Hitler. Since the Germans realized the possibility of revoking the sanctions, the authority of those who decided them no longer represented a real threat.

> In the report on the activities of the IfS conducted between 1933 and 1938, it was stated that "The differences between the cultures of pre-war Germany and Italy were many and sharp, but fascism is bound up with human complexes which existed in both countries, in fact, in all countries where the present form of economy and society prevails.[46]

From a methodological perspective, critical theory found its most congenial intellectual environment within the Marxist interpretative strand and the subsequent institutional changes. However, the Frankfurt perspective transcended the boundaries of Marxist orthodoxy, although continuing to operate within an autonomous perspective of rethinking fundamental Marxian concepts, such as the axis between productive base (in the aftermath of the European capitalist crisis of the 1930s) and ideological superstructure (state and ideology)—to which was added the contribution of a psycho-value sphere based on Fromm's revision of Freudian psychoanalysis. Fromm's sociopsychology studied the relationship between varying instinctual drives and changing socio-structural productive contexts: "Thus analytic social psychology enables us to understand fully the ideological superstructure in terms of the process that goes on between society and man's nature".[47] This provided the Frankfurt School with an additional theoretical basis to abandon the hypothesis of a one-directional replication between productive base and ideological superstructure. Thus, the way was opened for overcoming a deterministic-functional view between production and ideology, favouring instead the perspective of a bidirectional delimitation between the two domains aimed at considering coercive impulses

45 M. Horkheimer, "The Lessons of Fascism", 1950, p. 211.
46 IfS, "A Report on Its History, Aims and Activities 1933–1938", 1939, pp. 10–11.
47 E. Fromm, "Method and Function of an Analytic Social Psychology", [1932] 1970, p. 134.

as psychic motivators.[48] This will help explain how social deformities and regressions, of which fascism was an emblem, could, in turn, leverage internal normalization mechanisms.

1.2 The Frankfurt School and National Socialism

In light of the numerous historiographical and cultural interpretations of fascism already presented, the Frankfurt School emerged as a non-orthodox Marxist interdisciplinary approach to study. Sociological analysis, philosophical-methodological perspectives and new frontiers opened by studies on mass psychology collectively contributed to defining an innovative research agenda. Starting from Reich's psychoanalytic reflections of 1933, fascism was framed as a phenomenon expressing a "basic emotional attitude of man in authoritarian society, with its machine civilization and its mechanistic-mystical view of life".[49] It is evident that the Frankfurt School's interpretative approach would also address economic crisis aspects as contributing factors to the rise of fascism. As Fromm summarized: "Nazism is an economic and political problem, but the hold it has over a whole people has to be understood on psychological grounds".[50] Authoritarianism, destructiveness, and moral and intellectual conformism would be the main indicators defining the process of "escape from freedom".[51]

In attempting to trace the early signs of societal transformation, Horkheimer noted in *Dawn & Decline: Notes 1926–1931 and 1950–1969*—a diary written between 1926 and 1931 and published for the first time in 1934 under the pseudonym Heinrich Regius—what immediately appeared to him as evident signs of a political horizon obscuration: "the less stable necessary ideologies are, the more cruel the methods by which they are protected".[52] Horkheimer had already observed that the economic depression of Weimar's third phase would give rise to a series of political polarizations supporting Hitler's ascent. This was the final

48 Marx expressed his vision of the relationship between base and superstructure in a non-deterministic and unidirectional manner in the preface to *A Contribution to the Critique of Political Economy*: "[I]n the social production which men carry on they enter into definite relations that are indispensable and independent of their will; these relations of production correspond to a definite stage of development of their material powers of production. The sum total of these relations constitutes the economic structure of society—the real foundation, on which rise legal and political superstructures and to which correspond definite forms of social consciousness. The mode of production in material life determines the general character of the social, political and spiritual processes of life. It is not the consciousness of men that determines their existence, but, on the contrary, their social existence determines their consciousness". In K. Marx, *A Contribution to the Critique of Political Economy*, [1859] 1904, pp. 11–12. For an accurate interpretation of the functional relationship between base and superstructure in Marx, see M. Thompson, *The Domestication of Critical Theory*, 2016, p. 96 ff.

49 W. Reich, *The Mass Psychology of Fascism*, [1933] 1980, p. XIII.

50 E. Fromm, *Escape from Freedom*, [1941] 1965, p. 232.

51 Ibid.

52 M. Horkheimer, *Dawn & Decline: Notes 1926–1931 and 1950–1969*, [1934] 1978, p. 17.

phase of the Weimar Republic, that political experience from '18 to '33, born from the ashes of the German Empire following the resignation of Chancellor von Bethmann Hollweg on July 12, 1917. The episode notably came to an end with the political rise of the Nazis in the elections of September 14, 1930, when they were elected with 6.4 million votes.[53]

Weimar was born under poor auspices and ended in the worst way possible.

In the aftermath of Germany's defeat in the Great War, burdened by massive war debts and a working class increasingly resistant and exposed to the imminent threat of a Marxist revolution, Germany found a fragile political balance under a unified constitutional framework.[54] However, the institutional setup did not establish inviolable rules to pacify political conflict. Instead, a constitution could only be born through constant negotiation between parties, through which Weimar was placed in a condition of "contracted democracy"[55] and political compromise. In this historical phase, reflections on Germany's wartime defeat in World War I and its technological backwardness generated a heated debate. Discussions concerned the thematic relationship between means and ends in instrumental rationality. The Frankfurt School members extensively discussed this with reference to Weber.[56] Social tendencies toward technical advancement intertwined with a nationalist ideology, which, in turn, opened the doors to the Third Reich. Herf defined this combination as the expression of a "reactionary modernism"[57] within a "republic without republicans".[58]

Benjamin, in his essay-review "Theories of German Fascism" [1930],[59] had also seen in the German imperial war the discrepancy between the power of technology and the "[m]inimal moral illumination"[60] it provided. Benjamin understood that Nazism had completed a historical-cultural process, initiated with Weimar, of a reactionary use of technology and a total rejection of Enlightenment tradition. Technological advancement came to subjugate the *Volk*, rather than initiating forms of emancipation from the limits of the natural

53 Cfr. E. Eyck, *A History of the Weimar Republic*, vol. 2, 1963.

54 On the historiographical reconstruction of pre-Weimar and Weimar Germany, with particular reference to the turbulence within the Social Democratic Party and the subsequent reactionary turn of the revolution, see P. Broué, *The German Revolution 1917–1923*, [1971] 2005, pp. 43–258.

55 G. E. Rusconi, "La parabola della socialdemocrazia tedesca durante la repubblica di Weimar", 1979, p. 193.

56 On the debate concerning the role of technology, see F. Dessauer, *Streit um die Technik: Technik prägt Menschen*, 1959.

57 "My basic point is the following: Before and after the Nazi seizure of power, an important current within conservative and subsequently Nazi ideology was a reconciliation between the antimodernist, romantic, and irrationalist ideas present in German nationalism and the most obvious manifestation of means—ends rationality, that is, modern technology. Reactionary modernism is an ideal typical construct". In J. Herf, *Reactionary Modernism: Technology, Culture and Politics in Weimar and the Third Reich*, 1985, p. 1.

58 Ibid., p. 20.

59 W. Benjamin, "Theories of German Fascism", in *Selected Writings*, [1930] 2005, pp. 312–321.

60 Ibid., p. 238.

world. It is no coincidence, then, that the dialectical reversal of rationality would become one of the crucial issues in Horkheimer's and Adorno's subsequent reflections. A decade later, in a letter to Horkheimer in October 1941, Marcuse emphasized the insidiously accommodating nature of fascism to the new historical times: "This movement, we now see, has not changed the basic relationships of the productive process that is still administered by special social groups which control the instruments of labor regardless of the needs and interest of society as a whole".[61] Thus, for Marcuse, fascism was not a phenomenon emerging in radical opposition to the productive structure of the time. At the same time, National Socialism did not realize a "social and economic restoration"[62] of old ruling classes. In other words, it did not present itself as a mere replica of the old Prussian Reich. Instead, National Socialism maintained capitalist production forms, replacing the dominant elite with a new economic group. This new group was granted monopolistic control over the means of production and a totalitarian concentration of economic resources. Totalitarian control of society and technical rationality fused together in an authoritarian solution to the crises of 1920s liberalism. In a 1941 lecture, Marcuse highlighted two distinctive features of the fascist state: "(1) the totalitarian character of the *state,* and (2) the authoritarian character of the *society*".[63] Both elements acted as instruments of "the absolute repression of the individual with all his rights and abilities".[64] However, between Nazi-fascist authoritarianism and the preceding (and future) liberal form, the line of continuity would be a totalizing capitalist organization of social relations. Differences would instead concern the organicist (and irrational) naturalization of social relations which, in Nazism, became a complete sacrifice of oneself for the race before the nation.

As with other Frankfurt School theorists, Marcuse believed that the task of social sciences was to understand the nature and scope of fascism within its capacity to shape the exercise of democratic power and the surrounding culture. Moreover, Horkheimer had sought to highlight the influence of socio-environmental aspects on the characterization of authoritarian personality, such as the family nucleus in the repression/frustration of instincts.[65] While it is accurate that the Frankfurt School scholars will primarily focus their studies on National Socialism, it is nonetheless undeniable that their analyses will encompass a historical period extending from the late 1930s, particularly with Fromm, Horkheimer, Kracauer and Marcuse, through to the early 1960s with Adorno. During this time, both the economic-political and ideological-cultural scenarios underwent profound transformations. This

61 H. Marcuse, "State and Individual under National Socialism", in *Technology, War and Fascism,* [1941] 1998, p. 69.

62 Ibid.

63 Ibid., p. 70.

64 Ibid.

65 M. Horkheimer, "The Lessons of Fascism", 1950, pp. 209–242.

helps explain why representatives of the early critical theory, despite starting from systemic analyses, would eventually move toward meta-structural categorizations, as in the debate on state capitalism versus monopoly capitalism.

In all cases, however, the Frankfurt School maintained the idea that the multiple faces of fascism must be traced back to a single underlying matrix: the capitalist structure of economic production. Horkheimer's assertion that "Fascism has only revealed what was already inherent in liberalism"[66] encapsulates the connection between democratic authoritarianism and fascism in the strict sense. As ideal types, these concepts shared elements of each other along an incremental axis of violence and autocracy. The critique of the ideological and cultural superstructure thus embraced a rejection not only of fascist pseudo-philosophy but also of the consumerist vision of democratic societies predominantly shaped around the "American dream".

For the Frankfurt School, fascism was a phenomenon that, at least in Germany, traversed various political phases—from Weimar to the totalitarian state[67]—but whose production roots lay in Fordist capitalism. With the advent of post-war democracies, right-wing radicalism tendencies would not disappear but assume new forms and strategies. The current crisis of liberal democracies stands as the most authentic witness: the short-circuit in the triangulation between idealized forms of democratic norms (constitutions, deliberative models etc.) and the ever-increasing concentration of capital (as well as the impoverishment of the masses) will lead to a radical constriction of the liberal democratic paradigm. The Frankfurt School accompanied its studies on fascism with the analysis of individual and mass psychology. To this end, they held a deep interest in the new Freudian science. It was from the original syntheses between psychoanalysis and mass society on one hand and psychoanalysis and Marxism, on the other that long-term evaluative directions of societies emerged, accompanied by perspectives on collective social redemption.

Horkheimer's philosophy and the group of intellectuals gathered around the IfS had thus always envisioned that critical thought should aim for a theory of radical transformation of society.[68] Critical theory expressed a well-defined function: that is, to promote the process of modernization and emancipation,

66 M. Horkheimer, "On the Sociology of Class Relations", [1943], *Horkheimer Archiv.*

67 For an analysis of the various interpretations of 'total state' and the theoretical-political significance of totalitarianism in 1930s Germany, see C. Galli, "Strategie della totalità: Stato autoritario, stato totale, totalitarismo, nella Germania degli anni Trenta", 1997, pp. 27–62. The author notes that political reflection on "totality" highlights a paradoxical aspect of the concept: "that totality is also, at the same time, its own negation, partiality. That it is an inclusion which always implies—albeit in differentiated forms—exclusion" (p. 59). For an analysis of the concept of "totality" in C. Schmitt, see W. Scheuermann, *Between the Norm and the Exception: The Frankfurt School and the Rule of Law*, 1994, p. 11 ff.

68 Among the various writings, the one I find most significant is M. Horkheimer, "Traditional and Critical Theory", in *Critical Theory. Selected Essay*, [1937] 2002, pp. 188–243. For a more personal perspective on the subject, see the interview H. Marcuse, "Critical Philosophy: A Personal Perspective with Dr. Herbert Marcuse", [1979] 2011, pp. 226–233.

not only of fascist society but also of the one born after the Second World War. It aimed to develop critical thought toward achieving comprehensive reformist goals without the limitation of a predefined political ideology, as was the case with Marxism's critique of society and political economy. Critical theory addressed the particular, considering factual data as not extrinsic to its own conceptual aura or thought to be superior to facts.[69] From this perspective, it sought to propose an immanent critique of social reality expressed in the form of a negative dialectic of "conceptualized practices" in society.[70] The immanence of critique consisted of maintaining a methodological perspective aimed at highlighting the contradictions of the real relative to normative, rational and value ideals. The latter historically set standards for the validity of the society that had been constituted. Thus, the orientation of immanent critique sought to highlight the failure of society relative to its own terms of legitimacy. The object of investigation and criteria of evaluation ended up forming a unitary core differentiable only analytically.[71] This meant that critical standards, while sharing the same form of immanence with the behavioural regularity of social practices, differed from these because they were capable of realizing a genuine transformation of social practices. For these standards to have critical validity, they had to be both forms of knowledge and immanent presuppositions of self-evaluation as in accordance to a Hegelian perspective.

More Marxianly, however, critical theory conceived social practices as resulting from a structure of production—capitalism—and thus as practices that incorporated a general form of domination. Consequently, critical activity was directed toward unmasking the internal contradictions—the dynamics of domination—of current social practices. Unlike Hegel and Marx, however, critical theory did not merely present the variations of historical experience in terms of the articulations of spirit or capital, nor did it resolve dialectical contradictions. Rather, critical theory identified what it considered to be the necessary transformations of inadequate social practices. In immanent critique, the method was thus not viewed as separable from historical determination, nor was the latter separable from its dialectical articulation.[72] This meant that social critique was situated beyond both a relativism typical of the bourgeois irreducibility of subjective preference and an objective neutrality of analyzing the entity investigated, which, in turn, depended on an inappropriate separation between facts and values. Critique was understood as articulated based

69 Regarding these concepts, it is worth recalling the influence of G. Lukács's *History and Class Consciousness*, [1923] 1971, as well as K. Korsch's *Marxism and Philosophy*, [1923] 2013, both originally published in 1923, the year of the founding of the IfS.

70 A. Schmidt, "Praxis", 1974, pp. 264–306.

71 For a prospective examination of the philosophical problems that this position raises, see T. Stahl, "What Is Immanent Critique?", 2013, online. See also A. Buchwalter, "Hegel, Marx, and the Concept of Immanent Critique", 1991, pp. 253–279.

72 R. J. Antonio, "Immanent Critique as the Core of Critical Theory: Its Origins and Developments in Hegel, Marx and Contemporary Thought", 1981, p. 332.

on standards of social self-understanding. In this sense, the project of immanent critique took on a dual trajectory: from ideology to the critique of social reality and from the latter back to the former. The idea of immanent truth held together what exists (what is) with what is desirable (what could be).[73] Truth was neither hypostatized as an absolute ideal nor posited as the goal of instrumental reason. Against these two extremes, the idea of the determined negative was defended as the historically posited truth opposing the dominating force of the whole—akin to a sort of "metaphysic of the concrete".[74] The form of knowledge defined by the immanent method was thus anti-positivist and anti-metaphysical: that is, critique as an exercise in diagnosing the contradictions of reality and initiating processes of social emancipation. Critical theorists, reasoning on the ashes of the Enlightenment, did not believe that human progress was a linear and guaranteed given. On the contrary, they considered that the voluntariness of historical change could not be scientifically anticipated and that, as a result, the social critics had the task of pointing out the political short-circuits of their time.

The Frankfurt School thus developed a method of social critique that progressively clarified itself through the examination of the historical development of German National Socialism and fascism in general. Fascism emerged as a recurring theme, distinguishable in periodizations that, however, shared a series of background assumptions from the outset, such as a) the urgency of reworking fundamental Marxian categories, b) the recognition of the autonomy of psychic processes, and c) the idea of a historicity of a cognitive and productive basis. It is therefore in light of this perspective that the periodization suggested by Dubiel and later taken up by Benhabib should be integrated; this posits that the IfS followed an initial phase of "interdisciplinary materialism" (1932–1937) with a period of reflection on the concept of "critical theory" (1937–1940) and finally—as a third phase—a turn toward cultural criticism articulated around a "critique of instrumental reason" (1940–1945). The theme of fascism emerges as a common thread in these critical-methodological developments, straddling these periodizations and encompassing various specific thematic areas.

In this sense, Horkheimer's questioning of the epistemological foundations of the sciences, presented in the essay "Traditional and Critical Theory" (1937),[75] found a political retranslation in the critique of instrumental reason in capitalist society. With no pre-given objects of knowledge (i.e., constitutively already formed, as these are always the result of a constitutive historical activity), the capitalist system of production and its possible transformation were placed at the root of a critique of the commodification of society. Authoritarian ascent, mass and power, monopolistic transformations of capital

73 Ibid., p. 338.
74 Ibid., p. 341.
75 M. Horkheimer, "Traditional and Critical Theory", [1937] 2002, pp. 188–243.

and commodification of culture were the areas of illiberal regression of the psyche and civilization identified by the Frankfurt theorists according to an incremental axis of interest. Indeed, the understanding of the irrationality that had taken hold among German workers since the late 1920s was the subject of Fromm's studies on the psyche and those of Horkheimer and his collaborators on the family. These studies were accompanied by investigations into the changes in the structures of the fascist state and capitalism.[76] The theme of fascism and its ramifications in what would become the post-war democracies will help explain the continuity over time of some fundamental pillars of Frankfurt School reflection on the Marxian relationship between base and superstructure.[77]

The historical context of the final years of the Weimar Republic (1929–1933) saw the growing affirmation of Hitler's NSDAP. Economic volatility required the use of emergency powers granted by Article 48 of the Weimar Constitution. Brüning's anti-parliamentary policy did not succeed.[78] The Reichstag opposed this measure, and the Parliament was consequently dissolved. The elections held in 1930 saw the NSDAP make a significant leap forward, obtaining more than 18% of the votes. The resulting stalemate, due to the lack of a clear majority, hastened Germany's collapse. With public spending cuts and a disastrous social situation due to rampant unemployment, Brüning ended up alienating popular sympathies definitively. Hindenburg was re-elected in 1932, but this time he appointed von Papen as chancellor. This was a fatal mistake, probably the result of a political miscalculation that saw the opportunity for parliamentary inclusion and normalization of the NSDAP as a way to tame National Socialism. The Junkers and the German financial and industrial elite did not like Hitler but could no longer ignore his political strength.[79] At this point, the NSDAP felt legitimized to make precise political demands. One of these was the calling of new elections. On July 31, 1932, the NSDAP obtained more than 33% of the preferences. Despite having achieved a relative majority rather than an absolute one, due to further political turmoil, on January 30, 1933, Hindenburg was reluctantly forced to appoint Hitler as the new chancellor of the Reich. One of the first measures adopted by the new regime was the so-called *Gleichschaltung* (coordination/uniformation).

76 H. Dubiel, *Wissenschaftsorganisation und politische Erfahrung: Studien zur frühen Kritischen Theorie*, 1978, p. 24; S. Benhabib, *Critique, Norm and Utopia: A Study of the Foundations of Critical Theory*, 1986, p. 152 ff. The tripartition is attributed by Benhabib to the studies of H. Dubiel, Söllner, and W. Bonss, fn 5, p. 377.

77 In fact, Dubiel had included this theme in the proposed periodization, albeit with a different temporal framework and historiographical role than the one presented here. See H. Dubiel, *Wissenschaftsorganisation und politische Erfahrung: Studien zur frühen Kritischen Theorie*, 1978, p. 35 ff.

78 For a clear reconstruction of the events, see F. Gaeta, *Democrazie e totalitarismi dalla prima alla seconda guerra mondiale: Profili di storia contemporanea 1918–1945*, 1989, pp. 306–307.

79 It is worth noting that a similar underestimation error was made by the pre-fascist political elites in Italy in their attempt to tame the advance of Benito Mussolini in the early 1920s.

This involved a gradual dismantling of the institutions and values of German society in order to establish total control over society and the economy.[80] The endeavour succeeded. All parties (starting with the SPD), trade unions and even the centuries-old federal structure of the Länder were abolished. Political dissidents were eliminated. Social democracy was erased.

Regarding these events, the Frankfurt School adopted two differentiated strategic-interpretative lines. A first group, led by Horkheimer but supported by the decisive contributions of Fromm and Marcuse as well as Kracauer, oriented itself toward the analysis of the irrationalism of National Socialism using tools of social psychology and mass theory. A second group, consisting mainly of Neumann, Kirchheimer and Gurland, focused instead on legal-economic and institutional changes. We will later see how Neumann's final writings testified to the need to integrate these two lines of reflection into a single path. These two lines of investigation merely expressed different sensitivities, but both were founded on a common presupposition of interest: the rethinking of the state and the reorganization of society. From the rejection of a deterministic view of the Marxian relationship between economic base and ideological-cultural superstructure emerged for the first Frankfurt School a contextualized theory of knowledge and political action. In this sense, fascism would redefine the type of capitalism that would form from the 1930s onward. Certainly, what troubled Horkheimer during these years was precisely what he himself identified as the *Speerspitze des Faschismus* [spearhead of fascism]: "anti-Semitism".[81] The analysis of anti-Semitism was an integral part of the more comprehensive examination of fascism: not only the anti-Semitism of the *squadristi* loyal to the National Socialist party but also the kind that grew in children through the warmth of the home where parents themselves told the child about "the evil that exists outside" in a "wrong world".[82] Adorno would oppose this educational model when he warned the youth (and even more so educators) against the cult of a so-called "order" that avoids answering the question of the purpose that self-discipline aims to achieve.[83]

Studies on fascism by Pollock, Horkheimer, Adorno, Neumann, Kirchheimer and other Frankfurt School figures continued for well over a decade after the end of the Second World War, despite having begun in the early 1930s. Crucial themes such as the idea of state capitalism (i.e., the replacement of the free market with state control), the transformation of law and the emergence of a mass culture under National Socialism were examined. The proposed critique was of the economy and political institutions. The Frankfurt

80 F. Neumann, *Behemoth: The Structure and Practice of National Socialism 1933–1944*, [1942] 2009; O. Kirchheimer, "The Legal Order of National Socialism", [1941], pp. 456–475; A. R. L. Gurland, "Technological Trends and Economic Structure under National Socialism", 1941, pp. 226–263.

81 M. Horkheimer, "Sociological Background of the Psychoanalytic Approach", [1946], p. 1.

82 M. Horkheimer, "Eine besondere Art von Antisemitismus", [1949–50] 1987, p. 344.

83 Ibid.

School posed the following question: if fascism is identified with state capitalism and the latter is presented as the ultimate vanguard of capitalism, is it possible that state capitalism and fascism are simply surface variants of a common deep structure given by capitalism?[84] The historical-political development of Nazi Germany was first compared to both the transformation of the Wilhelmine society and the Weimar Republic and the various phases traversed by contemporary democracies. Limited to the historical periods preceding the advent of Nazism, the most relevant social transformations included social classes, the internal structure of the economy and the hierarchies of the command orders of the decision-making apparatus.

After the war, for Horkheimer and his followers, the illiberal nature of society became the legacy of the long development of pre-war fascisms. The irrational strategy of constructing Hitlerian society would continue to produce aberrations even in the democratic recovery of the post-fascist state, particularly in the form of mass democracy and cultural consumerism. The non-deterministic re-theorization of the Marxian relationship between base and superstructure allowed representatives of the early Frankfurt School to develop an analysis of the capitalist production system and its meta-structural transformations—state capitalism or monopoly capitalism—in terms of semi-independent variables (autonomous but correlated), where the psychic superstructure dimension would connect with the ideological-cultural one. The intellectual reflections embodied in the superstructure could not help but occupy a supra-state spectrum, thus rendering all possible consequences predictable. Even if only after the defeat of National Socialism and its ideological apparatus, US capitalism and Soviet deterministic Marxism continued to shape an ideological superstructure that persisted for decades until the fall of the Soviet regime, also contributing to the ideological transformation of the production structure.

If these were the guiding lines of Frankfurt School reflection, then an aberrant consequence was that Europe, from the post-war period to the present day, would no longer be able to develop a genuinely authentic culture. This happened precisely for the same reason that Europe could not build an autonomous ideological superstructure due to the lack of a productive structure representative of its own productive vision. The colonization of the production sphere at the base level thus ended up forming a diabolical pact with a cultural and ideological superstructure largely alien to the context. The latter manifested itself as a pale reflection of lifestyle models borrowed from the victorious countries of the second world conflict. The two hegemonic superpowers of the post-1945 era would divide the influence not only of labor organization but also, even more worryingly, of the very ways of thinking and

84 On this matter, see L. Fischer, "The Frankfurt School and Fascism", 2018, p. 802. Marcuse will return to this issue in a co-edited book: O. Bauer, H. Marcuse, A. Rosenberg (eds.), *Faschismus und Kapitalismus: Theorien über die sozialen Ursprünge und die Funktion des Faschismus*, 1967.

organizing the world of production. This would lead to a new form of alienation of European consciousness expressed in the lifestyles characteristic of the two blocs, Western and Soviet. In this respect, critical theory dismantled every dogmatic certainty about ideological axiological assumptions. Social critique was defended without disciplinary boundaries or temporal limits. Contemporary society, as well as the post-war one, was never considered out of danger of a relapse into forms of authoritarianism, even if disguised under unconventional appearances. Today, we can say that these forecasts proved correct. In this regard, we can consider the analyses of new forms of digital capitalism: customer profiling aimed at anticipating their fetishist desires and proposing desirable advertising objects. The centralization of power under fascism, monopoly capitalism and the role of propaganda have today taken on new forms that cut across the autocratic politics of the past. In light of what has been reconstructed, how can we determine a role for the critical intellectual in society? The primary goal of the IfS was to propose alternative figures to those Grünberg defined as "*Mandarinanstalten*" (mandarin intellectuals).[85] These were intellectuals who had placed their technical knowledge at the service of power. In some ways, this type resembled what Gramsci had already defined in the separation between the classical intellectual and the organic intellectual—the latter aimed at awakening the working class from the systemic passivity imposed by existing hegemonic powers.

However, neither of these Gramscian types represented the role that the Frankfurt School considered its own. The social critic did have the task of highlighting the contradictions of reality without resorting to the sentimentalism of ecstatic unity or the absence of dialectical mediation; however, they did not have the duty to act as a party vanguard or to overturn the hegemonic relationships between classes. In this sense, the moment of negation was configured as a realm for redeeming the very sensibility of reality, still beyond its realization. This would constitute the moment of critique in the proper sense—but not of approaching revolution—as was the case for Gramsci. Current times will instead see the progressive fragmentation of the structure in the transformation of production processes and the de-structuring of social classes and relations between capital and labor. These transformations will generate another form of social levelling similar in effect to that of fascism. The result will be the loss of critical self-awareness, leaving room for new forms of ideological authoritarianism to rise and dominate despite the civil achievements painstakingly obtained with the historical defeat of fascism. Contemporary mass society will end up replicating disturbing aspects derived from such superstructural levelling. A society deprived of internal articulations between interest groups and productive and social spheres will then be an easy prey to "integral or organic"[86] ideologies of the nation-state. Class struggle will be

85 C. Grünberg, "Festrede gehalten zur Einweihung des IfSs für Sozialforschung an der Universität Frankfurt a. M. am 22 Juni 1924", [1924], p. 4.

86 M. Mann, *Fascists*, 2004, p. 2.

replaced by the friend/enemy dichotomy, exercised toward those considered material contributors to society (the true workers!) and those who will instead be seen as unproductive enemies—both internal and external—of society. It is for this reason that the concerns of Polish economist Kalecki regarding new forms of fascism in the democracies of the 1960s must still be taken seriously today. Fascism will continue to replicate itself in the form of subversive extremism that will hold the premises around which democracies are built under check: "The fascism of our times is a dog on a leash; it can be unleashed at any time to achieve definite aims and even when on the leash serves to intimidate the potential opposition".[87] The mimetic capacity of fascism investigated by the Frankfurt School has revealed, in fact, "possibilities inherent in capitalism"[88] that identify new forms of economic and intellectual colonialism in unjustified restrictions on personal freedoms, aiming to operate based on a closure of free thought through predetermined choices. On these illiberal developments of contemporary democratic societies, our civil consciousness will be called upon to watch as a vigilant sentinel.

1.3 Toward a critique of society

In his inaugural lecture of 1931, as the new director of the IfS and professor of social philosophy at Goethe University Frankfurt, Horkheimer emphasized the importance of avoiding an "abstract"[89] understanding of the role of the Hegelian spirit in history where "economy . . . is the only true reality", and "the psyche . . ., law, art, and philosophy, are to be completely derived from the economy".[90] For Horkheimer, such a deterministic Marxism was merely a "badly understood Marx",[91] advocating for an increasingly close collaboration between philosophical and empirical sciences, where philosophers, economists, historians and also psychologists would work together. Renewing social philosophy, therefore, meant completing the post-Kantian overcoming of a philosophy entangled in the closures of the subject[92] and redefining an empirical and interdisciplinary framework that the IfS studies were to develop in the years to come. It was about understanding the very idea of society as something capable of focusing not only on the economic-political and productive aspects but also on the destructive implications within the subject and the

87 M. Kalecki, "The Fascism of Our Times (1964)", 2021, p. 132.

88 S. Kouvélakis, *La critique défaite : Émergence et domestication de la Théorie critique. Horkheimer—Habermas—Honneth*, 2019, p. 18.

89 M. Horkheimer, "The Present Situation of Social Philosophy and the Tasks of an Institute for Social Research", [1931] 1993, p. 12. Note the indication of "method" in the programming of research, where Horkheimer, quoting Grünberg, his predecessor at the head of the IfS, speaks of the "dictatorship of the director" (p. 11), anticipating his full decision-making autonomy.

90 Ibid., p. 12.

91 Ibid.

92 Ibid., pp. 21–23.

object. For Horkheimer and Adorno, Freud had correctly related the potential self-destructiveness of socialization to an unaddressed compensation for the ego's renunciations within the instinctual sphere.[93] Society thus came to be constituted economically and deconstructed psychoanalytically.

From its beginning, critical theory adopted the eminently Marxian idea of the illusory and apparent nature of the relationships established by capitalism. However, it reworked the internal structures and conceptual tensions. Commodity fetishism had indeed reversed the relationship between people and products and thus the vectors in social relations. This legitimized a critique not only of political economy but also of society as a whole. Analyses therefore questioned both the historical-productive assumptions of contemporary systems and the underlying assumptions of the entire philosophical apparatus concerning the conceivability of society and its transformations. In *Materialism and Metaphysics* (1933),[94] Horkheimer redefined the role of social critique through a purification of the reflection of classical metaphysical apparatus, which, following a certain identitarian view of Hegel's idealism, had sealed the *coincidentia oppositorum* between being and thought, unable to effect a transformation of the existing. On the contrary, Horkheimer's critical theory aimed to reject the apologia of the existing and the metaphysical transfiguration of the determined into the totality. For Horkheimer, the metaphysicians had shown indifference to the ethical problem of reality. Their philosophical gaze had merely aimed to leave the world as it was without making the leap to the philosophy of praxis. Thus, for Horkheimer, the materialistic transformation of classical metaphysics had become the keystone to placing the relationship between philosophy and the socio-historical perspective of communal living at the center of reflection: not only the economic but also the psychic dimension became an essential constellation for understanding politics. This would reaffirm the necessity of formulating new categories for understanding the existing and avoiding, on the one hand, the hypostatization of a metaphysical relapse of forms of understanding the real and, on the other, the slippage into the self-determining data of scientific positivism.[95] "Neither with Kant nor with Lenin" would be Horkheimer's unspoken motto. Indeed, while Kant had already outlined the methodological presupposition and limit of all idealism in the preface to *The Critique of Pure Reason*—with its a priori derivation of knowledge of objects from the thinking subject—Lenin's empirio-criticism placed total trust in the immediate knowledge of Being.[96] In this case, however, one remained outside a historical-temporal dimension. The new method had to avoid ahistorical and thus metaphysical categorizations, as well as abandoning

93 M. Horkheimer, T. W. Adorno, Institut für Sozialforschung (eds.), *Soziologische Exkurse*, [1956] 2013.

94 M. Horkheimer, "Materialism and Metaphysics", [1933] 2002, pp. 10–46.

95 Ibid., p. 16 ff.

96 Ibid., p. 28.

the intent of a transfiguration of the dynamism and contradictions of the finite into identity categories. Rather, critical theory had to proceed with the scrutiny of the ideological assumptions of bourgeois society and the recognition that "justice was one-sidedly defined in terms of freedom and freedom in terms of negation" in such a way that a "groundplan for a reasonable society" could be restored.[97]

The overall research directions of the IfS from 1933 to 1938 are traced comprehensively in the aforementioned typed report titled "International Institute of Social Research: A Report on Its History, Aims and Activities 1933–1938". This text was drafted in 1938–1939.[98] Beyond clarifying the objectives of training the ruling classes in line with an organic view of society, as well as defining the sense of a multidisciplinary approach to analyzing complex problems, the issue of fascism would be addressed here as one of the main subjects the IfS would tackle. Fascism would provide the testing ground not only for the need to adopt a multidisciplinary approach to understanding the society of the time and its constituent groups, but also for reflecting on the emblematic nature of the base-superstructure nexus as an inseparable link between mechanisms of economic production and their psycho-social implications. The theoretical analysis emerging from all these components would then translate into practical struggle, in order that "ideas be made in connection with the problem of the causes and the future overthrow of fascism".[99] Both theoretical elaborations and the antifascist militancy of the early critical theory would embrace these aspects.

1.4 The theoretical-philosophical premises

The specificity of the Frankfurt School's critique regarding the historical-political reconstruction of the Nazification process in German society was grounded in theoretical premises developed as early as the second half of the 19th century. The fundamental coordinates upon which these reflections would be articulated are to be found in three classical thinkers: Marx, Freud and Weber. While Marx laid the foundations for a critical understanding of political economy, Freud introduced categories for understanding the psychology of the self within a collective-relational framework. "The Other" thus comes to be positioned in binary terms of friendship or threat, and the charismatic leader would become comparable to the protective father figure in analogy to the psychology of the self. Finally, Weber's thought provided tools for conceptualizing the

97 Ibid., p. 22.

98 IfS, "International Institute of Social Research: A Report on Its History, Aims and Activities 1933–1938", 1939, pp. 1–36. This document expands on the programming of the IfS that continued until 1935 and is outlined in IfS, "International Institute of Social Research: A Short Description of Its History and Aims", 1935, pp. 1–15.

99 IfS, "International Institute of Social Research: A Report on Its History, Aims and Activities 1933–1938", 1939, p. 10.

modern bureaucratic state. The debates within the IfS followed these directions, synthesizing, on the one hand, aspects of social theory and practice and on the other, classical disciplines and new frontiers of knowledge—such as the new studies in psychoanalysis. On the side of political economy critique and state theory, the Frankfurt School aimed to rethink Marxian theory regarding the tendency of the rate of profit to fall in light of the survival of capitalism following the 1929 crisis.

- From Marx, the Frankfurt School inherited both the inspiration for a new method of interdisciplinary and empirical social research and the idea that fascism should be situated within a specific evolutionary phase of capitalist society: that of a crisis due to an excess circulation of commodities, which then led to centralization/planning of production.
- From Freud, they adopted studies on instincts and the destructive nature of drives, which would later inspire Adorno's studies on the authoritarian personality.
- From Weber, Horkheimer critically developed the image of instrumental rationality as a limitation of the technical-industrial society.

According to Weber, Enlightenment culture achieved a disillusionment with the world through the detachment of scientific rationality from mythological narratives. Human beings thus acquired technical tools of domination, leading him to lose that sense of meaningfulness in life present in the pre-modern world. The rationalization of the world was accompanied by the technicalization and bureaucratization of social life. The Protestant Reformation was able to consolidate the link between a new ethic and the spirit of capitalism oriented toward unlimited instrumental accumulation: work as vocation and vocation as work would be synthesized in the term "*Beruf*" (work/vocation).[100] The reformed bourgeois society would bring to completion a new ethos: the attachment "to their work as to a life purpose willed by God".[101] However, for Weber, the issue with modernity was not capitalism itself but rather its distorted form due to a lack of rationalization.[102] In contrast, the Frankfurt School argued that the absence of values in economic action leads to a loss of meaning for the individual. In fact, Weber's own conception of reason could be seen as reductionist, as he viewed it primarily as subjective reason focused on the utilitarian

100 M. Weber, *The Protestant Ethic and the Spirit of Capitalism*, [1904] 2005, p. XXXI.

101 Ibid., p. 120.

102 While recognizing B. Franklin as the figure of the entrepreneurial printer, the most authentic expression of the Western capitalist principle is seen in the idea of profit as a purpose of life rather than as a means to fulfil material needs. Weber argues that the "unlimited greed for gain is not in the least identical with capitalism, and is still less its spirit". In M. Weber, *The Protestant Ethic and the Spirit of Capitalism*, [1904] 2005, p. XXXI. According to Weber, there would thus be the possibility of saving capitalism from the more irrational and aberrant forms it has reached.

calculation of means for the domination of the objective world: namely, nature.[103] As Horkheimer continued to argue until 1952: in "totalitarian systems of all kinds . . . [of] subjective reason . . . serve purposes that are not only inhuman but also mad and absurd".[104] In this case, Enlightenment reason transforms into destruction of individual and personal autonomy. The individual would be cast into a state of existential anonymity, into a social standardization that becomes easy prey for political authoritarianism and manipulation of man, now transformed into a homogenized mass. While Weber had initiated the analysis of the modern bureaucratic state, opening the way to the analysis of processes of reification of workers' consciousness, it would be up to Lukács, Korsch and Hilferding to lay the groundwork for the critique of post-capitalist society and political economy as developed by Pollock and the Frankfurt School.[105]

In *History and Class Consciousness* [1923],[106] Lukács would develop what Marx had anticipated in terms of the inversion of the relationship between men and commodities, expressed in the character of "a thing"[107] in interpersonal relations. The real problem thus becomes that of "fetishism",[108] or the commodification of social relations through the circulation and exchange of products. It is from the reversal between productive subjects and the circulation of commodities that the reification of consciousness takes shape. The task then becomes to reestablish the dialectic between subjectivity and objectivity within a historical process, thus revitalizing the possibility of real transformation. In modern capitalism, indeed, "the reified mind necessarily sees it as the form in which its own authentic immediacy becomes manifest and . . . does not even attempt to transcend it".[109] In *Eclipse of Reason* [1947],[110] Horkheimer would also recognize that the true task of philosophy as critical philosophy would be to recompose the split between the ideal and the real, between the subjective and the objective. In this polarization, the role of dialectical negation would be understood both as the negation of ideology and absolute subjective claims and as the dismantling of persistent claims of reality. The rejection of a definitive integration between "subject and object, word and thing"[111] would allow for the possibility to "salvage relative truths from the wreckage of false ultimates".[112] Horkheimer concludes this passage with an appreciation

103 M. Horkheimer, "Zum Begriff der Vernunft", [1952] 1985, p. 23.
104 Ibid., p. 27.
105 On the influence of Weber, Lukács, Korsch and Hilferding on the reflections of the early Frankfurt School, see H. F. Dahms, "Chapter 1: The Early Frankfurt School Critique of Capitalism: Critical Theory between Pollock's 'State Capitalism' and the Critique of Instrumental Reason", 2011, pp. 3–44.
106 G. Lukács, *History and Class Consciousness*, [1923] 1973.
107 Ibid., p. 83.
108 Ibid., p. 84.
109 Ibid., p. 93.
110 M. Horkheimer, *Eclipse of Reason*, [1947] 2004, p. 124.
111 Ibid.
112 Ibid.

of the critical-emancipatory value of negation as a denunciation of everything that hinders the free realization of man. With a neo-Enlightenment approach, it would be observed how scientific knowledge has now removed the chains of social coercion, thus making possible the "emancipation from fear"[113] and self-criticism of reason as liberating moments of humanity itself.

1.5 Rethinking the structure-superstructure relationship

After an initial phase of interdisciplinary critique of materialism and capitalism, the Frankfurt School scholars extended their account of society to other levels of analysis. Foremost among these was an examination of the masochistic tendencies of the socialized ego-psyche. The 1935 report on the activities of the IfS observed:

> The sado-masochistic character can be found in broad strata of our society, not as a mere sexual perversion or as an internal human quality, as is customarily assumed, but as a psychological structure which has come to dominate certain social strata as a result of the prevailing conditions of existence. Men of this type combine a drive for unconditional submission to a higher power with wild aggressive instincts.
>
> (IfS, *International Institute of Social Research. A Report On Its History, Aims and Activities 1933–1938*, 1939, p. 35).

Since the 1930s, the Frankfurt School held contemporary developments in social psychology in high regard. Consequently, their analysis of fascism fell within a theoretical framework of multidisciplinary analysis.[114] Specifically, their examination of National Socialism would encompass both the analysis of the economic-political structure and the reconstruction of a psycho-ideological superstructure. This latter aspect was not discarded merely as an expression of false consciousness but received renewed programmatic attention concerning the study of the psychological motivations supporting it.[115] The relationship between the world of labor and production (base) on the one hand and the individual (superstructure) on the other could no longer be conceived in standard forms of rationality consistent with Lukács's hope for a proletarian consciousness of production logic. In line with the rethinking of Feuerbachian materialism by the young Marx, the Frankfurt scholars would reconceptualize the relationship between base and superstructure in projective and expressive

113 Ibid., p. 126.

114 For the holistic and disciplinarily complex nature of M. Horkheimer's and H. Marcuse's interpretation of the concept of crisis, see S. Benhabib, *Critique, Norm and Utopia: A Study of the Foundations of Critical Theory*, 1986, p. 155.

115 M. Jay, *Marx and Totalit:. The Adventures of a Concept from Lukács to Habermas*, 1984, p. 204.

terms.[116] This meant recognizing the expansive character of productive forces—and thus the material conditions of historical development—without introducing a causal determinism of structure relative to social organization relations. The latter would be understood as exhibiting an adaptive character in relation to material changes in production conditions, also providing useful elements for the transformation of the productive structure. At the same time, the Frankfurt scholars would incorporate the discoveries of Freudo-Marxism by Fromm and the recognition of intermediate chains of transmissions between ideology and economic base. This would be the task of revisiting Freudian psychoanalysis from a Marxist perspective and the indirect consideration of the transformation between material impulses and the formation of ideas. Changes in the plastic functions of sexual energy and, generally, primary instincts would be seen in relation to the multifaceted aspects of libido sublimation and repression within the social organization of labor. Thus, the first generation of the Frankfurt School synthesized Marxian sociology and Freudian psychoanalysis, placing the latter within analyses of advanced capitalism.[117] The relationship between the world of labor, production and the individual could no longer be conceived according to purely rational parameters. Rather, the rationality of economic interests emerging from the structure would become discontinuous with the rational, instead revealing irrationality, the unconscious and the unreflective—phenomena typical of psychic mechanisms.

Reich, as early as 1933, had noted the need to bridge the gap left by Marx in the transition from the material (the brain's being) to the ideal (the emergence of consciousness), both regarding "how this takes place" and "the retroactive effect of this "consciousness . . . on the economic process",[118] observing how this would help identify "the 'subjective factor'"[119] of history absent in Marxist vision. This would be the task of Reich's synthesis of Marx and Freud in social sex-economy. It would seek to understand why "millions of people affirmed their own subjugation",[120] a fact incomprehensible if understood purely in terms of political and economic calculation. Rethinking the rationalist ego would thus involve recognizing the role of the unconscious in elements not

116 In the *Theses on Feuerbach*, Marx criticized the rigidity of materialism for failing to recognize its dynamism as a form of human practical activity; in the third thesis, he also expressed the bidirectional nature of the formative relationship between humans and their environment: "The materialist doctrine that men are products of circumstances and upbringing, and that, therefore, changed men are products of changed circumstances and changed upbringing, forgets that it is men who change circumstances and that the educator must himself be educated. Hence this doctrine is bound to divide society into two parts, one of which is superior to society". K. Marx, *Theses on Feuerbach* [1945], accessible online at: https://www.marxists.org/archive/marx/works/1845/theses/index.htm.

117 On this matter, A. Allen, *Critique on the Couch: Why Critical Theory Needs Psychoanalysis*, 2020.

118 W. Reich, *The Mass Psychology of Fascism*, [1933] 1980, p. 12.

119 Ibid.

120 Ibid., p. 29.

brought to consciousness by the individual in determining daily life choices and ancestral fears. The Frankfurt scholars would link this to a program of critique of social forms of ego repression, which, in Marcuse's case, would accompany the formulation of regressive and utopian hypotheses of social liberation. It was the same Nietzschean ego resentment that had anticipated the frustrations of Freudian psychic repression, later sublimated into broader artistic forms. It was therefore a matter of understanding whether Freudian prognostications of a non-redeemability of ego discomfort could turn in favour of forms of social progress unencumbered by death impulses. Despite the link between drive stabilization and frustration—within the framework of an anthropological perspective aimed at explaining the transition between the primitive stage and the process of civilization[121]—for Freud, there could be no psychic progress such that it was accompanied by an improvement in the material conditions of civilization. Only the eventual balancing between the pleasure principle and the reality principle seemed to become an achievable goal on the historical plane.[122] Thus, neither the satisfaction of material conditions through labor nor the redistribution of goods alone would be sufficient to guarantee the attainment of social happiness. As reiterated since 1927, coercion to work and drive renunciation had to be seen as the basis of every process of civilization, with psychic dominion having its own laws sensitive to economic-material conditioning.[123] For Freud, in *The Future of an Illusion* [1927], the sublimation of social repressions in artistic production would have been followed by all those forms of collective narcissism aimed at compensating individual renunciations with the sufferings of others, had these peoples been subjected to domination or, we might add with reference to what will happen in National Socialism, ethnic minorities, the disabled and homosexuals.

Freud somehow stopped where Marx had indicated a path to social progress. Indeed, while Freudian psychoanalysis could bring to consciousness the (ideological) illusions of the psyche and thus free it from the irrationalities of the unconscious (but not guarantee happiness in the course of civilization), Marx's socialist revolution was conceived as the result of a reversal of proletarian false consciousness—alienated consciousness—which, in turn, would require the overturning of bourgeois egoistic interests.[124] Freud and Marx shared another important characteristic that would place them at the center of Adorn's re-elaborations: a dynamic view of the human mind and the reality

121 I am referring to the pact that sons and brothers forge for parricide in S. Freud, *Totem and Taboo*, [1913] 2001.

122 Freud addresses this point extensively in two closely related texts: S. Freud, *The Future of an Illusion*, [1927] 1961 and S. Freud, *Civilization and Its Discontents*, [1930] 2002.

123 S. Freud, *The Future of an Illusion*, [1927] 1961.

124 Fromm defines Marxian alienation as a "sickness of man" where experience is no longer that of a subject confronting a world but of a subject living through his products. In E. Fromm, *Beyond the Chains of Illusion: My Encounter with Marx and Freud*, [1962] 2009, p. 38.

of productive forces.[125] Nonetheless, as Fromm would later observe in *Marx and Freud* [1962], psychoanalytic therapy would remain individual and unrepeatable, while Marx's doctrine—so we say—would impose itself collectively and generally. The very possibility of optimizing production mechanisms would be seen by the Frankfurt scholars as dependent on the ability to reorganize social relations of dominance. Some interpreters would argue that Marx's materialistic explanation followed the logic of a teleological rather than causal relationship, and the determination of the productive organization remained functional to the "the efficient use of . . . productive powers".[126] Other interpreters would consider Marx's issue of the structure-superstructure relationship as "the name for a problem, whose solution is always a unique, ad hoc invention",[127] also highlighting the paradoxical nature of any reductionism—under penalty of an unacceptable approach of Marx to the sense of "resentment"[128] in fascist culture.

In general, rethinking the relationship between base and superstructure would involve the possibility of tracing an analytical but not ontological independence between the two levels.[129] This would entail the idea that every variation in the base realm would be accompanied by a (non-homologous!) variation at the superstructural level and vice versa. In short, base and superstructure form an indissoluble knot where the productive organization inevitably correspond to a social division of labour and thus an associated ideology. Central to this is the psyche: that is, the idea of the de-transcendentalized Kantian subject impelled by Freudian drives polarized on a life-death axis (drive theory). In this sense, even at the ideological-superstructural level, the subject-psyche would show a degree of autonomy such that each assumed configuration reflects a redefinition of the structural organization level of labour and production. While Marx had included both the object of consumption and the method in the concept of production, leaning toward the priority of the fundamental base over superstructural forms of consciousness,[130] for Horkheimer, this relationship would be entirely re-examined and redefined in light of new Freudian discoveries about the psyche. A fundamental indication of the interpretation (and integration) of Marx's base-superstructure relationship is the already-cited inaugural address of Horkheimer as the new

125 Ibid., p. 8.
126 In A. Wood, *Karl Marx*, 2004, p. 105.
127 F. Jameson, *Late Marxism. Adorno or the Persistence of the Dialectic*, 1990, p. 46.
128 This perspective is expressed in ibid., p. 47.
129 It seems that when a sceptical interlocutor asked Marcuse how a unified theory combining Marx and Freud could be conceivable, he replied that it was not at all inconceivable but rather appeared fully as a "happy marriage . . . [since it was] two interpretations of two different levels of the same whole, of the same totality". Cited in M. Jay, *'In Psychoanalysis Nothing Is True but the Exaggerations': Freud and the Frankfurt School*, 2020, p. 42.
130 In the preface to *A Contribution to the Critique of Political Economy*, Marx refers to the necessity of addressing the contradictions between the forces and relations of production. In K. Marx, *A Contribution to the Critique of Political Economy*, [1859] 1904.

director of the IfS.[131] Horkheimer refers to the psyche as a new mediating term between the world of labour and production on the one hand and the ideological-cultural plane on the other. It would be a matter of understanding how the psyche, in its relation to history, establishes links of transformation of the economic-institutional reality. As stated in *History and Psychology* [1932], the issue is to separate the psychic factors that:

> enrich the social and individual life process from those relatively static psychic characteristics of individuals, groups, classes, races, and nations that are determined by the overall social structure: in short, from their character.
>
> (M. Horkheimer, "History and Psychology", [1932] 1993, p. 119)

For Horkheimer, it was not a matter of questioning the priority of the economic-material and productive dimension over the definition of an ideological-cultural realm. Indeed, the historically given transformation of nature would equally realize a superstructural articulation of an ideological-cultural type. It is argued that the "The disclosure of psychical mediations . . . may lead not merely to a critique of the conception of the functional relations between the two, but indeed to a strengthening of the suspicion that the sequence may be changed or reversed in the future".[132] Thus, the link between base and superstructure is bi-univocal for Horkheimer, of internal co-implication, where the productive activity of the psyche is accompanied by the metabolic transformation of nature.

Regarding this complex, the dynamics of socialization should be considered. These terms belonged to Marx's philosophical lexicon and, though with variations, had also been used in subsequent Marxist elaborations. Within the concept of base, Marx had included both the totality of productive forces—that is, the capitals deployed for production (means-machines and labour-power)—and the relations of production, or the relations between classes operating during production. Both factors were considered in relation to a specific productive and historical context. If the relations of production could no longer hold the forces of production together—resulting in an internal contradiction—then the possibility of a new economic order would emerge.

Compared to fascism, for Horkheimer, the aspect of the social organization of the structure is implemented in Germany based on economic planning. This transformation of the structure is also reflected at the level of the superstructure in a sort of reciprocal mirroring. The authoritarianism of state

131 M. Horkheimer, "The Present Situation of Social Philosophy and the Tasks of an Institute for Social Research", [1931] 1993.

132 M. Horkheimer, "History and Psychology", [1932] 1993, p. 120.

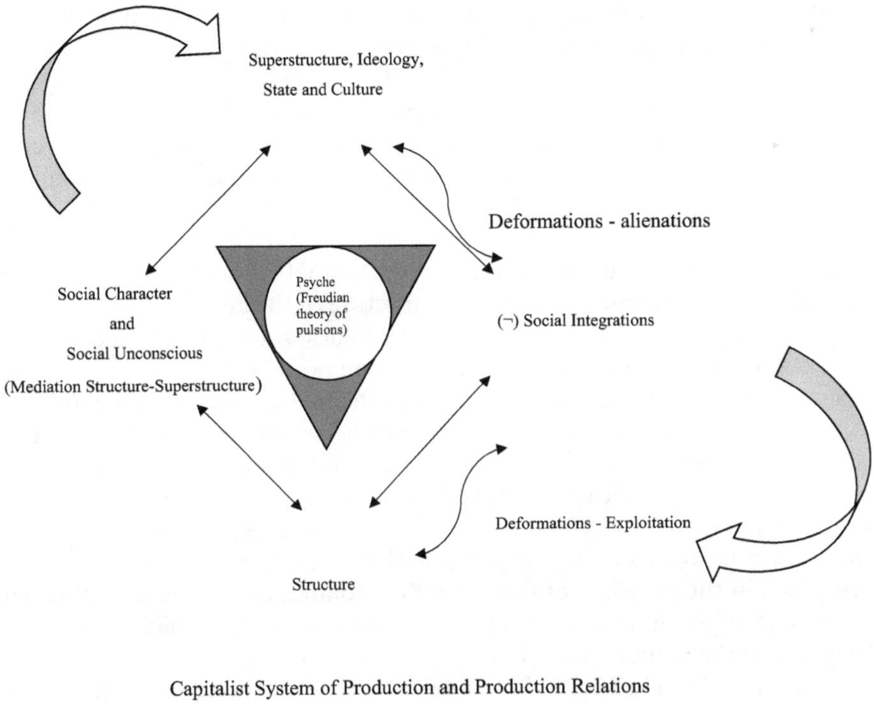

Figure 1.1 Structure-Superstructure Relation

capitalism, the bourgeois family and National Socialism triggers psychic processes of libido compression that, if successful in taming the ego, will also prepare the ground for violent actions. In this way, a narrative is developed that projects distorted psychic affections of a sadomasochistic nature. The correspondence of reality then generates a sense of self-satisfaction aimed at fulfilling self-destructive impulses. In Horkheimer, the overcoming of Kantian dichotomies is part of the completion of the philosophical project of idealism and the dualisms still present in Dilthey. Horkheimer outlines a new vision of sociology as a discipline straddling the knowledge of the psyche and the investigation of materialistic conditions of existence. All this is inscribed within a vision where the realm of thought reflects "the dynamic structure that history produces".[133] Elements of reflection and synthesis between socialist planned economy and state capitalism had interested Pollock since his first visit to

133 A. Schmidt, *Die Kritische Theorie als Geschichtsphilosophie*, 1978, p. 48.

Russia in 1927. In 1926, Benjamin had witnessed the enormous difficulties of Lenin's New Economic Policy (NEP, 1921–1928), noting that

> Of late, under the new "economic regime", these are the only items the state factories produce. The counters are mobbed. Other stores that are empty sell fabric only if paid for in coupons or—in cash—at prices beyond anybody's means.[134]

From a descriptive standpoint, the Frankfurt School scholars were to observe how fascism would come to modify the structure of the liberal bourgeois society, presenting itself as only an apparent ideological solution to the contradiction between forces and relations of production post-1929.

Simultaneously, in Europe, fascism implemented a program of centralization of control over the means of production, accompanied by nationalist and anti-Semitic propaganda. Repressive structure and the ideology of sadomasochistic submission to a leader were to be the two components that operate in complete synergy. The totalitarian state integrated these two elements into a cohesive whole in which the traditional authority of the patriarchal family was formalized in the principle of the *Führer*'s absolute power. The task of social disciplining of the individual, once carried out within the family sphere, was delegated to the authoritarian state.

For Pollock, Horkheimer and all those engaged in a long debate on the transformation of the Weimar liberal state, the concentration of power by the state would lead to the overcoming of a market economy that had become 'total', thus rendering the state itself authoritarian. Gurland, in a precursor of the analysis on the collapse of Weimar democracy and the transition to National Socialism, discussed a thesis on the subject in 1940 titled *The Collapse of German Democracy and the Expansion of National Socialism.*[135] Among the various problematic elements considered, it was observed that the economy inherited by Nazism in 1933 had already presented a distinctly "antagonistic"[136] character. The early manifestations of social intolerance were seen as pathologies of a society whose recrudescence led to the prominence of the totalitarian mentality (a reflection of the state and the economy): that is, to the birth of National Socialism and intolerant extremisms. Pollock's study of economic monopolism and state capitalism breaks the confines of a close link between the world of production and the form of the state. Not only fascism contributed decisively to the productive reorganization, but so too did Bolshevism and the American New Deal democracy.

For the Frankfurt School, the idea of a fully integrated society did not equate to socially realizing a metaphysics of the "whole", as was the case with

134 W. Benjamin, *Moscow Diary*, [1926–7] 1986, p. 28.

135 A. R. L. Gurland, *The Collapse of German Democracy and the Expansion of National Socialism*, PhD Thesis, 1940, *Horkheimer Archiv*, Na 1, 694, pp. 1–47.

136 Ibid., p. 2, online.

Hegel's ethical-social dimension, nor to embracing the idea of the party as class consciousness, as with Lukács. Rather, the "whole" was to be understood, in a Lukácsian sense, as the method of understanding social sciences or as a comprehensive framework of integrated social parts within a single analytical module: the dialectic of totality. These themes had been extensively addressed by Horkheimer during his rethinking of the relationship between traditional and critical philosophy. This epistemological stance completely eliminated the plausibility of any theory of reflection of the structure in the superstructure as maintained by the deterministic Marxism of dialectical materialism (DiaMat) and, more generally, by the Second International.

In *The Authoritarian Personality*,[137] Adorno considers that anti-Semitism was not merely a manifestation of antipathy toward a specific group; rather, it was an expression of a lack of integration between the economic-systemic plan and the subjective plane. In other words, the short-circuits of economic life and its crises would transform into a closure of social realization possibilities and—only then—into feelings of revenge against other groups. In *Soviet Marxism. A Critical Analysis* (1958),[138] Marcuse traces the fundamental distinction between the sphere of direction and organization of the structure by the socialist state on one hand and the irrationality and lack of planning in the capitalist state on the other. The relationship between ideological superstructure and productive structure had dampened the typical form of competitive relationship thanks to the also-superstructural medium of the socialist state. The conscious application of the objective laws of economics by the state thus allowed for a perfect congruence between the two planes—a harmony precluded by the capitalist state.

Regarding the relationship between capitalist production processes and cultural goods, the Frankfurt School scholars integrate Marx's critique of political economy into a critical-materialist approach to ideology and culture.[139] Adorno addressed the issue of the so-called culture industry—i.e., phenomena of mass culture, consumerism, and regression of expressive forms—that would later emerge as authoritarian expressions of knowledge. The function of ideology critique in relation to fascism is precisely clarified by Horkheimer and Adorno in the lecture titled "*Ideologie*", contained in *Soziologische Exkurse* [1956], where they affirm that the task of a critique of totalitarian ideologies will need to investigate the type of appropriate psychological configurations.[140] Totalitarian ideology is seen as operating based on the manipulation of the psyche, aimed at achieving results not transparent to the consciousness of citizens but useful to power. In this, the fascist propaganda of American preachers discussed by Adorno continues with the perlocutionary use of language. In the

137 See T. W. Adorno, E. Frenkel-Brunswik, D. J. Levinson, R. Nevitt Sanford, *The Authoritarian Personality*, [1950] 2019.

138 H. Marcuse, *Soviet Marxism. A Critical Analysis*, 1958, p. 195 ff.

139 On this point, see H. Dubiel, *Kritische Theorie der Gesellschaft*, 1988, p. 27 ff.

140 M. Horkheimer, T. W. Adorno and Institut für Sozialforschung (eds.), "Ideologie", in *Soziologische Exkurse*, [1956] 2013, p. 162 ff.

mass society of the culture industry, an identifiable relationship (unlike what happened in National Socialism) between ideological-superstructural and productive-structural planes is realized. The ideological immanence of mass culture will come to identify with the consumeristic productive process. In this way, the being and the ought-to-be of man coincide in a form of apology for the existent, where critical thought will no longer find a place.

For the Frankfurt School scholars, the reinterpretation of the relationship between base and superstructure will only occur through a renewal of the dialectic: a new economic-productive structure should be considered as in a dialectical-negative relationship—that is, in contradiction—with a pre-existing ideological superstructure. The realm of interstructural psychic dependencies, such as sadism and masochism, are seen as targets for structural modifications that provide a favourable ground for the genesis of apologetic ideologies. This dynamic of authoritarianism does not, however, foresee that the contradiction between base and superstructure will be resolved in favour of the productive base. The recovery of critical thinking by the Frankfurt School aims precisely to emphasize how the psychic level can draw on its own resources, resisting attempts at authoritarian manipulation of psycho-cognitive prerogatives.

1.6 Psyche, family and society

According to Negt's vivid expression, critical theory is "that form of Marxism that has experienced fascism as its decisive experiential content, or rather, that highly civilized fall into barbarism".[141] However, scholars disagree on both the scientific weight and the systematic nature of the interests that National Socialism occupied in the research of the IfS. Jay, in his important work on the early developments of critical theory, argued that although the IfS aimed to counter the fascist threat as early as the 1930s, Horkheimer merely identified its ideological character passively, underestimating its dynamic-destructive aspects.[142]

In addressing this assessment, it is necessary first to acknowledge that the IfS's interests were almost exclusively focused on the study of National Socialism, as no article on Italian Fascism appeared in the group's official journal—the *ZfS*—but only sporadic references (even though the term "fascism" had been widely used since 1923). A minor exception though was the collection of studies titled *Studien über Autorität und Familie* [*Authority and the Family*] [1936],[143] where Horkheimer tasked the sociologist Luini with presenting the

141 Cited in M. Wilson, *Das Institut für Sozialforschung und seine Faschismusanalysen*, 1982, p. 9, and also in S. Breuer, *Kritische Theorie*, 2016, p. 129; S. Breuer, "The Truth of Modern Society? Critical Theory and Fascism", 2017, pp. 75–103.

142 See, M. Jay, *The Dialectical Imagination: A History of the Frankfurt School and the Institute of Social Research, 1923–1950*, 1973, Ch. 5, pp. 143–172.

143 M. Horkheimer, E. Fromm, H. Marcuse (eds.), *Studien über Autorität und Familie, Forschungsberichte aus dem Institut für Sozialforschung*, [1936] 1963.

condition of the Italian family before and during fascism.[144] As suggested, the IfS's analyses of fascism were part of an overall research program on society from the outset. Furthermore, instead of the hypothesis of two separate periods contrasting the absence versus the development of fascism critique research, the thesis here defended is that the Frankfurt School incrementally developed an interest in fascism starting from the late 1920s.[145] It is also important to note that as early as 1929, with Fromm's study on the emergence of authoritarian character traits in German workers, the Frankfurt scholars began reflecting on the meaning of the end of Weimar and the consequent rise of National Socialism, urging critical theory scholars to develop empirical social science studies.[146] Following these thematic beginnings, Horkheimer would pursue a true programmatic commitment through the 1931 IfS inaugural speech, also initiating a study on the regression of society, starting from the authoritarian involutions of the family culminating into *Studien über Autorität und Familie* [1936].[147]

In response to these theoretical research needs, Marcuse wrote an essay in 1934 titled "The Struggle against Liberalism in the Totalitarian View of the State,[148] drafted in response to Hitler's 1932 speech at the meeting organized by Thyssen with Düsseldorf industrialists.[149] The research of these authors contributed to placing the study of fascism on consistent temporal tracks: one focusing on the analysis of the economic-structural framework and the other on the study of psycho-superstructural dimensions. Marcuse referred to National Socialism in terms of a "heroic-folkish" vision,[150] recognizing that liberalism had a sort of congenital authoritarian outcome due to the contradictions of capital. Authoritarianism was framed as an element inscribed in liberalism, defining the very structure of capitalism. As a totalizing system of organizing social and power relations: "The idea of the charismatic, authoritarian leader is already preformed in the liberalist celebration of the gifted economic leader, the 'born' executive".[151] The technical rationality of industry and bureaucracy was teleologically directed toward continuous productive and organizational efficiency, initially achieving a monopolistic destiny and later, in National

144 A. Luini, "Autorität und Familie in der italienischen Soziologie", [1936] 1963, pp. 808–823.

145 On the issue of authoritarianism in the '30, see C. Galli, "Strategie della totalità, Stato autoritario, Stato totale, totalitarismo, nella Germania degli anni Trenta", 1997, pp. 27–62.

146 E. Fromm, *The Working Class in Weimar Germany: A Psychological and Sociological Study*, [1929] 1980. On Fromm's merit for *an ante litteram* empirical turn, see J. Brunner, "Looking in the Hearts of the Workers, or How Eric Fromm Turned Critical Theory into Empirical Research", 1994, pp. 632–654.

147 M. Horkheimer, "Allgemeiner Teil", [1936] 1963, pp. 3–76.

148 H. Marcuse, "The Struggle against Liberalism in the Totalitarian View of the State", [1934] 1968.

149 A. Hitler, *Vortrag Adolf Hitlers vor westdeutschen Wirtschaftlernim Industrie-Klubzu Düsseldorf am 27 Januar 1932*, 1932.

150 H. Marcuse, "The Struggle against Liberalism in the Totalitarian View of the State", [1934] 1968, pp. 3–42.

151 Ibid., p. 18.

Socialism, a totalitarian consolidation of capitalist production relations. According to Marcuse, this process resulted in an organic-natural synthesis of class articulations in society already theorized by Othmar Spann under the idea of "organic universalism". Characteristics of this social form were expressed in the synthesis of naturalism and irrationalism, which, in turn, led to a mythologization of nature and an organicist view of the people in an ethnic (*völkisch*) sense. Nature and history came to coincide. The authority of the state and the pyramidal economic organization were accompanied by social and intellectual levelling, as well as a naturalization of man and his relations.

In 1936, Fromm further explored the issue of authority and its effects on the ego in the important essay "*Der autoritär-masoschistische Charakter*" ["The Authoritarian-Masochistic Character"].[152] Here, the relationship between pulsional repression and authority (superego) in the mediation of the authoritarian character is openly addressed. A fundamental distinction is drawn between monopolistic capitalism and totalitarian society/authoritarian character on one hand and democratic society/reciprocity of interest satisfaction on the other. While acknowledging that "authoritarian relations"[153] also exist in democratic society, Fromm highlights the drive toward the rationalization of relations in solidarity forms. This is supplemented by the aforementioned collection of essays edited by Horkheimer, *Autorität und Familie* [1936],[154] including, under a pseudonym, Kirchheimer's publications during his exile at the Paris branch of the IfS. Finally, in the same year, Horkheimer addresses central issues for understanding fascism in "Egoism and Freedom Movements: On the Anthropology of the Bourgeois Era" [1936].[155]

Here, based on the critique of the notion of egoism in its dual role of social construction and destruction, two anthropological-interpretive tendencies are reconstructed, thus defining the political horizon, expressing a repressive view and an educational view of human natural instincts: "[I]n the totalitarian states of the present", Horkheimer wrote, "all intellectual life is understood solely from the viewpoint of manipulating the masses",[156] while the potential for moral progress remains constantly under repressive power. It is the historical conditions that make egoism more or less good, not its nature in itself. It is no coincidence that by early 1936, Horkheimer had organized a Marx seminar for the IfS aimed at rethinking the historical reproduction of society and, ultimately, the monopolistic transformations of capitalism. In 1937, a seminar on monopoly capitalism (*Monopolkapitalismus*),[157] a precursor model of state capitalism, followed. Horkheimer's thesis was that the concentration of state power would end up subordinating the Marxian propulsive

152 H. Fromm, "Der autoritär-masochistische Charakter", [1936] 1987.

153 Ibid., p. 120.

154 M. Horkheimer, "Allgemeiner Teil", in M. Horkheimer (ed.), [1936] 1963, pp. 3–76.

155 M. Horkheimer, "Egoism and Freedom Movements: On the Anthropology of the Bourgeois Era", in M. Horkheimer (ed.), [1936] 1993, pp. 49–110.

156 Ibid., p. 55.

157 H. Grossmann, J. Gumperz, M. Horkheimer, K. A. Wittfogel, *Diskussionen aus einem Seminar über Monopolkapitalismus*, 1985, p. 429.

force of capitalist production, reorienting political economy critique to an internal critique of power. In the same year, Neumann published the work "*Der Funktionswandel des Gesetzes im Recht der bürgerlichen Gesellschaft*" ["The Changing Function of the Right in the Law of Civil Society"] [1937].[158] Here, it was demonstrated how fascism reintroduced a relationship of inequality among society members from a seemingly equal legal-institutional facade, eventually protecting a form of illiberal decisiveness—effectively the death of law in its function as a guarantor of symmetrically universal prerogatives for its participants. The isonomy between rulers and the ruled as equal subjects in a legal system is what Neumann recognized as the fundamental merit of modern natural law since Rousseau. Here, critical-normative elements are linked to a legal-naturalistic dimension. The positive freedom/democratic exercise of the power binomial, which justified Neumann's thesis that there should not be an inherently insurmountable opposition between law and sovereignty (i.e., between *ratio* and *voluntas*) had short-circuited first with the Weimar crisis and then with National Socialism. In this latter phase, only the leader's will would ascend to the status of law.

An official position from the IfS emerged in 1938 during both the presentation of the report on IfS, *International Institute of Social Research: A Report on Its History, Aims and Activities 1933–1938* [1939], and in essays in which Horkheimer used expressions such as "authoritarian order"[159] and "theory of fascism",[160] respectively.

As already mentioned, this text was never written. Instead, a wide range of studies appeared that—together—provided a detailed theoretical understanding of fascism and its various historical ramifications. The IfS indeed considered the following three disciplinary areas as useful levels for the theoretical understanding of fascism:

1 The socio-psychological component
2 The ideological-critical component of culture
3 The political-economic component[161]

In line with these indications, in the article "*Die Juden und Europa*", published in the *ZfS* in 1939, Horkheimer reorganized the research themes, stating:

> Whoever wants to explain anti-Semitism must speak of National Socialism. Without a conception of what has happened in Germany, speaking about anti-Semitism in Siam or Africa remains senseless. The new

158 F. Neumann, "Der Funktionswandel des Gesetzes im Recht der bürgerlichen Gesellschaft", 1937, pp. 542–596.

159 Respectively, M. Horkheimer, "Montaigne and the Function of Skepticism", [1938] 1993, p. 292; M. Horkheimer, "Die Philosophie der absoluten Konzentration", 1938, p. 384.

160 IfS, *International Institute of Social Research. A Report on Its History, Aims and Activities 1933–1938*, [1939]. *Horkheimer Archiv*, p. 36.

161 See H. Dubiel, A. Söllner (eds.), *Wirtschaft, Recht und Staat im Nationalsozialismus: Analysen des instituts für Sozialforschung 1939–1942*, 1981, p. 9.

anti-Semitism is the emissary of the totalitarian order, which has developed from the liberal one. One must thus go back to consider the tendencies within capitalism.

(M. Horkheimer, "The Jews and Europe" [1939], online).

Subsequently, in 1941, Pollock's already-mentioned work on state capitalism inaugurated the IfS's discussion on new forms of capitalism—a controversial and highly debated idea of centralized market organization. Pollock's state capitalism is configured as an inclusive category of the diverse political doctrines circulating at the time.[162] Horkheimer addresses the transformations of capitalism in three writings produced between 1939 and 1943[163] which anticipate and later recover Pollock's ideal type of state capitalism from 1941.[164] The transformations of the state and the underlying economic organization represented for Horkheimer historical moments inherent to the transformation of the liberal state. In the Frankfurt debate, these ultimately oppose both the ahistorical modelling of Pollock's state capitalism and the Neumannian reductionism of the non-state as presented in *Behemoth* [1942].[165] Horkheimer's alternation of state forms concerns the transition from monopolist state to state capitalism authoritarianism and, finally, to the fragmentation of state centralization and economic planning in the theory of rackets. In this latter case, the state assumes only a formal appearance, while the production and control of surplus value descends into a struggle among competing groups. Horkheimer emphasizes the continuity between the liberal state and fascism, asserting that the latter merely revealed what was already implicit in the former: namely, the illusory nature of the social contract as a political agreement among free and equal individuals.[166]

In 1941, Adorno followed up Horkheimer's program with a specific research proposal on anti-Semitism.[167] Adorno provides broad guidelines for analyzing the anti-Jewish resentment, whose origins had already manifested in the Enlightenment and German idealism.[168] The goal of this announced program is to directly address the fight against National Socialism, whose stubborn success was due, among other things, to the intellectuals'

162 F. Pollock, "State Capitalism: Its Possibilities and Limitations", 1941, pp. 200–225.

163 I am referring to the following triad of writings: M. Horkheimer, *Die Juden und Europa*, 1939; M. Horkheimer, *The Authoritarian State*, 1942; and the series of typescripts that partially flowed indirectly into M. Horkheimer, T. W. Adorno, *Dialectic of Enlightenment* [1947] and directly into M. Horkheimer, *Eclipse of Reason* [1947], as well as into M. Horkheimer, *On the Sociology of Class Relations*, [1943], *Horkheimer Archiv*.

164 F. Pollock, "State Capitalism: Its Possibilities and Limitations", 1941, pp. 200–225.

165 F. Neumann, *Behemoth. The Structure and Practice of National Socialism 1933–1944*, [1942] 2009.

166 M. Horkheimer, "On the Sociology of Class Relations", [1943], *Horkheimer Archiv*.

167 M. Horkheimer, T. W. Adorno, "Research Project on Anti-Semitism", 1941, pp. 124–143.

168 Ibid., p. 124 ff., in part. p. 131 ff.

failure to understand "its psychological, individual and social roots".[169] While Horkheimer's thought in the 1930s remained aligned with some central aspects of the Hegelian-Marxist tradition, using the idea of totality of society to counter positivism's epistemological claims, it is from *Dialectic of Enlightenment* [1947] that the notions of "totality" and "administered society" become coextensive terms.[170] In this work, Horkheimer and Adorno also use the expression "totalitarian capitalism", highlighting its thirst for "domination" and the inevitable outcome of "the extermination of humanity".[171] Much later, in a 1969 essay, Horkheimer states:

> The path of society that we finally began to see, and as we judge it today, is entirely different. We have come to believe that society will transform into a *totally administered world.*
>
> (M. Horkheimer, "Kritische Theorie gestern und heute", [1969] 1970. p. 340, emphasis added).

The oppressive and unidimensional character of the totally bureaucratized society reflects the conceptual shift from society as a whole to society as a bureaucratic-authoritarian totality—the latter being the premise of totalitarianism. The masses' thirst for totalitarianism had already been satisfied by the Great War[172] and the totalitarian regimes (Stalinist and fascist), which presented themselves as its ideological and political legacy. Thus, from their ashes, the silhouette of mass consumer society emerged. This, in turn, became the object of a totalitarian interest of power which, after 1945, took the form of a technological and consumeristic society embedded in liberal democracies.

Before these forms, although totalitarianism had been discussed in reference to fascism as a movement, it was the crystallization operated by the "fascist-regime"[173] in the process of recognizing the single party and the elites loyal to power that was totalitarian. The total state, defined by race and the subordination of the individual, constituted the salient feature of both Italian Fascism and German National Socialism, despite the specific and irreducible characteristics of each phenomenon. Totalitarianism and autocracy (in which the leader answers only to himself) proceeded in tandem, as "Totalitarian dictatorship, in a sense, is the adaptation of autocracy to twentieth-century

169 Ibid., p. 135.

170 For an analysis of the Frankfurt School's overcoming of the Marxian "totalizing" perspective in the study of society, see M. Jay, *Marxism and Totality: The Adventures of a Concept from Lukács to Habermas*, 1984, particularly pp. 196–276.

171 M. Horkheimer, T. W. Adorno, *Dialectic of Enlightenment*, [1947] 2002, p. 43.

172 On this matter, see E. Traverso, *Il totalitarismo: Storia di un dibattito*, 2002, in particular, p. 7 ff.

173 Ibid., p. 26.

industrial society".[174] This explained the critical theory's interest in issues regarding the reification of the world of social relations and consciousness and the relationship of German totalitarianism to the churches.[175] These would lead to discriminatory outcomes, as well as to the entrapment of work organization within a framework of given and insuperable pyramidal structures. Thus, the critique of society would take the form of a critique of the irrationality of work organization and the unlimited production of capitalist society. The rationalization of the latter would then be accompanied by the necessity of implementing a socialist transformation of the economy and labour.

1.7 Fascism and technology

The technological transformations of fascist society were significant, involving a shift from the individual rationality of pre-Weimar bourgeois liberalism toward a systemic standardization aimed at maximum productive efficiency. This transformation sought to clarify the dynamics of what appeared to be a managerial-type social revolution.[176] The fusion of technology and power, as well as the transformation of the capitalist's role into that of a *rentier*, legitimized the interest in the new managerial figures who had assumed control, albeit passively, over the fate of capital. This debate actually revisited an earlier theme originating in the 1920s and 1930s, developing around the figure of Fried (the pseudonym of F. F. Zimmermann) and his journal *Die Tat*. The journal had represented a form of national socialism based on the erroneous hypothesis of a continuity between autarky policies and the expropriation of the means of production.[177] For these intellectuals, it was also a matter of recognizing the radical subversion of the control relationship between the economy and politics: the end of free competition had meant a supremacy of political power over market laws.[178] This led to a progressive affirmation of totalitarianism.

Horkheimer, as early as 1936, had pointed out that "the bourgeois revolution did not lead the masses to the lasting state of joyful existence and universal equality they longed for, but to the hard reality of an individualistic social order instead".[179] It was from these premises that bourgeois figures with leadership qualities were able to assume the roles of charismatic lead-

174 C. F. Brzezinski, Z. K. Brzezinski, *Totalitarian Dictatorship and Autocracy*, 1965, p. 15.

175 P. Tillich, *The Totalitarian State and the Claims of the Church*, 1934, pp. 405–433.

176 J. Buhrnam, *Managerial Revolution: What Is Happening in the World?* 1941.

177 See C. Campani, *Pianificazione e teoria critica. L'opera di Friedrich Pollock dal 1923 al 1943*, 1992, pp. 181–182. Regarding the presence and media influence of other publications such as *Die Standarde*, which had a total of 110,000 readers among veterans, see J. Herf, *Reactionary Modernism: Technology, Culture, and Politics in Weimar and the Third Reich*, 1985, p. 25.

178 For a deeper exploration of the topic, see G. Marramao, "Ripensando gli anni Trenta", 1979, pp. 13–36.

179 M. Horkheimer, "Egoism and Freedom Movements", [1936] 1993, p. 62.

ers, thus becoming central references in fascist society. The idea that fascism had completed a long process of disintegration of the state, society and even the individual was something Marcuse conceptualized in his essay "Some Social Implications of Modern Technology" [1941].[180] In this work, he argued that National Socialism aimed to both lead the economy to a level of maximum rationalization and automation and direct this process toward forms of "totalitarian oppression".[181] For Marcuse, fascism had bent technology, production, transportation and communication apparatuses to its ideological purposes, proposing a specific technological model: that is, a distinct process of organizing social relations, dominance and control over its members. Technology had become a "partial factor"[182] of technology itself. The Marcusian man of technological rationality had become an interpreter of a radical upheaval in forms of individual and social thought organization, motivational mechanisms and expressive forms. Objectification of the self and alienation were the twin elements accompanying the progressive rise of instrumental rationality in technological society. These analyses contrasted with the fundamental issue that would inform the subsequent debate between Pollock and Neumann on the choice between state capitalism and monopoly capitalism. Gurland, in his essay "Technological Trends and Economic Structure under National Socialism" [1941],[183] also took a position on the subject. The newly appointed member of the IfS defended the thesis that technological innovations, while achieving a fusion aimed at rearmament between Nazi administrative apparatuses and economic monopoly elites, did not overturn the capitalist structure of the economy. In other words, profit had not been state controlled, and thus, large monopolies remained in control of production and the circulation of goods. If the saying "those who control the means of production are the actual capitalists" is true, National Socialism, by centralizing power, had effectively reduced the number of capitalists, excluding those subjects "who have no say in the management".[184] Thus, Gurland could rightly assert that "these very technological changes were fitted to the economic base so as to meet the profit requirements of monopolistic combines".[185] Therefore, the fundamental dynamic of capitalism, which required a continuous reinvestment of surplus value, remained unchanged. The change in the social use of rationality thus resulted in a subject characterized by aggressive impulses of "brute self-preservation".[186] The aggregation of individuals into a crowd had certainly led to some form of unity, albeit only constructed in terms of "atomic subjects

180 H. Marcuse, "Some Social Implications of Modern Technology", [1941] 1998.
181 Ibid., p. 41.
182 Ibid.
183 A. R. L. Gurland, "Technological Trends and Economic Structure under National Socialism", 1941, pp. 226–263.
184 Ibid., p. 261.
185 Ibid., p. 228.
186 H. Marcuse, "Some Social Implications of Modern Technology", p. 52.

of self-preservation".[187] Technological rationalization and the massification of society proceeded in parallel, transforming the self-liberating impulses of individuals into mechanisms of self-preservation for repressive power apparatuses. For Marcuse, this was evident in the hierarchical organization of enterprises as an expression of mature technological rationality, whose origins could be traced back to the Industrial Revolution. While individual action had been essential to achieving self-assigned goals in a free-market regime, with the rise of large-scale industry, individuality itself had become superfluous.[188] Thus, mass culture had eliminated not only the economic subjectivism of private initiative but also traditional forms of production such as art, philosophy and, more generally, knowledge.

Within capitalist societies, a sort of pact was forged between the advanced form of mass technological society (characterized by internal oppressive pressures) and the verticalized authoritarian political control with the *Führer* at its apex. The ideology of science and technology fused with that of National Socialism: that is, with the image of German supremacy over other people and territories. The synthesis of these two levels, the technical-material and the political-ideological, led to the generation of a form of social conformity in which individuality, dissent and divergent thinking were eliminated in favour of large-scale mechanized levelling, which, in turn, led everything to a totalizing vision of the party, the group and the race. While professing the idea that there was no freedom outside society, fascist society was erected on the principle of suppressing social freedom. This seems to be the paradox inherent in the repressive and disciplinary nature of National Socialism and fascism more generally. What was even more interesting to understand was that this hyper-rationalization of the role of the individual in society ended up flipping into its opposite: the irrationalism of totalitarian domination. Indeed, the oppressive rationalization process of society transformed people into mere appendages—tools—of high industrial operation, as well as agents serving security (Gestapo), in the objectifications and mechanisms of the social machine. The technical structure of fascist society thus proved functional to its own technological redefinition.

This transformation became even more apparent in light of the consideration of a new Germanic mentality that Marcuse discussed in a typescript that remained unpublished for a long time: *The New German Mentality*, a text probably drafted in 1942 in California during the preparation of the study "State and Individual under National Socialism".[189] Here, Marcuse emphasized that National Socialism had replaced the old values and ideals of German

187 Ibid.

188 Ibid., p. 63.

189 H. Marcuse, "The New German Mentality", [1942] 1998; H. Marcuse, "State and Individual under National Socialism", [1942] 1998, pp. 67–93.

culture by proposing a new linguistic and conceptual apparatus aimed at embracing two fundamental spheres:

- A pragmatic layer oriented toward facts, efficiency and mechanization
- A mythological layer that introduced elements of spiritual paganism, racism and social Darwinism

Marcuse argued that National Socialism had annulled the metaphysical perspective of Western thought by achieving its dissolution through totalitarian technological rationality.[190] It had also instilled the idea of life as competition directed toward "efficient use of his means".[191] Nationalism had thus inscribed spiritual relations in an economic framework, in what Marcuse considered a process of naturalizing the economy. The new German mentality was thus seen as the result of a process of 'totalitarian rationalization' of society that had set aside any moral scruples. Since this mentality identified with a form of social organization exceeding the historical configuration of fascism itself, it would not be exhausted by National Socialism, being destined to survive it. Even more curious was the fact that Nazism was able to combine technological rationality with the irrational language of propaganda and imperialist aggression. For Marcuse, these two elements had proceeded together, with one being functional to the other; indeed, the mythological language of National Socialist propaganda would take the form of technical rationality.

The insistence of National Socialism on the importance of facts over ideas and interpretations had transformed the former into uninterpretable data and the latter into suspect ideologies. For this reason, Marcuse argued, defeating Nazism would not be enough to implement antifascist propaganda centred on well-constructed counter-arguments. The appeal to universal human rights would not resonate with the "fascistized" individual. National Socialism needed to be stopped with direct intervention: that is, through an incontrovertible military defeat and the subsequent dismantling of its political organization. Nazi bureaucrats could only be removed through a complete replacement. Thus, the response to Nazi propaganda had to consider three elements that Marcuse identified as a) the language of facts, b) the language of memory, and c) and the language of re-education. The language of facts has been already discussed.

The language of memory, instead, was an attempt to dismantle such cognitive dependence on factual evidence by invoking the memory of events. Finally, the language of re-education presented itself as the third pillar of a profound and hopefully enduring process of renewing German society in the wake of the military defeat of National Socialism. These countermeasures aimed at realizing a new possible post-fascist society were contrasted by Marcuse's work on

190 Ibid., p. 153.
191 Ibid., p. 158.

the "33 Theses", which remained unpublished until a few years ago.[192] In this work, various themes that would later appear in the book *One-Dimensional Man* were anticipated.[193] Marcuse expressed a kind of scepticism about identifying concrete forces capable of bringing about truly emancipatory social change. The end of Hitler's National Socialism would not by itself guarantee the advent of an era of social progress and advancement of individual freedoms. On the contrary, Marcuse saw two other forms of totalitarianism vying for power in the vacuum left by fascism: Soviet Marxism with its aberrations and the post-fascist capitalist society, both American and European (Thesis 1).[194] Marcuse would also outline aspects that still seem to characterize the East-West political confrontation today: both political models that emerged victorious from the Second World War would not only postpone the possibility of engaging in a mutual armed conflict in the near future but also share a deep hostility toward socialist forms of development and, more generally, toward revolutionary forms of power renewal (Thesis 2).[195] Any attempt to achieve a transformation in this direction would produce the opposite and particularly acute effect of increased and centralized control powers in the Soviet regime.

In a certain sense, the same sense of tragedy that persisted even after the end of Nazism would be the subject of reflection for Adorno. In his 1942 essay "Reflections on Class Theory" (which had not yet been published at that time), he reflects on the transformation from a class society to a consumer society and the disappearance of internal social articulations. It is thus argued that "By abolishing the classes in this way, class ruse comes into its own".[196] He then specifies that the last phase of capitalism is indeed that of a monopoly from an economic-structural perspective, but also that of the transformation of classes into gangs from the perspective of the social organizational superstructure. Adorno concludes by stating that "in the image of the manifest act of usurpation that is practiced nowadays by the leaders of capital and labor acting in consort, it is the history of gang wars and rackets".[197] If the National Socialism of the SA or SS, as well as the party and other related organs, were a clear testimony of this, the strengthened powers of savage capitalism and cynical communism would represent some of the most inhumane features of modern times.

1.8 Fascism after National Socialism

Horkheimer's critique of Weber's instrumental reason focused on the notion that "When the idea of reason was conceived, it was intended to achieve more

192 H. Marcuse, "33 Theses", [1947] 1998, pp. 215–228.
193 H. Marcuse, *One-Dimensional Man*, [1964] 2002.
194 H. Marcuse, "33 Theses", [1947] 1998, p. 217. Marcuse would address Soviet Marxism much later in H. Marcuse, *Soviet Marxism: A Critical Analysis*, [1958] 1969.
195 Ibid.
196 T. W. Adorno, "Reflections on Class Theory", [1942] 2003, p. 100.
197 Ibid.

than the mere regulation of the relation between means and ends: it was regarded as the instrument for understanding the ends, *for determining them*".[198] The subjectivism of the purposes of reason, the formalism of thought—these are the limits of modernity and its inability to grasp the immanent objective structures of reality. Within this framework is the exaltation of individualistic egoism characteristic of liberalism, which, according to Horkheimer, in progressively distancing itself from the conditions of advanced industrial societies, failed to find any anchor of salvation ("no effective rational principle of social cohesion remains"),[199] except in the exaltation of the "idea of national community (*Volksgemeinschaft*)"[200] initially and, later, in its demand for respect "by terror".[201] According to Horkheimer, this dynamic accounted for a "tendency of liberalism to tilt over into fascism".[202] However, the fluidity of the transition from liberalism to fascism was not limited to the past. It also pertained to the perspective of the congenital infiltration of fascist elements into liberal democratic systems. Therefore, both Adorno and Horkheimer in the 1960s and 1970s were concerned with highlighting the element of violent and barbaric dysfunctionality in the management crises of modern industrial societies. For these scholars, fascism would not simply present itself as the dysfunctional alter ego of a fully administered society[203] or, more limitedly, of a totally administered society,[204] something "devoid of morality and spirituality".[205] Rather, fascism would represent the violent extremization of such a society, remaining to this day a dangerous legacy of the past operating from within contemporary democracy.[206]

The capitalist organization of society in practice will manifest through historically differentiated declinations, yet always adhering to a totalizing demand of subjective, individual and collective relations. The pervasiveness of the

198 M. Horkheimer, *Eclipse of Reason*, [1947] 2004, p. 7.
199 Ibid., p. 14.
200 Ibid.
201 Ibid.
202 Ibid. The most articulate explanation of this passage is offered by Horkheimer in his discussion of the decline of individualism: "Thus the individual subject of reason tends to become a shrunken ego, captive of an evanescent present, forgetting the use of the intellectual functions by which he was once able to transcend his actual position in reality. These functions are now taken over by the great economic and social forces of the era. The future of the individual depends less and less upon his own prudence and more and more upon the national and international struggles among the colossi of power. Individuality loses its economic basis". Ibid., p. 95.
203 M. Horkheimer, "Kritische Theorie Gestern und Heute", [1969] 1970, p. 340. Horkheimer gave this speech at the Cini Foundation in Venice on September 19–20, 1969.
204 On the definition of "society" or "administered world" as a filiation from Pollock's idea of "state capitalism", see H.-E. Schiller, "The Administered World", 2018, p. 834.
205 M. Horkheimer, "Es geht um die Moral der Deutschen", [1973], p. 483.
206 "I believe that the survival of National Socialism within democracy is potentially more dangerous than fascist tendencies against democracy". In T. W. Adorno, *Was bedeutet: Aufarbeitung der Vergangenheit* [1959], online.

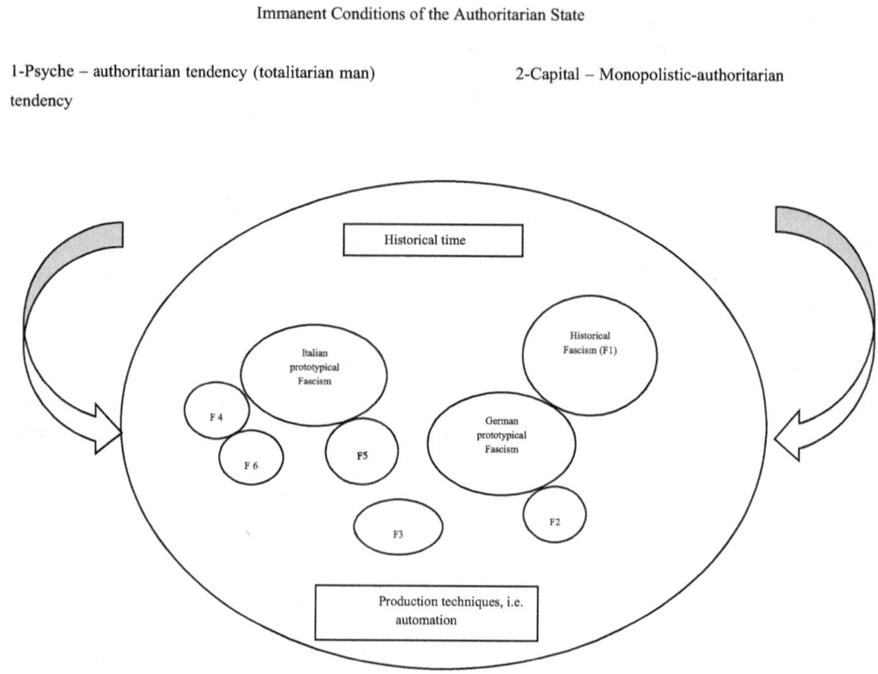

Figure 1.2 Critical Theory: Philosophical-Historiographical Thesis on Fascism

capitalist organization of society will be accompanied by the fascist authoritarianism's claim to total control. For Adorno, capitalism totalized precisely those subjective social relations ensnared in the grip of a society administered by the rules of capital. It will be the detachment from this world of inverted relations that will liberate the progressive and emancipatory force of a new society.[207] As Adorno, with an anti-Hegelian tone, would say: since "the whole is false",[208] presenting itself in a contradictory and irrational manner, there will necessarily follow a critique of instrumental reason and its loss of autonomy: that is, its inability to legislate for itself in the free organization of social life. Given that the reason supporting such reified relations is instrumental, it has transformed its own means into ends. Bureaucracy has thus become its ultimate goal. In this way, it has consummated the condemnation to a heteronomous destiny:

207 On the concept of totality in critical theory and its illustrious antecedents in idealism and Marxism, see L. Heitmann, J. Blumenfeld, "Society as 'Totality': On the Negative-Dialectical Presentation of Capitalist Socialization", vol. 3, 2018, pp. 589–606. For the examination and contemporary relevance of the Adornian concept of a totally administered society, see M. Cooke, "Totalitarianism and the Welfare State", 1998, pp. 16–26.

208 T. W. Adorno, "Diskussionsbeitrag zu 'Spätkapitalismus oder Industriegesellschaft?'", 1968, p. 586.

that is, to an alienating condition of control over the social nature of human beings. But herein lies the paradox: in the attempt to subjugate nature, reason has made the individual its "tool of repression".[209] In this sense, fascism has presented itself as the pseudo-ideological guise of the paradoxical nature of instrumental reason, whose crisis has distant origins. Fascism has extremized the demands of liberalism by reducing "human beings to social atoms".[210] During the 1940s, within the Frankfurt School circle, the idea was already clear that industrial capitalism had given way to a new form of managerial capitalism. For Burnham, an intellectual outside the Frankfurt School but author of one of the most influential texts of the time—*The Managerial Revolution* [1941][211]—it was about understanding a period of epochal revolutions where the Second World War had highlighted a convergence of technological transformations and interests that went far beyond Germany's power ideal.

The upcoming chapters will address the philosophical-theoretical implications of the overall position advanced by the Frankfurt School regarding the critique of National Socialism. As introduced, the philosophical-historiographical peculiarity of the ex post reconstruction of the early Frankfurt School's perspective was its interpretation of fascism as a category built on historically defined theoretical-immanent assumptions, characterized by specific forms of capitalist production and a specific psychic trait—the propensity for authoritarianism—rejecting both extremes of an "eternal" and meta-historical view of fascism, as well as the idea of it being a historically unique event. Due to its theoretical immanent status and historical existence, the category of fascism was extended by the Frankfurt School scholars to also encompass reflections on the political regression of Western democracies, both European and otherwise, in the aftermath of the Second World War.

209 M. Horkheimer, *Eclipse of Reason*, [1947] 2004, p. 110.
210 Ibid., p. 108.
211 J. Buhrnam, *The Managerial Revolution*, 1941.

2 State, law, capital

The 1930s and 1940s witnessed profound structural political upheavals following the collapse of the liberal market economies of the late 19th century. The intellectual debates of the time were dominated by the question of whether Marx's theory on the tendency of the rate of profit to fall was correct, or, in other words, what consequences could be anticipated for the survival of capitalist societies.[1] Central to these discussions was the reorganization of national production into wartime economies. Through a critical reconstructive analysis, it will be argued that the remedies to the capitalist crises of the time transformed state powers into coercive, private and illiberal entities. This change was well illustrated by the famous debate between Pollock and Neumann. The two expressed opinions aimed not only at shedding light on their own historical period but also at drawing long-term considerations on the authoritarian tendencies inherent in contemporary democracies. The debates within the Frankfurt School examined the reshaping of powers and the German economy in the post-Weimar period. The Frankfurt School scholars highlighted the fact that the increase in coercion during the totalitarian turn led to control over the private sphere, where the limitation of individual freedoms was accompanied by planning in production and the circulation of goods. The formation of elite groups and the verticalization of power under supreme leaders (the *Führer* or the *Duce*) facilitated processes of total control over society. The reciprocal competition between coercion and privatization thus found a new reconfiguration. The authoritarian transformation of the state had reduced the relative independence of free enterprises and private property as potential constraints on political power. At the same time, these renewed market conditions had favoured economic interest groups in complicity with the regime. State power was privatized within exclusive circles. Networks of rackets driven by nationalist ideology emerged.

1 K. Marx, *Capital. A Critique of Political Economy*, vol. 3, [1894] 1996, p. 138 ff. For an overview of the Marxist debate on the economic transformations from the early 1900s to the 1929 crisis, see E. Alvater, "Il capitalismo si organizza: il dibattito marxista dalla guerra mondiale alla crisi del '29", vol. 3, 1980, pp. 823–876.

DOI: 10.4324/9781003630340-3

Overall, neither coercion nor the ideological safeguarding of privatization operated on mutually exclusive terms. They jointly defined a specific configuration of power along two parallel lines: one related to the ideological control of private property and the other to the privatization of power. The rise of fascism in Europe was marked by the crisis of the liberal economy and the abandonment of the utopia of its supposed autonomous self-regulation of the market. Economic liberalism had developed at the turn of the 19th and 20th centuries during what Polanyi termed "the Hundred Years' Peace" (1815–1914).[2] During this period, four elements contributed to maintaining the stability of the European order (with the exception of brief conflicts): a widespread balance of power, an international monetary system anchored to the gold standard, a stable market and the freedoms guaranteed by the liberal state.[3] When, in 1929, the Wall Street stock market crashed, and in 1933, the gold standard was abandoned, that world fell apart. It was at this point that fascism definitively established itself as a mass movement and a new model of state centralization.

The three fictitious commodities defined by Polanyi—labour, land and money—were removed from market dynamics. Not only money but also labour and land became functional to satisfying nationalist interests of states, whose planning was increasingly geared toward a war economy and whose territorial expansion became a product of conquest. The solutions adopted by the new regimes mostly ended up destroying the democratic freedoms supported by the 19th-century laissez-faire system. Socialist and fascist ideologies (and, more mildly, as we will see, the American New Deal) believed that the answer lay in creating a transitional war economy in which the state would direct production and realization policies. Authoritarian regression was taking on global proportions. In Romania, Codreanu founded the Iron Guard in 1927, a self-declared fascist and revolutionary movement, while in Japan, from the 1930s onward, a more pronounced nationalism emerged.[4] However, both totalitarian planned economies and democratic interventionist economies agreed on one point: the condemnation of classical liberalism due to its unforgivable underestimation of the disastrous consequences of relying on a market incapable of self-regulation. For classical economics, Say's Law applied.[5] This law assumed that the total product would be realized in the market, rejecting the hypothesis of a crisis of overproduction. Just as production was aimed at creating products, so capitalist savings were reinvested in advance of wages and machinery (Ricardo). According to this law, the market would always be able to absorb production costs: demand would return to equilibrium with supply and the market with production forces until full employment was achieved.

2 K. Polanyi, *The Great Transformation*, [1944] 2001, pp. 3–21.

3 Ibid., p. 3.

4 For an examination of the different ideological trends in planned economies during the 1930s, see L. Villari, "Processi di razionalizzazione nei sistemi fascisti", 1979, pp. 135–152.

5 The same conviction will persist, albeit based on different arguments, in the neoclassical tradition of Jevons, Marshall and others.

This was the illusion on which the market economy relied until the Wall Street crash. From that moment, economists' problem became conceiving controlled systems capable of avoiding the unpredictability of capitalist crises. Societies' economies needed to be reorganized according to a rational scheme. For this purpose, state intervention would be necessary to introduce market corrective measures. Such measures would have to take the form of either state rationalization within the free market or full-scale economic planning, as actually occurred in the USSR. From a typological classification perspective, planned economies concerned either a form of partial planning (preserving private property) or total planning. Production control had to be accompanied by the possibility of decentralized or centralized planning. In the first case, the value of the commodity reflected a subjective idea based on psychological motivations for choice, while in the second case, it depended on an objective idea.[6] As we will see with reference to debates developed by the first generation of critical theory, the issue was the precise definition of what, in the wake of the Great War, was understood in terms of "late capitalism" (*Spätkapitalismus*) following Sombart's definition in the monumental work *Modern Capitalism* [1902–1927].[7] In relation to these definitions, the Frankfurt School's question became how to understand the transformations of the economy and state in the 1930s.

For Pollock, these years began to shape a form of state capitalism, whereas for Neumann, Pollock's hypothesis appeared as a conceptual aberration. For Neumann, it was a matter of defining what remained an autocratic transition within capitalism—a "totalitarian monopoly capitalism"[8]—still circumscribable within a market model governed by private property. While Pollock saw National Socialism's economy as introducing a new phase of economic planning, Neumann viewed Hitlerian totalitarianism merely as a late stage of capitalism and not as a

6 Decentralized planning leaves individual initiatives in the production sphere unchanged. It does not eliminate the defining (and contradictory) elements of capitalism; instead, centralized planning takes over decisions regarding prices, wages and overall production, thereby excluding from its scope those particular decisions that are not economically decisive. While the decentralized model posits that the state should confine itself to defining employment and income allocation policies (as well as choosing sectors for development and investment while allowing enterprises to compete freely in the market), the centralized model is structured around a hierarchical decision-making framework that controls the entire process of production and distribution. In the decentralized model, enterprises remain subordinated to the state through the policy of interest rates set on loans provided by banks. Thus, the re-monetization of the economy is not disconnected from state control of planning. See A. Bettelheim, *Les Problèmes Théoriques et Pratiques de la Planification*, [1946]. If the objective choice refers obviously to Marx, the most representative work of the time for subjective orientations is O. Lange, F. M. Taylor, *Economic Theory of Socialism*, [1938] 1956.

7 W. Sombart, *Modern Capitalism*, [1902–27] 2019–3.

8 F. Neumann, *Behemoth: The Structure and Practice of National Socialism 1933–1944*, [1942/1944] 2009, p. 261.

new type.[9] Historically, the point became evaluating whether Nazi planning also fell within a planned economy. It was clear from the outset that the Soviet Union had opted for centralized planning. Lenin, with the establishment of *Gosplan* in 1921, understood the need to implement a planned economy with the help of experts who were not just Bolsheviks. In 1929, the first five-year economic plan was launched, which would subsequently lead Stalin's USSR to surpass the NEP perspective, transforming the country into the world's second industrial economy by the early 1940s. Soviet planning aimed to achieve a perfect transition from capitalist anarchy to socialist justice. The human and political costs were enormous. Already in the 1930s, very few of the professors and intellectuals who had participated in *Gosplan* remained—not to mention the sophisticated planning theories they had developed. With Stalin's rise to power, Soviet policy shifted toward complete Bolshevik control of economic and state apparatuses. A centralized planned economy erased any trace of the NEP initiated by Lenin as well as any development initiatives linked to capitalists. In this way, Stalin intended not simply to stabilize society through a planned economy but to effectively stabilize the economy through a totalitarian conception of party power.

On the liberal democratic side, where planning was rather assimilated to corrective state interventions in the economy, Keynes was one of the few who did not fall for the reassuring promises of Say's Law. He understood that capitalist economics was fundamentally based on the role of money and the disproportion between savings and investments. Modern capitalism was characterized by crises of overproduction, demand and supply. Additionally, Keynesian man was no longer a fully informed subject. Against the classical *Homo oeconomicus*, Keynes proposed the entrepreneurial subject capable of sensing opportunities and risks in capitalism and deciding what to do accordingly. Beyond subjective factors, Keynes maintained the importance of criticizing the "assumption of equality between the demand price of output as a whole and its supply price which is to be regarded as the classical theory's 'axiom of parallels'".[10] Besides the examples of policies related to Keynesianism, cases of decentralized planning also included economic liberalism theories, such as the *Ordoliberalismus* of the Freiburg School, which would later support the free market after the war. Even in such market theorization, there was the idea that the non-natural character of laissez-faire lay in the necessity of supporting free trade with state interventions, avoiding cartels or overproduction phenomena. Thus, even when governments did not transform into dictatorships, aligning themselves with a "third way" as in the case of the New Deal (1933–1937), corrective state intervention in economic planning became an essential factor in market rebalancing. In the United States, during the years

9 For an extensive examination of the relationship between the transformation of the state, capitalism and law in the thought of the early Frankfurt School, see W. Scheuermann, *Between the Norm and the Exception: The Frankfurt School and the Rule of Law*, 1994.

10 J. M. Keynes, *The General Theory of Employment, Interest and Money*, 1936, p. 13.

from 1929 to 1933, the unemployment rate reached 27% of the population, and international trade had decreased by 25% in volume and 60% in value.[11] Roosevelt's New Deal policy identified the problem primarily as the collapse of demand. Therefore, support had to be provided to workers' purchasing power (aggregate demand) and employment policies through public works financing. However, while Roosevelt was interested in redistributive measures, Keynes considered that such resources were only usable for consumption or investment. In short, for the British economist, the problem of capital crises lay in overproduction. Therefore, the state had to ensure maintaining a large economic volume, leaving the market free to decide.[12] In Roosevelt's policy, increased liquidity was achieved with the abandonment of the dollar's gold standard and the issuance of banknotes by the FED (Federal Reserve). Securing a financial measures margin, the United States also protected itself from the advance of fascism.[13] In relation to such epochal changes in economic and social structures, Horkheimer, in a paper presented at the 11th Sociology Congress in Geneva in 1933 titled "*Zum Problem der Voraussage in den Sozialwissenschaften*" ["On the Problem of Prediction in the Social Sciences"][14] observed that various social processes were increasingly subordinated to "human planning"[15] and that "the transition from a purely natural functioning and thus inappropriate of the social apparatus"[16] would hopefully transform itself into "lucid cooperation of social forces".[17] Only by achieving "a unitary planning",[18] Horkheimer concluded, would "predictions . . . acquire a higher degree of certainty".[19] Thus, he adopted the thesis regarding the illusory nature of a market economy capable of finding autonomous equilibria without public intervention support. However, the idea of planning was soon accompanied by the awareness of a progressive authoritarian regression in national and international politics. Economic planning and the consolidation of fascist ideology would reinforce each other.

2.1 Thinking about crisis after Marx: contributions from the IfS

As Dubiel asserted regarding the crisis of European society in the 1920s and 1930s, "[W]hen critical theorists spoke of 'crisis', they had in mind the

11 F. Caffè, *La crisi del liberismo*, 1979, p. 28.
12 J. M. Keynes, *The General Theory of Employment, Interest and Money*, 1936, pp. 333–371.
13 E. Rauchway, *The Money Makers: How Roosevelt and Keynes Ended the Depression, Defeated Fascism, and Secured a Prosperous Peace*, 2015.
14 M. Horkheimer, "Zum Problem der Voraussage in den Sozialwissenschaften", 1933, p. 411.
15 Ibid.
16 Ibid.
17 Ibid.
18 Ibid.
19 Ibid.

totalitarian forms through which the endangered capitalist order stabilizes itself".[20] In 1929, the IfS published and promoted two texts that opened fundamental discussions on the crisis of capitalism and the state. (The IfS also published a third text by F. Sternberg, *Der Imperialismus*, which did not receive equal attention.)[21] The texts in question were the economic and political works of Grünberg's two assistants: Grossmann, author of *The Law of Accumulation and Breakdown of the Capitalist System*, and Pollock, author of *Die planwirtschaftlichen Versuche in der Sowjetunion, 1917–1927 [The Planned Economy Experiments in the Soviet Union, 1917–1927]*.[22] Grossmann was regarded as a highly refined interpreter of Marx, while Pollock had been the administrative head of the IfS since 1927 and, from 1931, co-director and representative for economic research. One of his tasks was to develop a critique of capitalism.[23] With Horkheimer's appointment as the new director, this task was abandoned by Pollock and left to the spontaneous and diverse interests of the IfS members, who followed its development until the authoritarian regressions of National Socialism. The two essays by Grossmann and Pollock were situated within the tradition of the so-called revisionist controversy [*Revisionismusstreit*] initiated by Bernstein's articles in *Neue Zeit*—as well as in his foundational work *The Preconditions of Socialism* [1899]—and continued with Luxemburg's writings on the collapse of capitalism.[24] Grossmann's and Pollock's writings were thematically connected, both addressing the issue of economic planning. Grossmann's question was: "Is regulation, planning of the economy on a capitalist basis, feasible?"[25] The reference was to Hilferding's idea of a general cartel as a means of organizing production, which represented the "highest stage of planning under capitalism".[26] The answer was that such an option was "completely impossible".[27] For Grossmann, there was an inseparable relationship between production and distribution. The exchange value of commodities depended on the socially necessary labour time in a given historical phase. Thus, economic

20 H. Dubiel, *Kritische Theorie der Gesellschaft*, 1988, p. 25.

21 F. Sternberg, *Der Imperialismus*, [1926] 1971.

22 Respectively, H. Grossman, *The Law of Accumulation and Breakdown of the Capitalist System*, [1929] 2021 and F. Pollock, "Die planwirtschaftlichen Versuche in der Sowjetunion 1917–1927", in J. Gleixner, P. Lenhard (eds.), *Friedrich Pollock Schriften zu Planwirtschaft und Krise*, [1929] 2021, pp. 23–468.

23 R. Wiggershaus, *The Frankfurt School: Its History, Theories, and Political Significance*, [1986] 2007, pp. 750–751. For a reconstruction of the debates within the IfS concerning the critique of liberal capitalism and the possible options for societal transformation (ranging from the Bolshevik revolution to state capitalism, fascism, rackets theory etc.), see M. Gangl, *The Controversy over Friedrich Pollock's State Capitalism*, 2016, pp. 23–41.

24 These writings (to which Cunow responded) were published between 1896 and 1898, as well as in E. Bernstein's seminal work *The Preconditions of Socialism* [1899] 2012. See also R. Luxemburg, *The Accumulation of Capital*, [1913] 2003.

25 H. Grossman, *The Law of Accumulation and Breakdown of the Capitalist System*, 2021, p. 501.

26 Ibid., p. 500.

27 Ibid.

collapses interpreted by bourgeois theories of society, including Hilferding's view, ended up seeing only what appeared to be transitionary crises of distribution without questioning the entire valorization process (understood both as production and as commodity circulation). Grossmann emphasized the inescapability of the effects of the declining rate of profit as a radical tendency of capitalism linked to the process of progressive accumulation and capitalist competition. Thus, the scholar's task should be to show how the capitalist reproduction process, as a result of causes arising from the economic process itself, necessarily takes the form of cyclical, therefore periodically recurring, movements of expansion and contraction and, finally, leads to the breakdown of the capitalist system.[28] However, it would be incorrect to attribute to Grossmann the hypothesis that the collapse of capitalism would occur automatically and deterministically. Grossmann referred to the underlying assumptions of the tendencies toward collapse. These required a specific interpretation of Marx's theory of value, which, in turn, provided an explanation for price transformations. For Grossmann, a correct interpretation of the theory of value needed to Marxianly consider the presence of counter-tendencies to its tendency to decline.

Two levels of analysis were identified: the first, abstract and related to the deep structure of the economy, the second, more concrete, in which commodities were placed in a context of relationships encountering forces that slowed down the systemic collapse. The two planes were not to be reversed in the interpretation of the capitalist system nor related to the causes of crisis. According to Grossmann, the failure to understand this point led to fanciful interpretations of political economy that ended up providing ineffective remedies to the irrationalities of capitalist production. Grossmann, agreeing with Marx, saw the cyclical production of crises among the relations of production and labour, as in the case of creating a reserve army or capital devaluation, as evidence of the reproduction of exploitation structures for capital accumulation. The starting point was the contradiction between use value and exchange value, from which the crisis of capital was derived. The dynamic of progressive accumulation/competition based on ever-increasing investments in fixed capital and labour exploitation ended up producing underconsumption. Thus, here is where Grossmann, in line with Marx, considered the ultimate foundation of crises to be located.

For Grossmann, a rebalancing between material needs and valorization between use value and exchange value could not occur within the capitalist system. In order for the negative externalities of capital crises to transform the quality of the organization of production, a shift to class struggle and the initiation of a society organized on socialist principles became necessary. This transformation would, in turn, require a radical redefinition of the process of reproducing surplus value and, more generally, the organization of the system

28 Ibid., p. 108.

of production and capital accumulation. Pollock, on the other hand, sought to understand the extent of the transformations produced by the crisis: "What is coming to an end is not capitalism, but only its liberal phase".[29] Ten years later, he would see the idea of state capitalism as the theoretical possibility of reconciling capitalism with economic rationality through the intersection of state powers and planning. Pollock would also reflect on the introduction of mechanisms for rebalancing production and distribution operating both within a socialist planned economy and, later, within the framework of a vision of the intersection between the free market and command economy.[30] Thanks to the idea of state capitalism, he would propose that socially necessary goods identified by the state could coexist with a free market based on competitive laws. It would be only in this latter case that planning and free competition would be placed within a comprehensive state power framework.[31]

In the essay *On Marx's Monetary Theory* [1928], whose theses dated back to the 1923 dissertation,[32] Pollock had alluded to planning as a decisive moment in the crisis. Here, various economic fluctuations (prices, markets etc.) found resolution in the balance between socially necessary labour time and exchange or in socially necessary needs. It was from this reflection on the theory of value that Pollock would develop the idea of a planned economy, eventually leading to the concept of state capitalism. In this initial phase, Pollock could still consider himself fully aligned with the "broad field of Marxism",[33] since the main research objective was to think about how to replace an outdated market economy with a planned economy: i.e., with socialist economic planning. From this, the already-mentioned essay on Soviet planning from 1917–1927 originated.[34] At the centre was the question that had occupied debate since Weber, regarding which standards of rationality to consider for defining the economy and society in the formation of the modern state. While Weber had considered that the maximization of marginal profit achieved in the free market was superior to that of "a planned economy" (and thus that the free market economy was more rational),[35] Pollock believed the opposite: the times highlighted the incorrigibility of the internal distributive imbalances of the market. In *Die planwirtschaftlichen Versuche in der Sowjetunion* [1929], however, Pollock did not intend to present a theory of planning but only to provide a

29 F. Pollock, "Bemerkungen zur Wirtschaftskrise", 1933, p. 350.

30 On the notion of the market in Pollock as a synthesis between production and circulation, as well as the substantial conceptual continuity in the use of the term up to the 1940s, see C. Campani, *Pianificazione e teoria critica. L'opera di Friedrich Pollock dal 1923 al 1943*, 1992, pp. 78–79.

31 On this matter see P. Lenhard, "Capitalismo di Stato e automazione", in N. Emery (ed.), *Automazione e teoria critica a partire da Friedrich Pollock*, 2018, p. 85.

32 F. Pollock, *Zur Marxschen Geldtheorie*, 1928.

33 P. Lenhard, "Friedrick Pollock und der 'westliche Marxismus': Einleitung zum ersten Band der Gesammelten Schriften", 2018, p. 18.

34 F. Pollock, *Die planwirtschaftlichen Versuche in der Sowjetunion, 1917–1927*, 1929.

35 M. Weber, *Economy and Society*, [1921] 2019.

descriptively detailed account of the newly initiated Soviet planning. He considered Lenin's idea, expressed in *State and Revolution*,[36] about the transition from a monopoly economy to a state economy as the final stage of capitalism and a precursor to socialist planning to be an analytical error. The substitution of material needs and wartime requirements for the formal objectives of capital valorization did not seem to guarantee long-term economic planning. In this 1929 work, there was indirect reference to the possibility of reconciling market and planning by overcoming the opposition between market/capitalism and planning/socialism.[37]

We will later address how the idea of state capitalism would take on a specific political-economic meaning in Pollock, although his revisionist model would not produce a more reassuring profile regarding the exercise of power and control over citizens' lives. In general, even among non-Marxist scholars, there would be an increasing awareness of the impossibility of thinking about the economy in terms of equilibrium and thus addressing a model of an organized rather than a competitive economy. Although pursuing different political-organizational outcomes, both Schumpeter and Keynes would come to a similar political-economic awareness.[38] The instability of capitalism, entrepreneurial initiative and the creation of monopolies will all become factors of constant modification of economic relations. The transformation of capitalism at the end of the 1920s would signify the crisis of commodity valorization in European societies (primarily German), relative to the increasingly frequent failure to realize the exchange value of commodities. This will open a research interest motivated by the transitional developments of Soviet economic planning still in an embryonic phase.

Indeed, while in the early 1920s, the state's intervention in organizing the Soviet economy had been limited to a purely financial and credit role, starting in 1925–1926, state resources shifted toward industrial development. It was at this point that the anti-planning groups of the *Narkomfin* would be definitively defeated.[39] While centralized economic planning remains in the background, planning conducted by *Gosplan* would promote technological and energy transformation and thus the overall industrial advancement of the country.[40] Starting in 1932, with the essay titled "The Present State of Capitalism and

36 V. Lenin, *State and Revolution*, [1917] 1993.

37 C. Campani, *Pianificazione e teoria critica. L'opera di Friedrich Pollock dal 1923 al 1943*, 1992, p. 117.

38 On the instability of capitalism as a "system" (in terms of business conditions) but not as an "order" (in terms of institutional survival conditions) and on the transition to socialism, see Schumpeter's 1928 essay: J. Schumpeter, "The Instability of Capitalism", 1928, p. 363 ff.; also see J. M. Keynes, *The End of Laissez-Faire*, 1926.

39 E. H. Carr, R. W. Davies, *A History of Soviet Russia: 4 Foundations of a Planned Economy, 1926–1929*, vol. 1, part 2, 1974, p. 336.

40 Ibid., p. 390.

the Prospects of a New Planned Economy",[41] Pollock further develops the proposal for economic planning on explicitly capitalist grounds. Here, the issue of a non-automatic overcoming of public intervention in response to the 1929 crisis would be raised. The latter will be considered against the backdrop of a general lack of industrial investments and rampant unemployment, as well as the effects of the centralization of political powers and state interference on the economy. Pollock would indeed see in the overcoming of "partial organizations" within a "total organization . . . the planned reorganization of the economy".[42] Although Pollock does not yet express a preference for either the capitalist version (unstable in replicating the condition of capitalists reduced to rentiers benefiting from services not fairly reciprocated by society) or the socialist version, later, he will nonetheless consider it of "little" effect as long as "the influence of the interested strata . . . is not sufficient to allow for an overthrow of the current social order".[43] The rise of totalitarian regimes will thus emerge as a possible outcome of the monopolistic concentration of capital.

In 1933, Pollock published "*Bemerkungen zur Wirtschaftskrise*" ["Remarks on the Economic Crisis"].[44] Here, he expressed the idea that the current crisis of capitalism, manifesting in the clash between production forces and the transformation of relationships, would not lead to a radical revolution of society and the production system. On the contrary, regardless of the outcome, both hypotheses would leave "the foundations of the capitalist system intact".[45] The results of Pollock's analyses in the early 1930s led to the exclusion of the possibility of a collapse of capitalism. The idea of an initial outline of state capitalism serves to provide a way out of the post-liberal crisis. However, this transition still remains within a model centered on state monopolism, constituting its extreme case. For Pollock, the crisis does not lead to a proletarian revolution but instead produces economic-political contractions favouring the rise of fascist authoritarianism. Unemployment, financial collapse, discord and paralysis within the workers' movement, as well as a general material and intellectual impoverishment, provide fertile ground for the rise of dictatorships.[46] In this sense, Horkheimer came to view fascism as the natural offspring of the crisis of liberalism. Once philosophical rationalism was rejected, the semblance of "a relatively progressive antirationalism" transformed into a "universalistic version closely associated with a totalitarian theory of the state".[47] According

41 F. Pollock, "Die gegenwärtige Lage des Kapitalismus und die Aussichten einer planwirtschaftlichen Neuordnung", 1932, pp. 8–27.

42 Ibid., p. 15.

43 Ibid., p. 27.

44 F. Pollock, "Bemerkungen zur Wirtschaftskrise", 1933, pp. 321–354.

45 Ibid., p. 335.

46 C. Campani, *Pianificazione e teoria critica. L'opera di Friedrich Pollock dal 1923 al 1943*, 1992, p. 193.

47 M. Horkheimer, "The Rationalism Debate in Contemporary Philosophy", [1934] 1993, p. 221.

to Horkheimer, this point recalled the transition from the liberal state to the "capitalist-monopolistic" state;[48] the latter, in turn, leads to a fascist authoritarian regression. The constant element accompanying these transformations was that of the individualist liberal society, whose principle of egoism remains intact up to fascism, albeit with the following variations: the loss of the "principle of happiness in associated life" [*den Leben der Allgemeinheit*][49] and the inversion of private satisfaction of instincts into self-sacrifice for the social totality. As Horkheimer emphasized in *Rationalismusstreit* [*Rationalism Dispute*] [1934]: "[I]n place of personal power stands only obedience; in place of wealth, poverty; in place of libertinism, chastity".[50] If in *Bemerkungen zur Wirtschaftskrise* [1933], Pollock had marked the turning point in the analysis of economic planning by opening the way to the idea of state capitalism, it was the analysis of socialist planning in the 1920s that would provide a foundation for constructing hypotheses on future political trajectories. The analysis of Soviet planning had distant biographical origins. Pollock had indeed been in the Soviet Union in 1927 during the tenth anniversary of the Bolshevik Revolution at the invitation of Ryazanov, the new director of the Marx-Engels Institute in Moscow. The latter was in contact with the IfS for the realization of a complete edition of Marx's works. Pollock was interested in Soviet economic planning because it had indeed limited the damage of the 1929 collapse. However, for Pollock, the Soviet Union remained trapped in a series of backward conditions that had severely limited its ability to plan and design in the long term. In implementing a socialist planned economy, the Bolsheviks had not sufficiently considered the starting condition from which the transformation of the economy would have to be realized: namely, the indispensable pursuit of an "alliance"—the "*Smytschka*"—[51] with the mass of peasants. Furthermore, they had naively believed that for the establishment of a socialist regime and thus the consequent elimination of the free market and private property, it would suffice to proceed with the collectivization of banks. However, the conditions of industrial underdevelopment (especially in heavy industry) prevented the formation of a modern, bureaucratically organized state. The result was that the Soviet Union ended up missing the set goal of economic-industrial growth. For Pollock, this was not sufficient reason to reject the validity of the planning model, but only to fully realize that "the planning efforts . . . will inevitably encounter enormous difficulties".[52]

As will become evident from the following sections, the discussions on capitalist crises in the 1930s revealed the dynamics of a profound structural change

48 Ibid.

49 M. Horkheimer, "Vorbemerkung des Herausgebers (Kurt Mandelbaum, Gerhard Meyer, 'Zur Theorie der Planwirtschaft')", 1934, p. 230.

50 M. Horkheimer, "The Rationalism Debate in Contemporary Philosophy", [1934] 1993, p. 254.

51 F. Pollock, *Die planwirtschaftlichen Versuche in der Sowjetunion, 1917–1927*, 1929, p. 36.

52 Ibid.

in the liberal state. Concerning the issue of privatization versus coercion, the crisis of privatized capital led world economies to respond with an increase in public spending. A revitalized economy would require the interference of public powers in the market. Consequently, the power of the private market would be transformed into the coercive power of the state: i.e., its ability to shape the market. But here a difference emerges: if, on the one hand, the coercive turn of democratic state capitalism safeguarded the benefits of public society from the private market through non-destructive interference in the free market, the total state would reconvert capitalist production to the needs of fascist ideology. If the democratic state were to coercively limit privatizations in the name of overall social benefit, the fascist state would seize private capital. Critical theory will present this phenomenon in terms of the theory of the rackets of the Nazi state. According to this view, the Third Reich was nothing more than an empty shell, a political carcass where private gangs (the party, the army, the church) competed for state power through an internal struggle with no holds barred.

2.2 The Weimar crisis and the rise of National Socialism

The debate on the emancipatory function and the protection of freedoms within a legitimate system of rules sparked extensive discussion in Germany following the economic crisis of 1929, during the decline of Weimar liberal democracy and the rise of Hitler to power in 1933. At the heart of this debate was the question of the emerging National Socialist order, with its "totalizing control" over society (*Gleichschaltung*), and the consequent transformation of the bourgeois-liberal *Rechtsstaat* (rule of law). The *Rechtsstaat* had served as a threshold criterion for determining which laws and political actions could be publicly justified and which could not. Within this framework, some of the most significant contributions came from Neumann and Kirchheimer, who addressed these critical issues during this transformative period. Both scholars were critically engaging with the ideas of Carl Schmitt, particularly his works *Der Hüter der Verfassung* [*The Guardian of the Constitution*] (1931) and *Legality and Legitimacy* (1932).[53] In these writings, Schmitt tackled the crisis of Weimar constitutionalism and the burgeoning tension between inviolable liberal guarantees and the plebiscitary legitimation of political power.[54] Schmitt observed how the formation of a total state, constructed around total parties, had led to the gradual dismantling of democratic-parliamentary freedoms.[55] The politicization of the liberal impartiality of public life contributed to the

53 C. Schmitt, *Der Hüter der Verfassung*, [1931] 2016; C. Schmitt, *Legality and Legitimacy*, [1932] 2004.

54 For an extensive examination of this point see C. Galli, *Genealogia della politica. Carl Schmitt e la crisi del pensiero politico moderno*, 1996, pp. 641ff.

55 Ibid., p. 644.

deconstruction of parliamentary guarantees, while the proliferation of political parties introduced ideological competition. Here, constitutional legitimacy became reconnected to the totalizing role of constituent power—specifically, the people in their undifferentiated equality. According to Schmitt's logic, this necessitated the expulsion of the internal enemy, leading to the polarization of political confrontation into a dyadic friend/enemy conflict. Once a direct link between power and constituent people was established, aimed at marginalizing the bureaucratic apparatuses of the state—especially parliamentarianism—Schmitt turned his attention to the problem of representation: specifically, the direct exercise of the popular will.

In this context, the idea of a state of exception and the use of special powers entrusted to the guardian-president became the hallmark of the political disintegration of Weimar constitutionalism. As the guardian-president, he embodied the undifferentiated equality of the mass will, legitimating forms of commissary dictatorship in the name of the constituent people. The guardian-president predated the parliamentary division of powers since he operated at a constituent (rather than constituted) stage of power legitimation. On these and other crucial issues concerning the transformation of Weimar, Schmitt was undoubtedly one of the most astute and authoritative interpreters of his time. The writings of Kirchheimer, including *Legality and Legitimacy* [1932][56] and *Remarks on Carl Schmitt's Legalität und Legitimität* [1932],[57] co-authored with N. Leites, were key responses to Schmitt's ideas. Kirchheimer argued that a new bureaucratic power was emerging in Germany, alongside a search for a form of political legitimation. The power granted to the president by Article 48 of the Weimar Constitution to adopt emergency measures without the Reichstag's consent raised questions about the relationship between the legitimacy of power and the legality of decisions. The very definition of the *Rechtsstaat* established a necessary relationship between administrative acts and the country's laws. Kirchheimer acknowledged that both German and broader European democracy were undergoing profound transformation; however, he critiqued Schmitt's levelling vision of political diversity, arguing that it opened the door to a purely instrumental view (*Mitteleinstellung*) of democracy. The outcome of this process was a radical transformation of law, especially criminal law, a field in which Kirchheimer was a specialist. He identified 1933 as the year marking the transition from an already authoritarian legal system (particularly with the phenomenological school of Kiel) to a legal system that had now become explicitly racist with the progressive rise of National Socialist power.[58] Following this core of writings, a series of essays appeared in the *ZfS* 9(2), 1941, in which

56 O. Kirchheimer, *Legality and Legitimacy*, [1932] 2019.

57 O. Kirchheimer, N. Leites, *Remarks on Carl Schmitt's Legalität und Legitimität*, [1932] 2019.

58 See O. Kirchheimer, "Criminal Law in National Socialist Germany", 1939, pp. 444–463; O. Kirchheimer, "Recent Trends in German Treatment of Juvenile Delinquency", 1938, pp. 362–370. One of the characteristic features of this school, influenced by Scheler's eidetic materialism rather than Husserl's idealism, was its reliance on notions such as the "social

first Kirchheimer and later Pollock examined the philosophical-political and philosophical-legal implications of the rise of National Socialism. In his essay "Changes in the Structure of Political Compromise" [1941],[59] Kirchheimer analyzed the changes in mechanisms for mediating private interests through public forms of power. If, in the pre-Weimar liberalism of the early 20th century, parliamentary debate had served as a venue for resolving disputes, including those of an economic and private nature, with the advent of the *Führer*, the power of mediation shifted directly into his hands and those of a few oligarchic groups connected to him. According to Kirchheimer, this development impeded the possibility of anti-Hitlerian critique.

In the following issue of the *ZfS* 9(3), 1941, Pollock questioned whether National Socialism had introduced a new system of rules.[60] Kirchheimer, in a more assertive manner, analyzed the legal order of National Socialism.[61] For Pollock, a "new order" meant a "new social and economic system in contrast to monopoly capitalism".[62] If it is true that monopolistic capitalism had presented itself as a new order compared to the feudal system, Pollock questioned whether it also constituted a new order in relation to competitive capitalism. The answer to this question depended on the identification of investigative parameters, which emerged in concepts such as rulers/ruled, the role of the individual and societal integration.[63] It was emphasized that despite the advent of National Socialism, private property had been formally maintained. Quoting Gurland, it was argued that property controls benefited a few select groups.[64] This indicated that the function of private property had changed and, with it, the system of wealth redistribution and totalitarian capitalist monopoly. This transformation was also profoundly reflected in the new form of social integration brought about by National Socialism. Instead of an interaction/relationship among individuals within a free market, there was now mass adherence to an ideologically totalizing association—the *Arbeitsfront*—which defined asymmetric power relations between leaders and followers. Money gave way to power and ideological affiliation, with the latter now guaranteeing access to means of production and unlimited profits. According to Kirchheimer, National Socialism established a form of technocratic rationality as the foundation of law. This rationality, in turn, sacrificed the inviolability of the individual and their rights in favour of a ruthless and oppressive juridical practice. In this regard, the gap between morality and law had never been as wide as in the legal system of National Socialism. In fact, Kirchheimer had

sentiments of the people" to judge potential crimes, rather than reconstructing the factual circumstances and the objective responsibilities of the individual.

59 O. Kirchheimer, "Changes in the Structure of Political Compromise", 1941, pp. 264–289.

60 F. Pollock, "Is National Socialism a New Order?", 1941, pp. 440–455.

61 O. Kirchheimer, "The Legal Order of National Socialism", 1941, pp. 440–455.

62 F. Pollock, "Is National Socialism a New Order?", 1941, p. 440.

63 Ibid.

64 Ibid.

already published an essay in 1935 under the pseudonym Dr. Hermann Seitz, analyzing the legal-institutional structure of the Third Reich.[65] In this essay, he reiterated his critique of Schmitt's idea of the *Rechtsstaat* as a mask for private-liberal interests while also examining the transition from competitive to authoritarian monopoly capitalism.[66] For Kirchheimer, if the concept of the *Rechtsstaat* was identified with rational standards of objectivity and impartiality, under National Socialism, it had become "the quintessence of Adolf Hitler's German rule of law".[67]

In the new system, the ideological deformation on the impartiality of the law had not simply been linked to the very possibility left to the *Führer* to bridge legal gaps with his word-as-law verb. Similar deformation had also been linked to the legislative ability of judges to introduce new rules as long as they reflected National Socialist ideology.[68] It is evident how this had contradicted a fundamental principle of the legal system: namely, the maxim *nulla poena sine lege* (no punishment without law),[69] legitimizing retroactive sentences and, in the specific case of criminal law, centering on the presumed will of the accused (*Willensstrafrecht*) rather than on certain evidence. The introduction of this modification to the penal code was a clear manifestation of a determined political vision. Similarly, as Kirchheimer noted in his 1935 essay, the transformation of the civil code not only contributed to the definitive destabilization of different normative and decision-making levels (municipal, regional, state), reabsorbing them into the model of the total state, but also redefined the relationship between the people and power, unifying differences and subordinating them to Hitler's supreme command.[70] This led to the onset of a series of profound social transformations, one of the most significant being that "the acquisition and maintenance of economic power no longer rests simply on the exercise of a formal-legal title to property".[71] This change was directly reflected in inheritance law, particularly concerning agricultural properties, where restrictions were introduced, such as the prohibition of property transfers to non-Aryans and the ban on subdivision, limiting inheritance to the male heir only. According to Kirchheimer, the jurist's task was to bring an end to the National Socialist legal system as quickly as possible and to pave the way for a new system—socialist in the proper sense—for a new Germany.[72]

While the possibility of change remained a distant option, the present reality involved the instrumentalization of private law and the rule of law in accordance with Nazi ideology. The process of privatization and the exercise of

65 O. Kirchheimer, "State Structure and Law in the Third Reich", [1935] 1996, pp. 142–171.
66 Ibid., p. 143.
67 Ibid., p. 144.
68 Ibid., p. 146.
69 Ibid., p. 158.
70 Ibid.
71 Ibid.
72 Ibid., p. 166.

totalitarian coercion merged into a single dimension of legal construction and exercise of power. Private property ceased to function as a counterbalance to illegitimate forms of state coercion. On the contrary, it became a complementary tool useful for achieving the objectives of the Nazi regime. Privatization served the same purposes as the authoritarian coercion of the Third Reich.

2.3 Pollock and state monopoly capitalism

In the article "*Die gegenwärtige Lage des Kapitalismus und die Aussichten einer planwirtschaftlichen Neuordnung*" ["The Current Situation of Capitalism and the Prospects of a Planned Economy"] [1932], Pollock addressed the issue of the monopolistic transformation of modern economies.[73] He argued that the crisis of the liberal economy could only be resolved through a new, centralized and planned economic reorganization. On the other hand, Pollock had previously engaged with the topic of economic planning, presenting it as a solution to the crisis of market capitalism, foreshadowing an alternative to the system's collapse. For Pollock, clear indications of a societal shift (both in Germany and Europe) toward a planned economy were intertwined with the dual aspects of a war economy and, later, the so-called *Wehrwirtschaft*, meaning a defense and military rearmament economy, which he revisited much later in the article "Influences on Preparedness on Western European Economic Life" [1940].[74] In this context, Pollock defined *Wehrwirtschaft* as a transformation of the German economy starting from 1935, marking a phase of economic recovery based on rearmament. As a transitional economy, it was structured on two levels: as a "gearing of what was a peace economy to the threat of war" and as a "transformation of traditional capitalism",[75] albeit in not yet fully definable terms. The link between the economy and rearmament (*Wehrwirtschaft* or preparedness) was maintained through private property, which, though limited by state power, retained some semblance of function.[76] The topic of economic planning was of significant interest within the Frankfurt School circle, generating intense debates, particularly among Pollock, Mandelbaum and Meyer. The *ZfS* published six articles on the subject between 1932 and 1933, four between 1934 and 1936, and two between 1938 and 1939.[77]

73 F. Pollock, "Die gegenwärtige Lage des Kapitalismus und die Aussichten einer planwirtschaftlichen Neuordnung", [1932].

74 See *Neuere Literatur zum "New Deal"*, 1936, pp. 404–410; F. Weil, *Neuere Literatur zur deutschen Wehrwirtschaft*, *Zeitschrift für Sozialforschung*, 1938, pp. 200–218 and F. Pollock, "Economics of War. Influences on Preparedness on Western European Economic Life", 1940.

75 Ibid., p. 317.

76 On the decisive influence of these developments on the formulation of subsequent models of state capitalism, see C. Campani, *Pianificazione e teoria critica. L'opera di Friedrich Pollock dal 1923 al 1943*, 1992, p. 211 ff.

77 Ibid., p. 198, fn 28.

For Pollock, state monopoly capitalism could persist for an indefinite period, with private property coexisting alongside the coercive use of power. What had ended was not capitalism itself, but the liberal capitalism of the free market. Pollock's study thus examined the fundamental structure of crises, viewed in terms of the conflict between productive forces and relations of production.[78] State capitalism did not intend to replicate the Soviet socialist model of economic planning, as the former did not aim to abolish private property, unlike the latter. In this sense, the state's role was to guide and direct production in sectors where there was a mismatch between supply and demand, while still allowing the free market to determine prices within a competitive framework. Pollock's concept of state capitalism, aligned with the perspectives of Hilferding and Tugan-Baranowski[79] on the causes of economic crises—seen as imbalances between production and consumption (crises of disproportionality between productive sectors)—offered a political solution to the irrationalities of the market. The radical transformation element, however, coincided with the end of unregulated private capitalism (deemed irrational) and the rise of public capitalism—state capitalism, to be precise. Pollock left the question of defining this new form of state open until the 1940s, culminating in his work *State Capitalism* [1941].[80]

In the following year's issue of *ZfS*, scholars Mandelbaum and Meyer highlighted the necessity of resorting to planned economies, advocating for a socialist and "classless" turn.[81] They sought an escape route from the 1929 crisis, calling for the political transformation of the traditional liberal economic structure and thus for the task of philosophy, which Marx had already identified as paramount: the economic-political critique of society. However, these authors failed to grasp what Pollock saw as the true socio-political novelty of the time: namely, the emergence of a new form of political power defined as state capitalism. In some ways, Pollock's idea drew on the debate sparked by Hilferding's theory of the end of the free market, presented in *Finance Capital* [1910].[82] Here, Hilferding introduced the most advanced phase of capitalism—what more orthodox Marxists sceptically labelled imperialism, characterized by the predominant trend of mergers of enterprises into a single general cartel.[83] For Hilferding, the end of free competition and the

78 See O. Kirchheimer, N. Leites, *Remarks on Carl Schmitt's Legalität und Legitimität*, [1932] 2019, pp. 64–100.

79 M. I. Tugan-Baranowsky, *Theoretische Grundlagen des Marxismus*, 1905.

80 F. Pollock, "State Capitalism: Possibilities and Limits". In the same issue of *ZfS*, 9(2), 1941, three other essays of notable relevance to the topics discussed here can also be found: A. R. L. Gurland, "Technological Trends and Economic Structure under National Socialism", 1941, pp. 226–263; O. Kirchheimer, "Changes in the Structure of Political Compromise", 1941, pp. 264–289; M. Horkheimer, "Art and Mass Culture", 1941, pp. 290–304.

81 K. Mandelbaum, G. Meyer, "Zur Theorie der Planwirtschaft", 1934, p. 261.

82 R. Hilferding, *Finance Capital*, [1910] 1981.

83 Ibid. This text, as is well known, would be echoed in 1917 by V. I. Lenin's *Imperialism, the Highest Stage of Capitalism*, [1917] 1963.

increasingly close ties between banks and large industries led to a monopolistic economy. Finance capitalism thus envisaged the creation of a central bank accumulating power, which would, in turn, encourage the formation of cartels. These cartels dominated the remaining productive market, centralizing powers and subordinating enterprises to themselves. This trend in capitalism eventually rendered obsolete several key Marxist concepts, particularly the theory of commodity valorization and the consequent creation of surplus value as an uncontrolled effect of the free market and a consequence of wage labour exploitation.[84] In short, the question was the interpretation left open by Marx regarding the causes of cyclical capital crises. In the end, the nationalization of many economies passed through what Hilferding had already defined as the rationalization of the market inherent in "organized capitalism".[85] That the free market of laissez-faire was over was certainly a common assumption shared by Grossmann and Pollock. However, while the former categorically excluded the possibility of regulating capitalist production, the latter saw it as a means of internal transformation and productive reorganization. Each interpretation was based on a specific reading of the underlying causes of the falling rate of profit in Marx, which, in turn, had generated the Wall Street crash of '29. For Grossmann, the decrease in surplus value in relation to the increase in organic capital embraced the more orthodox Marxian thesis of a production crisis: that is, the contradiction between productive forces and relations of production (where value remained unchanged). In contrast, Pollock attributed the reasons for cyclical crises to realization crises. However, for Pollock (unlike what we have seen for Grossmann), the issue at hand was not so much the crisis as a disproportion between generalized demand and supply (underconsumption crisis), but rather the imbalance between various production areas, leading to the migration of capital from one sector to another (crisis of imbalance between productive areas). Rationalizing these productive disharmonies meant planning ahead for needs and their satisfaction through an economic planning model. These transformative trends of capital were first reconsidered by Pollock in light of a new economic policy adopted by states[86]—the Soviet socialist economic planning—and then, in light of what would become the theory of state capitalism.

2.4 Pollock and state capitalism

In the report on the activities of the IfS for the years 1933–1934, the Frankfurt School scholars still believed that "the current methods of planned economy

84 Of a different opinion are the reflections of J. Zoninsein in "Rudolf Hilferding's Theory of Finance Capitalism", 2000, p. 280.

85 R. Hilferding, "Die Aufgaben der Sozialdemokratie in der Republik", [1927] 1982, pp. 212–236.

86 F. Pollock, *Die planwirtschaftlichen Versuche in der Sowjetunion, 1917–1927*, 1929.

have not created more rational conditions".[87] However, between 1939 and 1942, the thematic interests and dominant positions of the Institute changed. For Pollock, the issue of the crisis of imbalance between production and consumption (and not specifically of the relations of production and capital as the Marxists emphasized) could be resolved with the rise of a power oriented toward enhanced state control over the economy and a gradual dissolution of the presumed objectivity of economic laws. The review articles by Weil on the New Deal and the organization of the economy in Germany provided useful insights for Pollock to develop the concept of "state capitalism" in the homonymous essay [1941].[88] This notion would echo Lenin's theoretical framework in his work *Imperialism* [1917].[89] Lenin had seen imperialism as the monopoly stage of capitalism and the transformation of competition into monopoly as a socialization and reparation of production among previously competing business cartels. While imperialism referred to the highest stage of capitalism, marked by the separation between financial capital (money) and industrial capital, a further development in the form of the "rentier state" or "usurer state"[90] would lead to a more complex articulation of monopoly.

At the outset of his essay, Pollock declares that "nothing essentially new is intended in this article"[91] in terms of contributing to the study of capitalism. On these subjects, he acknowledges the intellectual heritage not only of the aforementioned Hilferding but also of Trotsky and Fried.[92] For Pollock, the advent of new forms of economic organization and planning was to be attributed to the inevitable counteractions of oligarchic powers controlling the economy. Finance and industry had grown to such a massive scale that they could claim the entire profit for themselves, offloading the risk onto the mass of taxpayers.[93] However, the introduction of the concept of state capitalism initiated a process of reflection on the transformation of the role of capitalism in society. With the loss of tight control by capitalists over capital and

87 IfS, "International Institute of Social Research: A Short Description of Its History and Aims", [1935], p. 17, online.

88 F. Pollock, "State Capitalism: Its Possibilities and Limitations", 1941, pp. 200–225. For a reference discussion, see: M. Gangl, "The Controversy over Friedrich Pollock's State Capitalism", 2016, pp. 23–41 and, more specifically, regarding the subsequent analysis of the relationship between dialectics and enlightenment, see M. Gangl, G. Raulet (eds.), *Jenseits instrumenteller Vernunft—Kritische Studien zur "Dialektik der Aufklärung"*, 1998. In the same issue of *ZfS*, 9(2), 1941, three other essays of notable relevance to the topics discussed here can also be found: A. R. L. Gurland, "Technological Trends and Economic Structure under National Socialism", 1941, pp. 226–263; O. Kirchheimer, "Changes in the Structure of Political Compromise", 1941, pp. 264–289; M. Horkheimer, "Art and Mass Culture", 1941, pp. 290–304.

89 V. Lenin, *Imperialism, the Highest Stage of Capitalism*, [1917] 1963.

90 Ibid., p. 101.

91 F. Pollock, "State Capitalism: Its Possibilities and Limitations", 1941, pp. 200–225.

92 R. Hilferding, "State Capitalism or Totalitarian State Economy", [1940] 1962, pp. 334–339; L. Trotsky, *Die verratene Revolution*, 1936; F. Fried, *Das Ende des Kapitalismus*, 1931.

93 F. Pollock, "Die gegenwärtige Lage des Kapitalismus und die Aussichten einer planwirtschaftlichen Neuordnung", [1932], pp. 8–27.

the exclusivity of private property, the state began to assume control over prices and profits, while the entrepreneur—much like in decentralized planned economies—would reinvest profits in state bonds. Banks thus became "mere government agencies".[94] For Pollock, these measures led to the capitalist acquiring a fixed income tied to the payment of state interest.[95] The capitalist was thereby transformed into a "pure rentier".[96] The disappearance of the capitalist's role in a planned economy society did not apply only to the case of totalitarian state capitalism. This also occurred in all those forms of democratic state capitalism where the people held sovereign power. Following Hilferding's lead, Pollock argued that state capitalism could theoretically be applied to both authoritarian forms (as in German and Italian Fascism) and democratic forms of power (as in the American New Deal).[97] If the problem lay in neutralizing authoritarian tendencies, for Pollock, this remained a contingent issue dependent on the political orientation of the groups in power at any given time.[98] The bureaucratization of the state and its apparatuses, as well as the increasingly pervasive rise of political parties in political-institutional life, remained factors common to the various forms of government considered. Pollock questioned how "such a thing as state capitalism exists or can exist".[99] First of all, state capitalism should not be understood as the state taking full possession of capital but rather as the state assuming only some of the central prerogatives of the economy.[100] Additionally, for all forms of state capitalism (whether democratic or totalitarian), the following points remained valid:

1 The market is deposed from its controlling function to coordinate production and distribution. . . . With the autonomous marked, the so-called economic laws disappear.
2 These controls are vested in the state, which uses a combination of old and new devices, including a "pseudo-market", for regulating and expanding production and coordinating it with consumption.
3 Under a totalitarian form of state capitalism, the state is the power instrument of a new ruling group, which has resulted from the merger of the most powerful vested interests, the top-ranking personnel in industrial and business management. . . . Under a democratic form of state capitalism, the state has the same controlling function but is itself controlled by the people.

(F. Pollock, "State Capitalism: Its Possibilities and Limitations", 1941, p. 201)

94 F. Pollock, "State Capitalism: Its Possibilities and Limitations", 1941, p. 208.
95 Ibid., p. 210.
96 Ibid.
97 Ibid., p. 228.
98 Ibid., p. 218 ff.
99 Ibid.
100 Ibid. The same point is reiterated in F. Pollock, "Is National Socialism a New Order?", 1941, pp. 440–455. Here, the expression "command economy" is also used, which Pollock states was explicitly borrowed from a Nazi writer.

In other words, for Pollock, state capitalism became the most suitable expression to indicate the persistence of a profit-oriented system in which, nevertheless, the logic of realization was subordinated to a programming of national interest, the definition of which was based on a "principle of planning".[101] Consequently, "prices are no longer allowed to behave as masters of the economic process",[102] as the economic relationship between supply and demand was associated with a general plan of needs to be met.

As a search for a rationalized system of surplus value redistribution, Pollock's conviction was that state capitalism functioned as a meta-phenomenal category capable of including under one umbrella various state forms different from those Hilferding had referred to. Pollock raised the issue of rethinking the relationship between base and superstructure by reversing the perspective of influence between the two levels, thus paving the way for the critique of instrumental reason later discussed by Horkheimer and Adorno.[103] If, during Grossmann's 1929 reflection[104] and the IfS seminars of the 1930s, the problem had been to understand the relationship between the law of the tendency of the rate of profit to fall and the constitution of a new social order, for Pollock, the issue now became one of formulating new categories for a society no longer comprehensible based on an exclusive use of Marx's traditional concepts.[105] Pollock's perspective on state capitalism thus acquired an element of originality, ceasing to be a mere ahistorical generalization of the change in the relationship between power and capitalism. In connecting critique and transformation, Pollock was guided by the idea that capitalism could remain unchanged despite the variation in its surface characterization: from a competitive mechanism to a state mechanism. For Grossmann, capitalism was destined to fail because the point of systemic rupture was inscribed in the contradiction inherent in Marx's theory of value.[106] For Pollock, however, systemic collapse was only configured in relation to liberal and competitive capitalism, which had already been transformed into something else. Understanding this change was as important as it was urgent, to initiate a process of political reflection aimed at excluding any attempt to restore forms of private capitalism. For Pollock, the state needed to assume certain strategic functions that were once the exclusive domain of the market: decisions on profit in the redefinition of

101 Ibid., p. 204.

102 Ibid.

103 M. Horkheimer, T. W. Adorno, *Dialectic of Enlightenment*, [1947] 2002. Cfr. T. ten Brink, *Economic Analysis in Critical Theory: The Impact of Friedrich Pollock's State Capitalism Concept*, 2015, pp. 333–340.

104 H. Grossmann, *The Law of Accumulation and Breakdown of the Capitalist System: Being Also a Theory of Crises*, [1929] 2021.

105 On the broader critical-philosophical framework, see the IfS discussion protocols on the difference between positivism and dialectical materialism from 1939, M. Horkheimer, *Nachgelassene Schriften 1931–1949*, 1985.

106 H. Grossmann, *The Law of Accumulation and Breakdown of the Capitalist System: Being Also a Theory of Crises*, [1929] 2021.

the needs/products relationship, redistribution and, more generally, surplus value. What the power of the state transformed was the free and autonomous character of the capitalist and the market; in other words, it altered "its controlling function to coordinate production and distribution".[107] These control and market orientation functions were directly assumed by the government apparatus, which, in turn, introduced corrections to "the so-called economic laws" of the free market.[108]

In relation to the debate this position generated, Pollock's model of planned economy did not seem to leave much room for the freedom of enterprise and accumulation typical of competitive capitalism, while it drew a line of continuity (albeit reworked) with the early mixed socialist models implemented by Lenin with the introduction of the NEP. General economic plans came to regulate consumption, production and savings activities, while prices were no longer autonomous variables of commodities as they were the result of top-down regulation. On the more strictly social side, this transformation marked the shift from forms of intersubjective confrontation, where individuals acted as economic exchange agents (in the role of buyers/sellers), to relations of subordination (commander/commanded). Here, belonging to the political elite, especially the authoritarian version, defined the social rank of command even within the economic sphere. Power prevailed over property. Pollock advocated a shift to democratic state capitalism. For Pollock, this would be the only conceivable way to guarantee the economic efficiency and social stability on which the recognition of civil and political rights could be based. In this sense, the control placed on private property by public authority was subordinated to a principle of democratic collective interest and not to authoritarian and elitist power as in the case of authoritarian state capitalism. Pollock, on the other hand, considered the planning of German war economy production as imperfect compared to a truly planned economy organized according to long-term production deadlines. Even the authoritarian Nazi state had not been able to direct a rational production plan according to a well-programmed plan. Therefore, the post-war period was to be a testing ground on which to test the model of democratic state capitalism. Nevertheless, even the democratic model of state planning was never fully implemented. Pollock's reflection continued, therefore, with a deeper examination of socio-political issues regarding the role of technology in the liberal societies of the post-war period. The most relevant of these was the study of mechanized industrial production and its implications for advanced capitalist societies (particularly in America).

In his work *Automation* [1956], Pollock defines the socio-economic effects of advanced mechanization in production and industrial distribution in 1950s USA. The term "automation", coined by D. S. Harder, vice president of the Ford Motor Company, refers to a wide range of industrial phenomena, from

107 F. Pollok, *State Capitalism: Its Possibilities and Limitations*, 1941, p. 201.
108 Ibid.

improvements in the production chain to increasingly sophisticated production controls.[109] Under the pretence of completely replacing the workforce, automation aims to achieve a situation in which "the product is not touched by human hands from the beginning to the end of its manufacture".[110] Pollock notes that such processes, even assuming an initial stabilization of the economy, will ultimately lead to a form of "technological unemployment"[111] which will fuel the reserve army of workers who, in the new labour market, will have acquired either no new skills or only obsolete ones. This observation reflects a full awareness of the tendency toward the hierarchization of market economies through the progressive development of increasingly organized industrial systems. In societies of this type, "A new sort of society, based upon authoritarian or military principles, might be evolved".[112] Therefore, in addressing the broader issue of the long-term vision of democratic state capitalism, one cannot ignore aspects related to the ever-present risk of possible illiberal regressions. Automation represents the cornerstone of that fully administered world that will reappear in Adorno's and Horkheimer's reflections.[113] Despite these risks, however, Pollock remains confident in the possibilities of a "social system" that the second industrial revolution will make available through long-term planning in accordance with "reason".[114]

2.4.1 The Frankfurt School debate on Pollock's state capitalism

It is no surprise that Pollock's position provoked numerous reactions within the Frankfurt School circle. Some critics argued that his method of investigation betrayed the perspective of immanent critique inherent in the Horkheimerian critical theory. In other words, the transition from liberal capitalism to democratic socialism was not traced back to internal contradictions within society, as required instead by a properly immanent critique method. Horkheimer's stance on Pollock's theses was ambivalent overall. On the one hand, there was concern that Pollock was conveying a totalitarian response to

109 "By 'automation' we understand the use of certain methods of automatically producing and preparing goods; of producing information; and of making calculations (e.g. book-keeping)—methods which are characteristic of our present stage of technical development". In F. Pollock, *Automation: A Study of Its Economic and Social Consequences*, [1956] 1957, p. 5.

110 Ibid.

111 This is the expression used by Pollock to indicate the marginalizing effects on large groups of workers excluded from the production process due to the new technological revolution of automation. Ibid., p. 194 ff.

112 F. Pollock, *Automation: A Study of Its Economic and Social Consequences*, [1956] 1957, p. 83.

113 M. Horkheimer, "Kritische Theorie gestern und heute", [1969] 1970. On the implications of Pollock's theory of automation, see also N. Emery, *For Nonconformism: Max Horkheimer and Friedrich Pollock: The Other Frankfurt School*, 2023, particularly pp. 171–178.

114 F. Pollock, *Automation: A Study of Its Economic and Social Consequences*, [1956] 1957, p. 253.

the delegitimization of fascism, and there was an inappropriate historical comparison between state capitalism and the political situation in Germany. On the other hand, however, Horkheimer acknowledged Pollock's merit in identifying a correct topic for discussion.[115] In a letter of congratulations to Neumann for his *Behemoth* [1942], Horkheimer expressed his agreement with Neumann's view "that Germany is not in a situation remotely resembling that of state capitalism" but added that "society is moving towards precisely that"[116] direction. He would later observe that Neumann's model lacked an analysis capable of also including anthropological issues.[117] Ultimately, Horkheimer's position would align more closely with Pollock's theory. Horkheimer's writings, such as *The End of Reason* [1941] and *The Authoritarian State* [1942], already reveal significant points of convergence between the two thinkers.[118]

However, explicit opposition to Pollock's thesis came from Neumann, Adorno[119] and Marcuse (as well as Gurland and Kirchheimer). Neumann rejected Pollock's hypothesis of a purely political transfiguration of power and the idea that the market, commodity value and "the homo oeconomicus" were "deaths".[120] For Neumann, there was no rupture between the economic system of National Socialism and that of liberal democracy: in both, capitalism and its laws remained operational, leaving open the possibility of crises even within authoritarian systems. The break between the two systems, as Neumann would argue during a 1951 lecture at the *Deutsche Hochschule für Politik*, consisted instead of the fact that "fascism emerged from the need of the holders of economic power for a strong state which, however, must not be subjected to the control of the people".[121] Fascism emerged as a reaction not to communism but to democracy. It is the latter, in fact, that aimed to "give rational and democratic shape to the economy",[122] while this was contrary to the goals of fascism. Adorno criticized Pollock for lacking a dialectical-immanent vision of the economy and society. Thus, there was the difficulty of understanding how, from an "undialectical assumption that a non-antagonistic economy is possible

115 An analysis of the theoretical controversy opened by Pollock can be found in M. Gangl, "The Controversy Over Friedrich Pollock's State Capitalism", 2016, pp. 23–41.

116 M. Horkheimer, "Briefwechsel Horkheimer an Neumann", August 2, 1941, in "Briefwechsel 1941–1948", 1996.

117 Ibid.

118 M. Horkheimer, "The End of Reason", 1941, pp. 366–388. M. Horkheimer, "The Authoritarian State", 1973, pp 3–20.

119 It should be noted that although Horkheimer's initial reaction was ambivalent—despite his agreement to the publication—his stance would progressively evolve into explicit support for Pollock's theses (See R. Wiggershaus, [1986] 2007, p. 280 ff.). In contrast, Adorno clearly expressed his opposition in a letter addressed to Horkheimer (in Wiggershaus, [1986] 2007, p. 282), only changing his mind starting in 1947.

120 F. Neumann, *Behemoth: The Structure and Practice of National Socialism 1933–1944*, [1942] 2009, p. 222.

121 F. Neumann, "Economics and Politics in the Twentieth Century", [1951] 1957, p. 256.

122 Ibid.

in an antagonistic society".[123] Finally, in his work *State and Individual under National Socialism* (1941),[124] Marcuse argued that

> [T]his movement [National Socialism], we now see, has not changed the basic relationships of the productive process that is still administered by special social groups which control the instruments of labour regardless of the needs and interest of society as a whole.[125]

For Marcuse, the Nazi state was not equivalent to a non-state, as Neumann suggested. Political violence and economic rationality continued to coexist thanks to a convergence of interests among the three groups contending for power (the party, the military, the industry) under the *Führer*, symbol of the pan-Germanic racial unity.

Beyond the initial critical reactions, the acceptance of Pollock's theses by Horkheimer and Adorno matured in *Dialectic of Enlightenment* [1947]. It was to their friend Pollock that the two dedicated the text. Moreover, the idea of a totally administered society took shape within a vision of history that saw a reification of thought regarding the rationalist premises of the Enlightenment. Much later, in 1968, Adorno himself revisited the issue during the introductory address at the XVI Congress of the German Sociological Society. Here, he clarified that the problem was not defining the current situation in terms of "late capitalism" or "industrial society".[126] Rather, the problem was understanding whether one could still speak of capitalism or "whether industrialization has not made the concept of 'capitalism' itself obsolete".[127] For Adorno, the issue was of substantial importance, not merely terminological. It concerned the understanding of the effects of what seemed to him to be a new post-political phase of industrial society. Here, class conflict and the dialectical opposition between the forces and modes of production would disappear in favour of a purely economic administration of society.[128] Adorno concluded that if industrial society could be discussed in relation to "the forces of production", then it must also be considered that the industrial model would permeate every single aspect of society—from bureaucracy to culture. From the point of view of "relations of production", however, the post-political industrial society would remain inscribed within a form of "capitalism".[129] Indeed, for Adorno, the worker, as envisioned by Marx, would still be positioned func-

123 Letter 219 from T. W. Adorno to M. Horkheimer, 8 June, 1941, in Th. Adorno-M. Horkheimer, *Briefwechsel*, Band II, 1938–1944, 2004, p. 139.

124 H. Marcuse, "State and Individual under National Socialism", [1941] 1998, pp. 67–93.

125 Ibid., p. 69.

126 T. W. Adorno, "Late Capitalism or Industrial Society?", [1968] 1987, pp. 232–247.

127 Ibid., p. 232.

128 B. Harcourt, "Rethinking Capitalism with Friedrich Pollock, Frank Neumann, and the Frankfurt School", 2020, online.

129 T. W. Adorno, "Late Capitalism or Industrial Society?", [1968] 1987, p. 238.

tionally in service to the machine concerning his possibility of social inclusion and the production "of profit".[130] The idea of industrial society would express a primacy "of the technocratic reading of Marx": namely, "of the productive forces" over the "social conditions"[131] of workers.

Neumann's negative judgment of Pollock remained unchanged. The scholar pointed out the limitations of a reflection that was too abstract concerning historicity. For Neumann, the ideal type category that the theory of state capitalism sought to represent violated "the principle that the model or the ideal type must be derived from reality and must not transcend it".[132] The consequence of Neumann's critique was the necessary recognition, already mentioned, of a broader totalitarian monopolistic capitalism whose historical prototype was National Socialism.[133] This was a monopoly, yes, but still within an economic market framework of the capitalist type.[134] This would be defined as capitalism devoid of the state, where violence would be exercised through the actions of cartels and ideological groups, just as in Hitler's Germany. The dynamics that generated it traced back to the conflict between the excessive accumulation of capital by monopolistic groups and the undermining of liberal democratic rules during the Weimar experience.[135]

For Neumann, speaking of state capitalism in Pollock's terms represented a "*contradictio in adjecto*".[136] This point had actually already been anticipated by Grossmann in 1929. In criticizing Hilferding's theory of the general cartel, it was argued that if the state were to become the holder of the means of production, then private capital would cease to exist. However, if private capital persisted, then its public regulation could not be conceived.[137] More abstractly, the problem with Pollock's conception was that the statization of Marxian exchange processes and the consequent regimentation of the free market would cause the transformation of the commodity's exchange value to coincide with its relative use value. This form of reductionism did not seem to Neumann compatible with the idea that state capitalism could assume a social-democratic configuration of modes of production and wealth redistribution. Since the state would take on the task of planning surplus value and profit, the market, in turn, could not realize processes of social emancipation. National Socialism, in this

130 Ibid.
131 Ibid., p. 241.
132 F. Neumann, *Behemoth: The Structure and Practice of National Socialism 1933–1944*, [1942] 2009, p. 224.
133 Ibid., p. 179.
134 H. Dahms, "The Early Frankfurt School Critique of Capitalism", 2000, p. 343.
135 M. Sharpe, "Capitalism and the Far Right: Revisiting the Pollock-Neumann Debate in the Era of Trumpism", 2021, p. 198.
136 F. Neumann, *Behemoth. The Structure and Practice of National Socialism 1933–1944*, [1942] 2009, p. 224.
137 H. Grossman, *The Law of Accumulation and Breakdown of the Capitalist System*, 2021, p. 563.

sense, despite the ideology of a united *Volk* [*Volksgemeinschaft*],[138] according to Neumann, had nevertheless allowed the existence and operation of a multiplicity of private interest groups and, thus, a relatively independent market.

In summary, Neumann's critique of Pollock identified two fundamental undesired effects. First, state capitalism was presented in millenarian terms, leaving no hope for possible transformations. It was deprived of the movement of history itself: i.e., the identification of internal contradictions within capital that would have allowed for social transformation. Second, Pollock never articulated a theory of transition from state capitalism to totalitarian monopolistic capitalism.[139] There was thus a gap to be filled in Pollock's political and economic analysis of Germany at the time.[140] In fact, the society that defined state capitalism was such that labour—instead of exercising a liberating function for the individual—had realized a condition of domination. The primacy of the political over the economic had eliminated the contradictions of the free market economy but with them also the dialectical progress of history and, ultimately, its very possibility of immanent transformation. In this respect, the socialist transition Pollock hoped for could not have been based on actual processes of social progress achievable through the overcoming of the competitive market of liberalism. Pollock's planned and classless economy society showed the most troubling face—the illiberal one—of a society in which political power became the uncontrollable master of the rules. Pollock specifically addressed this in his essay/lecture "Is National Socialism a New Order?" [1941].[141] This was the last of five lectures held at Columbia University between November and December 1941. Sponsored by the IfS, Pollock's lecture followed those of Marcuse on "State and Individual under National Socialism", Gurland on "Private Property under National Socialism", Neumann on "The New Rulers in Germany" and Kirchheimer on "The Legal Order of National Socialism".[142] Pollock thus extended to the specific case of Nazi Germany the theory of the transformation of modern political authority into state capitalism. For Pollock, under National Socialism, four power groups coexisted as they did for Neumann: big business, the military, the party and the bureaucracy. Although they exhibited conflicting interests, they shared common fears. This made them cohesive allies united by the com-

138 F. Neumann, *Behemoth. The Structure and Practice of National Socialism 1933–1944*, [1942] 2009. For a reconstruction of the debate between Neumann and Pollock and a deeper analysis of the latter's position in particular, see M. Postone, "Critique, State, and Economy", 2004, pp. 165–193.

139 The concept of totalitarian monopoly capitalism is in F. Neumann, *Behemoth: The Structure and Practice of National Socialism 1933–1944*, [1942] 2009, p. 226 ff.

140 See, in this regard, the reconstruction of the Pollock-Neumann debate in R. Wiggershaus, *The Frankfurt School: Its History, Theories, and Political Significance*, [1986] 2007, p. 283 ff.

141 F. Pollock, "Is National Socialism a New Order?", 1941, pp. 440–455.

142 O. Kirchheimer, "The Legal Order of National Socialism", 1941, pp. 193–225. On the editorial fate of these presentations, see F. Pollock, "Is National Socialism a New Order?", 1941, fn., p. 440.

mon goal of responding to internal and external enemies. For Pollock, wealth would not be sufficient to guarantee status or social ascent. The latter would always depend on power:

> The relation between property, income and societal power has thus been radically altered. Money alone gives only limited power or (as in the case of the Jews) no power at all. Political power, in turn, which is equivalent to the control of the means of production, may become the source of practically unlimited income.[143]

In conclusion, National Socialism had indeed established a new economic order where political authority had become the controller of the market. Given this framework of the planning of the economy, albeit rough, and the fulfilment of the needs of the citizens, however, it did not seem possible to identify an internal economic contradiction within the National Socialist system that would presage a near collapse of the system itself. Hitler's totalitarian regime was destined to last at least until there was an increasingly pressing need externally to implement a thorough internal reform aimed at re-establishing the priority of freedom over economic security (the latter being the propaganda banner of the regime). The identification of such a way out, however, did not seem convincing because it was extrinsic to a possible immanent mechanism of resolution.

2.4.2 Neumann and National Socialism: Behemoth vs. Leviathan

While Pollock and Kirchheimer had highlighted certain aspects of the fusion between capitalism and state centralization, it was Neumann who introduced a thesis of radical incompatibility between Nazi authoritarianism and capitalism. In 1942, he published the aforementioned masterpiece *Behemoth: The Structure and Practice of National Socialism, 1933–1944.*[144] For Neumann, National Socialism presented itself as a monopolistic and totalitarian form of capitalism that, while being in complete formal alterity with Pollock's typologies, could not be classified as a typological-totalitarian declension of state capitalism. As a command economy, although the state regulated credit, money, markets etc., it did not interfere directly with the economy. While the institution of private property remained guaranteed, it was, however, controlled by the regime's apparatuses. National Socialism did not nationalize industry; instead, it allowed the party and the economic elites aligned with the regime free rein for a union of power and profit. In terms of the socio-economic reality, Neumann saw a synergy among four totalitarian formations: the party, big industry, bureaucracy and the military. In this context, the exercise of power by the *Führer*

143 F. Pollock, "Is National Socialism a New Order?", 1941, p. 444.

144 F. Neumann, *Behemoth: The Structure and Practice of National Socialism 1933–1944*, [1942] 2009, in particular pp. 221–364 and pp. 459–470.

appeared as a search for compromise among the four lobbies. Neumann firmly rejected Fraenkel's interpretation of National Socialism as a "dualistic state" or "normative state', in which the Nazi seizure of power on the one hand formalized an apparent law, while on the other subjected every issue of legal legitimacy to the whim of political power.[145] For Neumann, the Nazi state was none of these things, as not only did it not present itself as a form of autonomous economic organization, but it also did not even show the characteristics of a state. As noted, Neumann's assessment of the Nazi state was fully shared by Marcuse. The latter, during those same years, questioned whether the idea of the revolutionary vocation of fascism was adequate to describe its propagandistic demands and production reorganization. Certainly, National Socialism implemented a plan of totalitarian intimidation, as all public and private life relations were affected by it. However, Nazism failed to realize the total state as its dominant groups continued to compete for power and the accumulation of wealth while the masses were manipulated to achieve private gains.[146] Thus, there existed a structural fracture within the state.

With this economic-political setup, the Germany of the Third Reich increasingly moved toward an economy serving total war. Consequently, an enormous amount of resources were absorbed, which effectively rendered the system inefficient. Furthermore, National Socialism did not demonstrate a genuine long-term political-strategic ideology. The tools of power it employed consisted of mere domination techniques operating outside any form of rule of law. Since National Socialism lacked a rule of law, for Neumann, it was not even a state: "The state, Hitler says . . . is the servant of the racial people. It is not an end but a means".[147] This reintroduced the theme of the transition to National Socialism, acknowledging Schmitt's merit in identifying the fatal tension between the democratic and liberal soul of the Weimar Republic.[148] Neumann even agreed with Schmitt's thesis "in condemning the Weimer constitution for its lack of decision".[149] Several scholars thus aligned with Schmitt and his critique of Weimar constitutionalism. The latter reflected a positivistic character, with relativistic and nihilistic outcomes.[150] The system of a supposed liberal-democratic harmony in Weimar symbolized the political failure of Germany during those years.

For Neumann, the totalitarian state and the synchronization of political life at all levels—as opposed to Weimar's pluralism—proved to be a failure both politically and theoretically-philosophically, not only for Nazi Germany

145 E. Fraenkel, *The Dual State: A Contribution to the Theory of Dictatorship*, [1941] 2017.

146 H. Marcuse, "State and Individual under National Socialism", [1942] 1998, pp. 67–93.

147 F. Neumann, *Behemoth: The Structure and Practice of National Socialism 1933–1944*, [1942] 2009, pp. 63–64.

148 Ibid., p. 43.

149 Ibid., p. 45.

150 "The relativistic conception of democracy is precisely the ground for the decisionist and socialist attacks", F. Neumann, *Behemoth: The Structure and Practice of National Socialism 1933–1944*, [1942] 2009, p. 47.

but also for Fascist Italy and Stalinist Russia. Indeed, National Socialism had achieved remarkable economic progress in a short time: eradication of unemployment, economic growth and price control. However, for Neumann, this did not mean that capitalism had transformed into a state-structured form of profit production (a form of bureaucratic collectivism or brown Bolshevism). Rather, it highlighted that a different economic-social organization system had been realized. The paradox of the new system was that it was based on "an economy without economics".[151] For Neumann, the totalitarian state did not serve as the ideological-organizational foundation of a form of state capitalism, even though it allowed power to prevail over the economic man and the laws of the economy. Contractual freedom and commodity exchange had disappeared. Cartel monopolies had replaced the free market.[152] For this reason, Neumann argued that National Socialism's economic vision did not follow any doctrinal path or long-term vision but was merely oriented toward a pragmatic approach of welfare-oriented choices made as needed.[153]

The social effects of this economic restructuring were also considerable. However, Neumann did not share the view held by many that National Socialism transformed a structured society into a classless mass society. The presence of classes could continue to coexist with an absence of social differentiation between groups.[154] For Neumann, the essence of National Socialism lay precisely in the consolidation of the ruling elite and the dissolution and fragmentation of interest groups: i.e., in the overall loss of mediation between public and private interests. In this way, National Socialism reinforced autocratic bureaucracies in power, allowing them to infiltrate every aspect of citizens' lives. National Socialism also transformed the private interest groups of democracies into authoritarian bodies, bureaucratic aggregates aimed at depersonalizing every social relationship. To this, National Socialism added two ideological principles: the ideology of the community and the principle of leadership.[155] In this reconfiguration of social levels was the massification of modern man, which, for Neumann, was not entirely the work of National Socialism. The latter had merely completed a process already underway with the industrialization of the market and production. The question Neumann poses at the end of his extensive discussion is: Can we consider that National Socialism rested on a well-defined political theory? Answering this question would have placed the interlocutor in a state of "great embarrassment".[156] The irrationalism characterizing National Socialism prevented the attribution of any credible political doctrine to support it. For this reason, even Hobbes's Leviathan did not provide an adequate key

151 F. Neumann, *Behemoth: The Structure and Practice of National Socialism 1933–1944*, [1942] 2009, p. 221.
152 Ibid., p. 261.
153 Ibid., p. 228.
154 Ibid., p. 366.
155 Ibid., p. 369.
156 Ibid., p. 459.

to interpretation. But Hobbes, Neumann reminds us, was also the author of *Behemoth*,[157] which chronicles the Long Parliament era, the two-decade period from 1640–1660 in the English Parliament characterized by the effective absence of the state and the outbreak of two civil wars. This second figure appears as the most fitting image to describe the political aberration of the Hitlerian regime.[158] Neumann insisted on the error of interpreting National Socialism as the political expression of German idealism and, in particular, of Hegelianism. The rationalism of the Hegelian state was incompatible with the vertical and authoritarian form of the Nazi state. Marcuse had fortunately addressed this issue in his text *Reason and Revolution*, published first in 1941 and again in 1954.[159] German National Socialism, like Italian Fascism, was, for Neumann, indifferent to adherence to any ideology. What mattered to the two scholars was the racist view of society and the idea of a nation-people whose interests were pragmatically placed above all other concerns. In this sense, for Neumann, Germany could not even be defined as a state, as the absence of a solid rule of law and the direct control of the ruling group over society prevented any coercive function from being assigned to intermediate control organs.[160]

What conclusions could be drawn from the interpretative opposition between Pollock and Neumann regarding the transformations of capitalism and the definition of the Nazi state? Firstly, both authors distanced themselves from Grossmann's position expressed in 1929 in support of the idea of a collapse of the capitalist system. Moreover, both Pollock and Neumann rejected the prophetic reading of a law rather than a reversible trend in the fall of the rate of profit. The distancing from a deterministic Marxist reading of the reasons for capitalist crises allowed for a critical and shared position regarding the transformation of liberal capitalism as a new form of economic-social organization. However, while Pollock saw the solution to capital instability in the formation of a meta-phenomenal category like state capitalism (indifferent to whether it was socialist, Nazi or democratic), Neumann viewed it as leading to a form of totalitarian monopolistic capitalism. Pollock was more interested in identifying the common root of differentiated political forms where the solution to economic-historical crises would emerge in the long term through a balance between the means of production and the means of consumption or between the sphere of production and the sphere of distribution.[161] In contrast, for

157 F. Neumann also reminds us that it was Ferdinand Toennies who first edited the text in London in 1889. In ibid., p. 459.

158 Ibid.

159 Ibid. H. Marcuse, *Reason and Revolution: Hegel and the Rise of Social Theory*, [1941/1954] 1955.

160 F. Neumann, *Behemoth: The Structure and Practice of National Socialism 1933–1944*, [1942] 2009, p. 470.

161 It is no coincidence, in fact, that Horkheimer himself, while appreciating Pollock's study, pointed out in a letter dated May 30, 1942, that his thesis regarding a permanent political stabilization of fascism did not "avoid the false impression of sympathy toward the 'totalitarian response'". Translated by the author. In M. Horkheimer, *Briefwechsel 1941–1948*, [1941–8] 1996, p. 46.

Neumann, the centralized control of the means of consumption was equivalent to initiating a process of centralization of the means of production, leading to the formation of a totalitarian regime. However, this did not eliminate the relative autonomy of capitalism and the market, as National Socialism, according to Neumann, had not created a totalitarian society in the full sense but only in terms of the market, a capitalist form of totalitarian monopoly.

In attempting to propose a synthesis useful for interpreting the two positions, one might ask whether Horkheimer's idea of the authoritarian state identified a new model of synthesis between state capitalism and totalitarian monopolistic capitalism. In many ways, indeed, in the mixture of elements of wealth and capital accumulation of the former (state capitalism) and the totalizing characteristics of the latter (totalitarian monopolistic capitalism), there were anticipations of aspects of fusion between economic monopolies and power oligarchies typical of contemporary post-war capitalism—especially financial capitalism—and its deconstructive impact on contemporary democracies. The common trait was the syncrasis between the individual powers of the (Hitlerian) state of *Behemoth*—which, for Neumann, included the party, the bureaucracy, banking/finance and the military—[162] and capitalism, understood as a constantly adapting production system. Only the relationships of synecdoche between one of its powers and capitalism as a generally understood production system were retained from the democratic state as a system of balanced powers. With the democratic state's continued claim to a "total planning"[163] of society, Pollock's idea of state capitalism continued to influence Horkheimer and Adorno. Indeed, the meta-analysis proposed by the two scholars regarding a possible internal authoritarian tension within contemporary liberal democracies increasingly focused on understanding the bidirectional colonization relationship between portions of the economic base and the state superstructure. This further historical transformation would pose new challenges not only socially but also in terms of understanding it. The break from traditional Marxism lay in the abandonment of an analysis profile of society as regulated by objective economic laws, now deemed inadequate, in favour of an approach focused on the psychic, anthropological and cultural understanding of power in its relations with the productive base.

2.5 Critique of Western civilization: *Dialectic of Enlightenment* [1947]

Against the backdrop of Pollock's model of state capitalism, one might ask whether it was still possible to maintain a reasonable hope for progressive socio-political emancipation as a desirable outcome of a critical examination of reality and its

162 P. Hayes, "Introduction", in F. Neumann (ed.), *Behemoth: The Structure and Practice of National Socialism 1933–1944*, [1942] 2009, p. VII.

163 M. Horkheimer, T. Adorno, *Dialectic of Enlightenment*, [1947] 2002, p. 21.

irreconcilable contradictions. On this point, Horkheimer seemed uncertain. Indeed, while in *Eclipse of Reason* he had promoted a vision of trust in social progress, several years earlier, in the essay written with Adorno in 1944 and reissued in 1947 with a small addition in the section on anti-Semitism (*Dialectic of Enlightenment*), he expressed pessimism regarding the capacities for self-correction and political improvement in a society that had not yet emerged from the wartime atrocities of National Socialism. However, Horkheimer and Adorno differed in their reconstruction of the reasons underlying the crisis of Western rationality. In *Excursus I* on Odysseus,[164] Adorno traced the short-circuiting of Western reason not so much to the force of domination it imposed, but to the identity character that led it to render identical things that were dissimilar. For Horkheimer, the point of the crisis of Enlightenment reason and its failure to preserve the autonomy of the subject over time lay in the instrumental nature it had permanently assumed as a means of preservation, though no longer as a source of defining a set of values.[165] The rationalization of society and power in the Enlightenment-Weberian model had led to an ontological separation between nature and culture. The recomposition of this dichotomy was unachievable within a logic of instrumental reason focused on self-preservation. Within this socio-political framework, the Western ideal of self-liberation from the chains of ignorance and poverty, achievable only through a process of self-critique of reason, would remain unattainable. Reason could no longer serve as a non-contradictory ally in the realization of self-produced rational protection. On the contrary, the antagonistic divide between nature and culture would lead to the self-destruction of reason itself and thus to the loss of personal autonomy.[166] In this sense, the psychology of Odysseus reworked in *Dialectic of Enlightenment* [1947] revealed an archetype of Western subjectivity: the inability to reconcile the other within the self, resulting instead in forms of institutionalized domination of the other in general. The regressive barbarism of National Socialism simply showcased the aberration of the other within the mimetic—instrumental or identity-based—logic of reason. The other was dominated because it was useful for eliminating the anxiety of the dialectical alterity that could never be fully reduced. Thus, not only was the other suppressed, but this also led to the loss of reason's mimetic capacity. The barbaric regression evident in the experience of fascisms became structurally rooted in the same model of Western rationality, remaining ever ready to re-emerge with the persistence of the model itself.

In *Dialectic of Enlightenment* [1947], Horkheimer and Adorno provided the psychoanalytic-Freudian categories of repression, drives and so forth, with an

164 M. Horkheimer, T. W. Adorno, "Excursus I: Odysseus or Myth and Enlightenment", in M. Horkheimer, T. W. Adorno (eds.), *Dialectic of Enlightenment*, [1947] 2002, pp. 35–62.

165 On this matter, see S. Benhabib, *Critique, Norm and Utopia: A Study of the Foundations of Critical Theory*, 1986, p. 164 ff.

166 For an analysis of the developments of this theme within critical theory starting from Weber, see D. Schecter, *The Critique of Instrumental Reason from Weber to Habermas*, 2010; S. Petrucciani, *La Scuola di Francoforte: Storia e attualità*, 2023, p. 27 ff.

interpretive connotation applicable to the understanding of a historical process of development of the contradictions inherent in reason. This reason would be realized as both a presupposition and an object of the process of critiquing power dominance and the authority of the personality. This aporetic outcome of the contradiction could not be resolved dialectically. In this, both Horkheimer and Adorno recognized the incomplete nature of the post-Hegelian dialectic of reason. The challenge would be to establish the terms in which non-identity could be rehabilitated as a process of critique of the existing order while remaining functional. At this point, divergent interpretive paths would open up among the Frankfurt School theorists. In particular, for Benhabib, utopia would play a role in resolving and maintaining non-identity.[167] The way out, however, could not be found by presupposing a scientific-discursive reason as an analytical framework to perform an immanent critique of reason. On the contrary, a non-discursive resolution and a modification of the relationship between critical theory and the sciences would be necessary. It is art and aesthetics that would provide a utopian turning point for the dilemmas of critical Enlightenment rationality. Adorno would become an interpreter of this type of program in the years immediately following *Dialectic of Enlightenment* [1947]. He will emphasize not only the change in objects of investigation, such as the critique of political economy and the diagnosis of the present time, but also the very goals of critique, which would become those of a utopian vision of history in its chronological and existential development.[168]

2.6 The theory of rackets

The transformation of Weimar society saw the emergence of gangs competing for power and economic resources. It was these gangs that defined the new German society, justifying Neumann's opposition to Pollock's theory of the Nazi state. Benjamin had already addressed the issue of gangs in terms of a "you"[169] emerging from the transition from the Weimar Republic to the fascist state. The Nazis privatized state powers by allowing ideological groups to privately exercise (il)legitimate force within society. The Frankfurt School theorists defined rackets as elementary natural forces of domination, capable of including not only criminal gangs but also mutual support groups, such as associations and lobbies.[170] These groups occupied a middle ground between the sphere of the family and that of civil society.[171] Within these groups, individuals found a

167 S. Benhabib, *Critique, Norm and Utopia: A Study of the Foundations of Critical Theory*, 1986, p. 169.

168 Ibid., p. 171ff.

169 W. Benjamin, "Theories of German Fascism", vol. 2, part 1, [1930] 2005.

170 A thorough discussion of the concept can be found in T. Fuchshuber, *Rackets: Kritische Theorie der Bandenherrschaft*, 2019. Here, the author presents Horkheimer's idea of rackets as a foundational form of power (*Grundform der Herrschaft*).

171 G. Scheit, "Rackets", 2018, p. 1554.

second family in which exchanges of goods and services were not regulated by contract but through personal favours, which indebted and subordinated the individuals who received the benefit. Rackets operated like monopolies; they were hierarchically organized around an internal sense of loyalty and affiliation.[172] From Horkheimer onward, critical theory took an interest in rackets not just in terms of empirical sociology but as a genuine critical theory of class and society. In a certain sense, the theory of rackets can be viewed as a theory of elites within a framework of social totality.[173] It was also a reflection on the transformation of Weimar society into a totalitarian state, where the economic principles of the free market were replaced by the violence of gangs under the formal and propagandistic ideal of a *Volksgemeinschaft* (people's community).[174] This overturning of social structures had deep ethical and intellectual roots. According to Horkheimer, it was precisely the "intellectual imperialism of the abstract principle of self-interest—the core of the official ideology of liberalism"[175] that, by exposing the fracture between such ideology and the material living conditions of society, identified the *Volksgemeinschaft* as the only form of social reconciliation, transitioning from idolatry to respect through the exercise of "terror".[176]

This transformation found dramatic outcomes in Nazism. The death machine established by the Nazis reflected both in military and civilian contexts a bureaucratic apparatus aimed at maximizing external conquest and internal extermination. In the death camps, the executors of the Final Solution saw themselves merely as a mechanism of automized procedures. They did not perceive themselves as agents of death but as specialists [*Fachmannen*] indifferent to human affairs, addressing these with the support of special treatments [*Sonderbehandlungen*] and special installations [*Spezialeinrichtungen*]—gas chambers—in places specifically designed for such purposes: extermination camps.[177] In contrast to a levelling ideology, the Nazi society was characterized by division and competition among rival groups, which Neumann, as mentioned, labelled—in contrast to Pollock's theory of state capitalism—a "non-state" [*Unstaat*].[178] Although Neumann never explicitly mentioned it in his *Behemoth*, he framed the Nazi state in terms of totalitarian anarchy and chaos, where the idea of gangs in perpetual competition was complemented by a pseudo-ideological superstructure of a homogeneous ethnic

172 Kirchheimer would define them as "monopolistic practices which are carried through by physical force, violence in trade disputes, or similar objectionable means", in O. Kirchheimer, *In Quest of Sovereignty*, 1944, p. 159.

173 T. Fuchshuber, *Rackets: Kritische Theorie der Bandenherrschaft*, 2019, p. 28.

174 For a contemporary reinterpretation of the concept starting from Horkheimer, see W. Pohrt, *Brothers in Crime*, 2015.

175 M. Horkheimer, *Eclipse of Reason*, [1947] 2004, p. 14.

176 Ibid.

177 E. Traverso, *The Origins of Nazi Violence*, 2003, p. 44 ff.

178 F. Neumann, *Behemoth: The Structure and Practice of National Socialism 1933–1944*, [1942] 2009, pp. 469–470.

unity [*Volksgemeinschaft*]. From these political-ideological premises emerged the anti-Semitism characteristic of Nazism.

The gangs in power became part of Horkheimer and Adorno's reflection in *Dialectic of Enlightenment* [1947], as well as in the draft by Horkheimer alone, *Die Rackets und der Geist* [*The Rackets and the Spirit*] [1939–1942],[179] initially intended for this occasion but later excluded. In this latter work, Horkheimer expressed not only the idea that rackets constituted the "fundamental form of domination"[180] but also that the relationship between rackets and social community was direct, unmediated, and thus realizable as *Volksgemeinschaft*. Such a link would not have been conceivable if one had remained faithful to a Hegelian view of the spirit consisting of mediations and dialectical differences. In *Dialectic of Enlightenment* [1947], this discourse will be revisited with reference to the idea of a Nazi will to power. The ruling elite would generate those aberrations of life domination through the use of instrumental rationality of technique. The Enlightenment aspiration for human emancipation through the use of reason would be inverted into its opposite, into manipulation and objectification within scientific rationality of what had been subjective instances of individual and collective self-liberation.[181] The betrayal of Enlightenment reason's aims would be completed with the rise of the scientistic positivism of subjectivizing reason aimed at formalization and calculation of its practical goals. What will be definitively lost, however, is the truth in its objective-immanent dimension. Truth, as the satisfaction of the self-reflected in itself, in contrast to the substantiality of being, would also encompass the transformation of the functions of the arts and culture in mass society. In *Eclipse of Reason* [1947], Horkheimer asserts that in today's liberal bourgeois society, the veritable function of the artwork as an expressive claim of a collective good is definitively lost. Culture transforms into a cultural product, musical performance into "leisure-time occupation, an event, an opportunity for star performances, or a social gathering that must be attended if one belongs to a certain group",[182] since "it transforms works of art into cultural commodities".[183] Instrumental reason defines an era characterized by multiple political forms: not only the aberrations of totalitarianisms but also the authoritarianism of scientific reason and its legitimate claims to truth and meaning transcending the horizons of the self.

179 M. Horkheimer, "Die Rackets und der Geist", [1939–1942] 1985.
180 Ibid.
181 For a comparison of the theory of rackets with contemporary populism, particularly in the US context, see M. Jay, *Trump, Scorsese, and the Frankfurt School's Theory of Racket Society*, 2020, online.
182 M. Horkheimer, *Eclipse of Reason*, [1947] 2004, p. 27.
183 Ibid., p. 28.

2.7 Horkheimer and the authoritarian state

Horkheimer recognized in Pollock the idea that state capitalism, as an ideal type, possessed a critical-immanent (and we might add "heuristic") profile, concluding that such "utopias",[184] in both their "beauty"[185] and "ugliness",[186] remain standards for judging reality. For Pollock, this idea represented the ultimate and non-transformable stage of capitalism per se. Horkheimer thus approached Pollock's perspective with cautious detachment, mindful of the need to emphasize aspects related to the immanent critique of society and the idea of a dialectical contradiction inherent in capitalism. However, the capitalist contradictions facing Nazism were not seen as fostering the transition to a new political order. On the contrary, the stabilization of the economy through the state-controlled market seemed to ensure the prolonged existence of Germany's authoritarian regression, even following the hoped-for collapse of the Third Reich. For Horkheimer, the static nature of the system described by Pollock provided the deepest sense of pessimism following the increasingly brutal rise of National Socialism. In reality, Horkheimer had already anticipated this idea in *Die Juden und Europa* (the typescript of which is dated September 1939).[187] Here, it was hypothesized that the transition from the crisis of the liberal system to fascism could be attributed to an internal transformation within capitalism itself. The overcoming of the collapse thesis of the economy through centralized control of surplus value led Horkheimer to formulate the hypothesis of a historically ahistorical, imperishable and ultimately illiberal positioning of capitalism, in which the totalitarian society would be seen as capable of surviving economically in the long term.[188] The rationalization of surplus value production led to the taming of the dialectical relationship between productive forces and relations of production, thus establishing identity relations devoid of emancipatory dynamism. Fascism, by transforming the harmony of interests between labour and capital into a national community [*Volksgemeinschaft*], had radicalized the differences between classes determined by surplus value. This transition was logical rather than brutal, unlike the transition from mercantile society to 19th-century liberalism. Having produced unemployment, social disorder and economic inefficiency, the market created the conditions for a reorganization of power first in a monopolistic sense, then for war and finally in an authoritarian direction. Thus, only a semblance of improvement in social conditions was achieved, as while the labour market saw a reduction in unemployment, the available tasks became state-imposed labour. Conflicts among working classes were not resolved at all: wage disparities, impoverishment and the loss of power of the middle class, especially among Jews, produced a society increasingly

184 M. Horkheimer, *Briefwechsel 1941–1948*, [1941–8] 1996, p. 115.
185 Ibid.
186 Ibid.
187 M. Horkheimer, "Die Juden und Europa", 1939, pp. 115–137.
188 Ibid.

atomized and intimidated by state power. It is based on these considerations that Horkheimer published *The End of Reason* in 1941,[189] while in 1941–1942 in Los Angeles, an article titled "The Authoritarian State" dedicated to Benjamin appeared in the special issue of the now-American *Studies in Philosophy and Social Science* (formerly *ZfS*).[190]

In the first of these texts, Horkheimer introduced the issue, later extensively developed with Adorno, of the Enlightenment delusion of an omnipotent reason which for Kant had served as the secret guide of history, as well as the foundation of the ideas of "freedom, justice, and truth",[191] but which, in its progress, ended up turning against itself, leading to its own "self-destruction".[192] Hence, Horkheimer's stark choice: "barbarism or freedom".[193] The connections to what would be more extensively developed in *Dialectic of Enlightenment* [1947] are evident, such as the link to the discussion of the acquisition of awareness of a progressive decline in civilization which "fascism has strengthened".[194]

The second contribution considers how the transition from monopolistic capitalism to state capitalism represents the final stage of bourgeois society and its process of capital appropriation before further authoritarian rigidity. Horkheimer expresses this viewpoint with the statement "[S]tate capitalism is the authoritarian state of the present".[195] The crisis is thus hypostatized and elevated to eternity. The authoritarian state, in analogy with Pollock's state capitalism, defines an ideal-typical socio-political category sensitive to the changed historical context. Horkheimer criticizes both the bureaucratization of power in Weimar social democracy, which failed both to express revolutionary demands and to transform itself into a council democracy, and the extremist tendencies of National Socialism and Soviet communism. Horkheimer succinctly asserts:

> The murky relationship between Lassalle, the founder of the German Socialist mass party, and Bismarck, the father of German state capitalism, was symbolic. Both aimed at state control. Government and opposition party bureaucrats from the left and right were pushed toward some form of authoritarian state.
>
> (M. Horkheimer, "The Authoritarian State", [1942] 1973, p. 7)

Not all such forms of state and economic organization express the same degree of completeness. For Horkheimer, "integral statism, or state socialism"[196] (that is, Soviet communism) is certainly the most successful form of authoritarianism

189 M. Horkheimer, "The End of Reason", 1941, pp. 366–388.
190 M. Horkheimer, "The Authoritarian State", [1942] 1973.
191 M. Horkheimer, "The End of Reason", 1941, p. 366.
192 Ibid., p. 388.
193 Ibid.
194 Ibid., p. 366.
195 M. Horkheimer, "The Authoritarian State", [1942] 1973, p. 4.
196 Ibid., p. 8.

because it has "freed itself from any dependence on private capital",[197] but fascism represents its "weaker" form because it is "mixed".[198] Lastly, liberal democracy is placed in a subordinate order as it represents a more distant development from the model of state capitalism and the collective redistribution of surplus value. Given this framework, the only possible way out is to find a council-based turn of the state, in which workers' councils assume democratic-radical governmental functions much broader than the Weimar political degradation of factory councils. In any case, each of these types fits into a dialectical development perspective that cannot be ignored. The proletariat, according to Horkheimer, must put an "unnatural end"[199] to the capitalist state system. The latter, by providing an objective basis for domination, creates the conditions for a "social revolution"[200] that, in turn, favours its overcoming through "emancipation".[201] The historical revolutionary process will not occur by reducing "the revolution to mere progress".[202] It will rather involve exiting a perspective solely linked to "the dimension of the cycle of progress and regression".[203] As Horkheimer concludes: "[A]s long as world history follows its logical course, it fails to fulfil its human destiny".[204] Horkheimer would also abandon the possibility of finding in the current situation a political model capable of ensuring the realization of the Enlightenment ideals of human emancipation. Thus, this drastic narrowing of the political horizon prefigures the impossibility of organizing a rational society. Instead, a pessimistic thesis regarding the course of history and the possibilities of improving the socio-political conditions of humanity become increasingly consolidated. Possible transformations of the state remain within an authoritarian framework and a negative view of the philosophy of history. This awareness then becomes fully articulated in the opposition between autonomy and self-sacrifice exemplified in the figure of Ulysses as presented in *Dialectic of Enlightenment* [1947].[205] Horkheimer conceptually transforms Pollock's idea of state capitalism by merging it with the idea of the authoritarian state as an alternative to Neumann's expression of "totalitarian monopoly capitalism", thus defining his new view of the illiberal state of the present both terminologically and conceptually.[206]

In reality, this is a view of power and the state aligned with the profile of the philosophy of history already outlined by Benjamin in the posthumously published

197 Ibid.
198 Ibid.
199 Ibid., p. 3.
200 Ibid., p. 18.
201 Ibid.
202 Ibid.
203 Ibid., p. 20.
204 Ibid.
205 M. Horkheimer, T. Adorno, *Dialectic of Enlightenment*, [1947] 2002.
206 On this point, see H. Dahms, "The Early Frankfurt School Critique of Capitalism", 2000, p. 347. The importance of constructing categories of thought that avoided both the old metaphysical tradition and the exaltation of empirical data was addressed in the previous chapter in the discussion of M. Horkheimer, "Materialism and Metaphysics", [1933] 2002, pp. 10–46.

essay "On the Concept of History" [1942/1950] edited by Horkheimer.[207] Even within a framework of mystical-salvific transfiguration of history, Benjamin had anticipated in his critique of certain materialist views of progress (both revolutionary and non-revolutionary) the tragedy of a past struggling to pass, which, in fact, revealed in its "remembrance"[208] [*Eingedenken*] the possibility of producing meaning for the future. Through three images, Benjamin articulated the planes of the transfiguration of time-history: the hunchbacked dwarf symbolizing historical materialism who "is to win all the time"[209] by pulling the strings of a puppet; Klee's *Angelus Novus*, who, in an attempt to embrace and redeem the stacked catastrophes of time, is increasingly driven toward "progress" by a "storm";[210] and finally, the cosmic-messianic path of remembrance as a salvific possibility in contrast to the non-redemption of man in the course of the historical process. For Benjamin, the option denied to Jews of "investigating the future" left open through remembrance the possibility that time might open a "strait gate through which Messiah might enter".[211] While sharing the fundamental pessimistic assumptions, Horkheimer did not adopt Benjamin's transfiguration of the historical process with its messianic appearance (problematic even for Benjamin himself). Instead, he remained faithful to a rationalist program of historical understanding, enriched by a critical-dialectical component capable of addressing those practical rationality short-circuits that the Enlightenment had failed to resolve.

In "*Vernunft und Selbsterhaltung*" [1942], a text also published in the special issue honoring Benjamin's premature death, Horkheimer anticipated the theses he would address more extensively in *Dialectic of Enlightenment* [1947].[212] Both texts inform us of a changed perception of history on Horkheimer's part and, in particular, of the fact that abstract Enlightenment reason will now be seen as having inverted into a technocratic functionalism and utilitarian calculation oriented toward redefining the contingent interests of the state—thus far from the task of realizing a human emancipation project. Abstract reason has become instrumental reason, and this has transformed into its opposite—the unreasonable—contradicting the very premises of abstract rationality. Translating this process into Marxian categories reveals the terms of the authoritarian character of Horkheimer's state: the annulment of the individual and the dynamic asymmetry between use relations and exchange relations: that is, the absorption of production and circulation into a centrally controlled economy.

207 M. Horkheimer, "*Vernunft und Selbsterhaltung*" ["Reason and Survival"], [1942] 1970. The essay appeared in the special issue of *ZfS/Studies in Philosophy and Social Science*, IX, 3, 1942, in honor of Walter Benjamin, who committed suicide in 1940 in Portbou, a town on the French-Spanish border. For a contextualization of the debate, see L. Ceppa, "Lo stato autoritario di Max Horkheimer", 1980, pp. 445–458.

208 W. Benjamin, "On the Concept of History", [1942/1950] 2005, p. 13.

209 Ibid.

210 Ibid.

211 Ibid.

212 M. Horkheimer, T. Adorno, *Dialectic of Enlightenment*, [1947] 2002.

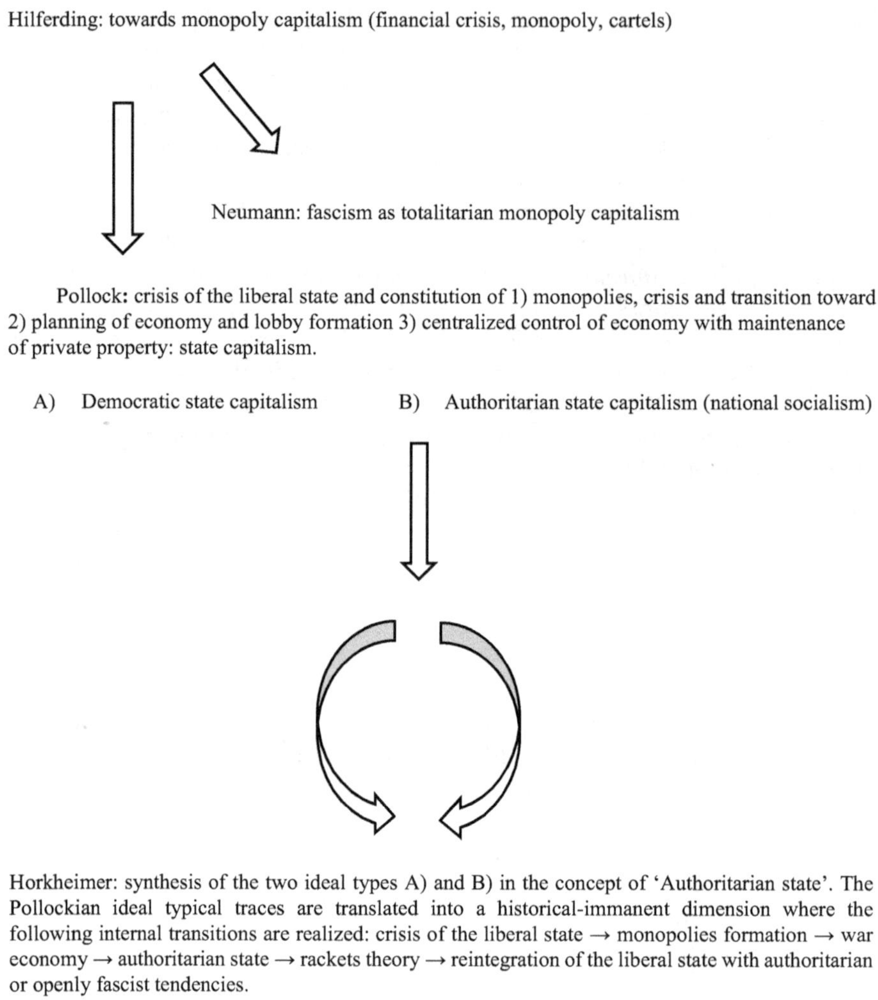

Figure 2.1 Transformation Models of the State and the Economy (1910–1945). (A) Democratic state capitalism. (B) Authoritarian state capitalism (national socialism).

For Horkheimer, economic demands become technical in nature,[213] as it could be argued, since internal contradictions within capital do not enter the state-controlled market. Consequently, society would become a disconnected whole as conflict and the dialectic inherent in any emancipatory process would become a reified and flattened totality along a one-dimensionality of so-

213 M. Horkheimer, "The Authoritarian State", [1942] 1973.

cial relations. Finally, individual consciousness, as well as collective consciousness, would be alienated in the verticalization of state reason, eliminating the possibility of developing an immanent critique of society.[214]

In *Eclipse of Reason* [1947], Horkheimer completes the philosophical reconstruction of the crisis of modern rationality.[215] By dismantling the objective dimension of reason, Enlightenment reason ended up transforming itself into a subjective-instrumental reason. Deprived of autonomously established objective purposes, instrumental reason has, in turn, become capable only of perpetuating "its co-ordinating activity"[216] without being able to set autonomous ends. As a result, "man has been stripped of all aims except self-preservation".[217] The world has turned into an infinite series of means that, paradoxically, have taken on the guise of masked objectives: "appearance of autonomous entities".[218] In this sense, the preservation of the self as an autonomy from nature has reversed into its opposite, the subordination to a world no longer under its control. The means-ends dialectic has thus led to the betrayal of its own initial assumptions: the dominant subject has become the dominated object, and his mind is "transformed into an automaton of formalized reason".[219] Consequently, art and human cultural expressions have also lost their connection to truth and politics, turning into mere "cultural good".[220] This cognitive framework bears witness to the intense conceptual reworking of the positions expressed by the Frankfurt School during the 1930s and 1940s. The analyses proposed have started from the consideration of the crisis of the liberal state of the early 1900s and have extended to include the subsequent transformations of institutions and national policies. However, before proceeding to a detailed examination of the transformation of the post-war technocratic state and its psychoanalytic implications, the issue of the Frankfurt School's intellectual militancy against Nazi-fascist authoritarianism must be addressed.

2.8 Exiles in America: anti-fascist activism (1943–1951)

The fortunes of the Frankfurt School coincided with the rise of National Socialism. After a brief stay in Geneva in 1933, the IfS moved to New York in 1934, establishing itself at Columbia University. Despite being under constant surveillance by American counterintelligence services and the FBI, the Frankfurt scholars endeavoured to distance themselves from accusations of pro-communism by working toward a democratic resolution of post-war

214 On the connection between societal contradictions and immanent critique, see M. Postone, "Critique, State, and Economy", 2004, p. 170 ff.
215 M. Horkheimer, *Eclipse of Reason*, [1947] 2004.
216 Ibid., p. 63.
217 Ibid., p. 69.
218 Ibid., p. 70.
219 Ibid., p. 88.
220 Ibid., p. 55.

German and European issues.[221] However, American authorities' scepticism never fully dissipated, making it quite difficult for Horkheimer to secure funding from local foundations, such as the Rockefeller Foundation or the American Jewish Committee, even though the aim was to develop studies on fascism. In America, IfS members managed to combine two objectives: on one hand, they were able to develop research in social psychology on anti-Semitism and authoritarianism; on the other, they engaged in anti-fascist activism by collaborating with American intelligence. Horkheimer had always expressed opposition to active political militancy among IfS members, believing their sole purpose was scientific. However, starting in 1938, the ongoing economic crisis impacted the finances of the IfS to the extent that even the salaries of some key figures, including Neumann, Marcuse and Kirchheimer, were drastically reduced. This event led them to seek alternative sources of income. An opportunity for these individuals arose in 1943, following the United States' entry into the war against Hitler's Germany, when the American government established the research and analysis branch (R&A) within the Office of Strategic Services (OSS)—an intelligence agency of the State Department tasked with producing reports analyzing German society and politics under National Socialism. Active until 1949, this unit involved the aforementioned Neumann, Marcuse and Kirchheimer, as well as occasional co-authors such as Gurland, Gilbert and Herz. All these scholars, despite their affiliation with the IfS and socialist sympathies, offered diverse analytical profiles and historical-political considerations. Neumann, besides being a renowned scholar for his discussed work *Behemoth*, had also been a lawyer for the Social Democratic Party (SPD) and a political activist. In 1948, he was appointed professor of political science at Columbia University, and his reception in the United States was considerably warmer than that of his other Frankfurt colleagues. Marcuse, after gaining study experience under Heidegger, became one of Horkheimer's early collaborators. In 1941, he published his already-mentioned monograph on Hegel. Finally, Kirchheimer was a criminal lawyer with experience in the Prussian administration who had undergone extensive analysis of German National Socialism. The involvement of prominent Frankfurt School figures coincided with the Wehrmacht's setbacks in Tunisia and Stalingrad. On June 25, 1943, Neumann wrote a report titled "German Morale after Tunisia",[222] highlighting the emerging belief that the Reich had already lost the war. It became essential at that point to differentiate between the morale of individuals within democracies and that of those within dictatorships: in the former case, the erosion of individual sentiment had become a political issue, whereas in the latter,

221 See, in this regard, A. Stephan, *Im Visier des FBI. Deutsche Exilschriftsteller in den Akten amerikanischer Geheimdienste*, 1995, and the essay by D. Bondì, "Max Horkheimer in esilio. La sorveglianza politica e l'idea di Democrazia", 2019, pp. 347–374. On the experiences and intellectual legacy of the Frankfurt School in America, particularly with reference to Marcuse and the New Left, see M. Jay, *Permanent Exiles: Essays on the Intellectual Migration from Germany to America*, 1985, and T. Wheatland, *The Frankfurt School in Exile*, 2009.

222 F. Neumann, "The Free Germany Manifesto and the German People (August 6, 1943)", [1943] 2013, pp. 95–99.

totalitarian sentiment "cannot be effectively attacked by the ordinary methods of psychological warfare".[223] This meant that only through the total defeat of Nazism—that is, through the dismantling of the entire administrative and ideological apparatus—would it be possible to rehabilitate individual moral sentiment and the overall transformation of society in a democratic direction. The military setbacks of the Axis forces could not yet provide the illusion that "morale itself is in danger of collapse".[224] Nazism had understood from the outset that the system of societal control had to be based on the establishment of a regime of terror. On one hand, this indicated the paths to submission to the power system; on the other hand, it discouraged forms of rebellion through extreme punishments and tight social control.

Following the publication of *Behemoth* in 1942, Neumann was tasked with directing the central European section and the civil affairs division of the US War Department.[225] This unit produced a significant number of reports, not only analyzing the internal structure of Hitler's state but also providing recommendations on how to transform Germany democratically in the future post-war reconstruction phase (reactivation of rights, freedoms and political pluralism). In this regard, the political directions from the exiled Frankfurt scholars focused on a hoped-for socialist turn in the post-war German state through the nationalization of industry. They also expressed general opposition to the Morgenthau plan, which proposed a territorial dismemberment of Germany.[226] Neumann was assigned the task of collaborating with the Nuremberg military tribunal under Judge Jackson, responsible for prosecuting Nazi leaders for war crimes and other charges that were then difficult to formulate legally. This involved not only gathering evidence on the perpetrators of the crimes but also assessing specific roles and responsibilities within the command chains. A separate issue was the Holocaust, regarding which Neumann was unfairly accused of underestimating the most egregious outcomes of anti-Semitism. This led him to resign from the position shortly after the proceedings began.[227]

A different issue was the transformation of German society in the 1930s. As previously noted, it was a new totalitarian society that levelled individual ideas and initiatives. Thus, Churchill's observation that Nazi Germany represented a kind of evolution of Wilhelmian imperialism was promptly considered by Frankfurt analysts as completely misleading. The role of command, once held by the landed aristocracy of the Junkers, no longer served as the axis of Prussian militarism. Nazi Germany had carefully planned the replacement of the previous elites with new figures while also maintaining a privileged relationship with industrial capitalism (particularly with Krupp's steel industry, which was crucial for the war effort). The report written by Marcuse and Gilbert emphasized this aspect, arguing that Prussian militarism had specific geographic, economic, social and

223 Ibid., p. 63.
224 Ibid., p. 64.
225 Ibid., p. 12.
226 Ibid.
227 L. Fischer, "The Frankfurt School and Fascism", 2018, p. 801.

ideological characteristics.[228] Large capital investments were directed at maintaining land profits, leading to a radical transformation of the Junker class.[229] Their properties were overvalued, and, unable to maintain them, they needed to form an alliance with heavy industry. While the aristocracy's landholdings survived due to protectionism, what the Junkers conceded to capitalist industry was free initiative in an expansionist foreign policy.[230] Starting from Weimar, the rights acquired under the Bismarckian era were erased. Prussia became a parliamentary democracy in 1918, and the Junkers lost their privileges and power. Nevertheless, they remained an influential group that, even under the Republican *Reichswehr*, could occupy elite positions in the military and the economy. Hindenburg's election in 1925 certainly worked in their favour, although they lost the decisive roles of the past, independent of party control. The process of excluding the Junkers was completed by Nazism through a radical centralization of power, a war economy, the advancement of the petty bourgeoisie in the social hierarchy and the emergence of a new ideology focused on technocratic growth at the expense of agricultural power and mass manipulation. In the report "German Social Stratification" of November 26, 1943, Marcuse identified three main groups responsible for power co-management at different levels: the Nazi Party, the ministerial bureaucracy and the military.[231] This analysis was complemented by a comprehensive collective essay by Gurland, Kirchheimer and Neumann on the fate of small enterprises in Nazi Germany.[232]

The subsequent question concerned the possibility of identifying fault lines within the seemingly monolithic Nazi bloc. In this regard, the three scholars co-authored a particularly interesting report titled "Possible Patterns of German Collapse" on September 21, 1943.[233] This text compared the causes of the German collapse in 1918 with those of the current situation. The conclusion was that while German military defeat was certain, the timing of such an event remained uncertain. An accurate prediction was therefore not feasible.[234] From a comparative perspective, the social situation was indeed quite different from that hypothesized in 1918. The material conditions of the people had improved, and, above all, the totalitarian form of political control left no room for opposition to express itself or organize. In this context, the Allies were obligated to exercise great caution in planning a military intervention, as it would jeopardize the social situation. Therefore, initiatives such as the

228 H. Marcuse, F. Gilbert, "The Significance of Prussian Militarism for Nazi Imperialism: Potential Tensions in United Nations Psychological Warfare (October 20, 1943)", [1943] 2013, p. 61 ff.

229 Ibid., p. 64.

230 Ibid.

231 H. Marcuse, "German Social Stratification (November 26, 1943)", [1943] 2013, p. 74 ff.

232 A. R. L. Gurland, O. Kirchheimer, "The Fate of Small Business in Nazi Germany", [1943] 2010.

233 F. Neumann, H. Marcuse, F. Gilbert, "Possible Patterns of German Collapse (September 21, 1943)", [1943] 2013, pp. 106–117.

234 Ibid., p. 108.

text of "Manifesto Issued by Free German Committee in Moscow" published in full in the *New York Times* on August 1, 1943, were considered politically ineffective.[235] On the other hand, the German Communist Party had been suppressed by the Nazis in 1933, and while it remained active both inside and outside Germany, it no longer had the political and organizational capacity to present itself as a genuine opposition force. The Frankfurt analysts informed the American State Department of the virtually non-existent possibility of overturning the Hitler regime.[236] The prognosis was that some forms of radical opposition would re-emerge following the triumphant entry of the Allies into Germany, which would spark hopes of a revolutionary attempt.[237] In other words, the process of denazification would need to be planned to avoid the rise of additional authoritarian leaders. Crucial reading in this direction are the reports by Neumann, Kirchheimer and Herz on the treatment of Nazi leaders and the principle of responsibility for executing orders,[238] as well as Marcuse's evaluations regarding new power subjects in post-Nazi Germany, particularly unions and the Communist Party.[239] Overall, the militant activism of some prominent figures of the early Frankfurt School contributed decisively to providing assessment parameters and political action input to the Allies and the post-war pacification process in Germany. The Frankfurt scholars played a fundamental intellectual and political role in the study and combat of National Socialism. Primarily as theorists, they developed a series of analyses concerning the transformations of capitalism and German society. They offered positions that helped the Allies understand previously unknown phenomena such as the political effects of propaganda, the vertical authoritarianism of the Third Reich, Aryanism and ideological racism. However, it was in grappling with the reality of historical facts that these contributions provided a key to understanding complex phenomena, necessarily imbued with a multiplicity of disciplinary knowledge. The Frankfurt scholars involved in OSS monitoring activities thus played a role in line with Horkheimer's methodological approaches, reinterpreting the synthesis of theory and practice into militant anti-fascist activism.

235 F. Neumann, "The Free Germany Manifesto and the German People", [1943] 2013, pp. 143ff.

236 H. Marcuse, "The German Communist Party (July 10, 1944)", [1944] 2013, p. 167ff.

237 H. Marcuse, "Dissolution of the Nazi Party and Its Affiliated Organizations (July 22, 1944)", [1943] 2013, p. 261 ff. For contributions related to the processes of denazification at the social, political and legal levels, see pp. 229–396.

238 F. Neumann, "Problems Concerning the Treatment of War Criminals (September 25, 1944)", [1943] 2013, pp. 457–463; O. Kirchheimer, J. Herz, "Leadership Principle and Criminal Responsibility (July 18, 1945)", [1943] 2013, pp. 464–474.

239 H. Marcuse, "Status and Prospects of German Trade-Unions and Works Councils (May 27, 1946)", [1943] 2013, pp. 557–590; H. Marcuse, "The Potentials of World Communism (August 1, 1949)", [1943] 2013, pp. 591–610.

3 "A new 'anthropological' type"

Psyche, technology, culture[1]

Beginning in the early 1920s with the publication of Freud's *Group Psychology and the Analysis of the Ego,* [1921][2] and continuing throughout the 1930s, numerous psychoanalytic discoveries and analyses emerged addressing issues related to collective living. In his 1921 work, Freud explained the need to overcome the dichotomy between individual psychology and mass psychology, presenting a framework that distinguished between the individual's subordination to paternal authority within the family and the collective's submission to the power of the leader. For Freud, man is not a "herd animal", but rather a "horde animal, an individual creature in a horde led by a chief".[3] Thus, the dynamics of the primal Darwinian pack led by a dominant male were reflected in the mass. The figure of the leader was seen as the one who calmed the mutual aggressiveness of the mass members. However, explaining the regressive nature of the mass did not require abandoning individual psychology; rather, it involved accounting for the gregarious nature of the group psyche through the socialization of individual instinctual mechanisms. Freud thus "socialized", so to speak, individual psychology—the sexual drive, libido—arguing that "from the very first Individual Psychology is at the same time Social Psychology".[4] However, he was careful not to let psychoanalysis lose its focus on the analysis of the individual. The link between the individuals who make up the mass and their unreflective subordination to a leader is of an affective-projective nature. Individuals become a mass through abandoning the ideal of the ego and replacing it with the "same object".[5] The mass is therefore constituted on the basis of an erotic-libidinal (not rational!) bond, in which the leader embodies the figure of the primal father, providing "the group ideal, which governs the ego in the place of the ideal of the ego".[6] The

1 The expression appears in the preface by M. Horkheimer to T. W. Adorno, E. Frenkel-Brunswik, D. J. Levinson, R. Nevitt Sanford, *The Authoritarian Personality,* [1950] 2019, p. lxxi.
2 S. Freud, *Group Psychology and the Analysis of the Ego,* [1921] 1949.
3 Ibid., p. 89.
4 Ibid., p. 2.
5 Ibid., p. 80.
6 Ibid., p. 100.

DOI: 10.4324/9781003630340-4

image of the leader and the primal pack had already been extensively addressed in psychoanalytic and anthropological comparative studies in *Totem and Taboo* [1913].[7] Here, it was shown that the horror of incest in the modern psychotic was a trace of the suppression of the dominant father by children and brothers typical of primitive peoples. The exclusion of females from the rest of the clan by the primordial father/leader had generated a process of instinctual liberation through a path of civilization and stabilization by the suppression of the dominus. This had led to a rationalization of domination that had, in turn, helped "universalize libidinous relationships"[8] by socially translating them into the division of labour (thus pacifying them within a social framework). In the process of civilization, the principle of reality was established, which, in turn, generated frustration, oppression, inhibition of the drives of the id and, ultimately, unhappiness. Instinctual repression, as individuals internalized the principle of reality by limiting their instincts, ended up governing the very instinctual structure, transforming "culture" in "nature".[9] It is in the wake of this process that society turned to forms of authoritarian domination, subordinating individual needs to social ones. Consequently, the psychic life of the individual was still considered to be constituted by relationships with social otherness, only opposing narcissistic phenomena of the exclusion of the other's intervention. Already in *On Narcissism* [1914], Freud had identified a close connection between the idealization of the ego and the "understanding of group psychology",[10] allowing the possible opposition between the two to fade. Mass psychology should not be taken as an original category but as a social drive that developed within the individual according to proximity forms of aggregation such as the family. While the pioneering studies on crowds by Le Bon, cited by Freud, had highlighted the regressive and hypnotic nature of group behaviour, these aspects were now linked to the lives of primitives and the psychotic fantasies of neurotics.[11] The repression of jealousy impulses ensured expectations of fair treatment both within the family unit and in the social sphere. Freud thus demonstrated the psychological foundations of political power: in other words, how it was possible to draw a common line between the individual's desire for equal treatment with siblings and the citizen's desire to be considered an equal among equals. The internalization of authority thus legitimized consent to the authoritarian political leader. Despotic power found support in the psychological adherence of individuals to its exercise. The figure of the authoritarian father and that of public political authority activated the same psychological mechanism learned within family

7 S. Freud, *Totem and Taboo*, [1913] 2001.
8 H. Marcuse, "Freedom and Freud's Theory of Instincts", [1956] 1970, p. 22.
9 Ibid., p. 11.
10 S. Freud, *On Narcissism*, [1914] 2012, p. 101.
11 Reference here is to G. Le Bon when he affirms that "The substitution of the unconscious action of crowds for the conscious activity of individuals is one of the principal characteristics of the present age", in *The Crowd: A Study of the Popular Mind*, [1895] 2002, p. iii.

relationships. However, both Le Bon and Freud had treated these psychic structures in a syncretistic and ahistorical manner. Freud did not account for class dynamics or the definition of aggressive pulsionality starting from a defined productive structure.

The integration of psychological categories with economic-productive concepts would instead be the task of the Freudo-Marxist research program, of which the first critical theory became an intellectual heir. Beginning with Reich, a second-generation Freudian, some of Freud's fundamental categories were extensively reconsidered. This was especially the case with the superego and its redefinition in historical-social terms in terms of "character". As a proponent of a synthesis between Marxism and Freudianism, Reich focused on investigating authoritarianism from the perspective of family formation. While Freud laid the groundwork for a social psychology by identifying the psychic structures of the socialized individual within the family and the mass, Freudo-Marxism later emphasized the dependence of psychic structures on material conditions and their change over time. In this regard, the bio-physiological conditioning of infantile instincts described by Freud as sensitive to affectivity developed in the family would be framed within an economic and social context of mediation of parental affectivity: the "analytical social psychology seeks to understand the instinctual apparatus of a group, its libidinous and largely unconscious behaviour, in terms of its socio-economic structure".[12] Freudo-Marxism would thus turn to a comprehensive rethinking of the relationship between the psychic superstructure and the structure of the productive forces and economic organization. In line with a coherent development of Marxian categories, Freudo-Marxism would conceive the development of psychoanalytic categories in terms of a "theory of instincts" aimed at "clarify[ing], in detail, the psychological effects of production conditions upon the individual; . . . that is to say, the way that ideologies are formed 'inside the head'".[13] As Fromm would specify almost a decade later, if the consciousness of social being is the hallmark of historical materialism, the consciousness of psychoanalysis concerns the unconscious and the theory of instincts. In both cases, they are "materialistic sciences"[14] as they start from a theory of material needs and not from pure ideas. Reich's irreverence toward established political-cultural standards cost him not only his expulsion from the Communist Party but also his expulsion in 1933 from the German Psychoanalytic Society and, subsequently, in 1934 from the International Psychoanalytical Association. Reich would publish *The Mass Psychology of Fascism* in

12 E. Fromm, "The Method and Function of an Analytic Social Psychology", [1932] 1970, p. 451.

13 W. Reich, "Dialectical Materialism and Psychoanalysis", [1923] 1972, p. 45.

14 E. Fromm, "The Method and Function of an Analytic Social Psychology", [1932] 1970, p. 451.

1933, the year of Hitler's coronation as Chancellor of the Reich.[15] This text would profoundly influence the developments of social psychology research at the Frankfurt School.[16] While Freud had posited that drives should find confinement in the repressive mechanisms of aggression, Reich, on the other hand, believed that only through a social liberation of libido and sexuality could the individual finally open up to forms of subjective self-realization. In this respect, the political retranslation of sexual liberation would lead to manifestations of sexual-revolutionary rebellion rather than to mild social reformism incapable of modifying the deep structures of interpersonal relationships. Thus, if Freud's socio-anthropological pessimism did not intend to maintain a psycho-emancipatory gap concerning the oppressive dynamics of cultural development, then a rethinking of Freud's theory of the death drive was necessary. This began with an article Reich originally published in the *Internationale Zeitschrift für Psychoanalyse* [1932] and later included in *Character Analysis* [1933].[17] The aim was to examine how the mania for destruction contained a derivative rather than primary element of the removal of the sexual drive. Repressed libido generates aggression. Thus, for Reich, only a rehabilitation of libido as a life force could curb the emergence of destructive instincts.

In alignment with his project to renew Freud's concept of the unconscious, Reich introduced the notion of "orgone biophysics", which he used to demonstrate that "Freudian unconscious, *the antisocial element in the human structure, is a secondary result of the repression of primary biological impulses*".[18] However, it was in the 1920s, through the clinical problem of resistance, that Reich began to develop the concept of the "character structure" as a comprehensive historical explanation for mental illness, in contrast to the specific consideration of Freudian neurosis (such as in the case of tics). It was no longer a matter of attributing the domestication of violent unconscious drives to an ahistorical dimension like the superego; rather, it was necessary to assign the control of the drive dimension to a characterological superstructure.[19] It was precisely

15 W. Reich, "Dialectical Materialism and Psychoanalysis", [1923] 1972, p. 43. For some scholars like Breuer (2016 and 2017), the IfS only began to take a programmatic interest in the subject starting in the 1940s—almost a decade after the NSDAP's electoral victory and twenty years after the rise of fascism in Italy. Breuer's judgment appears even harsher when he highlights the omission of any evaluation of the political effects produced in Germany by the NSDAP in the early issues of the *ZfS*, edited by Horkheimer. As will be shown in this chapter, these interpretations of a delayed interest by the early Frankfurt School in fascism do not hold up to the facts. The following sections will demonstrate how the IfS developed a series of studies on authority first and, later, a program of critique of fascism, as early as the late 1920s. See S. Breuer, "The Truth of Modern Society? Critical Theory and Fascism", 2017, p. 78.

16 In particular, Horkheimer refers to Reich's theory on the fixation of drives as a pathway to sadism in M. Horkheimer, "Egoism and Freedom Movements: On the Anthropology of the Bourgeois Era", [1936] 1993, pp. 49–110.

17 W. Reich, *Der Masochistische Charakter*, [1932], pp. 303–351.

18 W. Reich, *The Mass Psychology of Fascism*, [1933] 1980, p. VII.

19 P. A. Robinson, *Freudian Left*, 1990, p. 9 ff.

this rethinking of the superstructure in terms of ideology becoming replicated character that allowed Reich to reconsider the Marxian relationship between base and superstructure. Although ideology was the product of the forces of production in play, its crystallization in character ensured a persistence that extended far beyond the structural transformations of the production world itself. Ideological-characterological learning already occurred within the family, even as social transformation subsequently followed its course. Similarly, the sexual repression of the child anticipated an education in authoritarianism that he would later encounter and even support in society. Repression and the structuring of character thus provided new directions for rethinking the relationship between base and superstructure. This also explained the subject's inability to rationally transcend the false consciousness formed through the inversion of interests pursued by capitalist society. Similarly, in his 1932 work published in the *ZfS—Psychoanalytic Characterology and Its Application to the Understanding of Culture*—Fromm observed how the bourgeois (capitalist) anal character could be found within the proletarian class despite the scarcity of personal capital. In this work, in fact, it was argued that the libidinal structure underlying these traits is conditioned by the family and other traditional cultural factors,[20] which slow down its realignment with the ongoing transformation of the productive structure.

In line with these initial discoveries, Reich addressed the theme of the masses' voluntary subordination to political authority in *The Mass Psychology of Fascism* [1933] and the relationship between power and consent as irrational outcomes of sexual repression. Reich's core idea, later taken up by Horkheimer, considered the identification of the masses with the leader as a substitute for fulfilling needs through their sublimation into an ascetic ideal. Moreover, in the case of fascism, Reich saw it as the product of a cross-cutting sexual repression across its various forms of political organization, so much so that even in Russia, the transition to state capitalism "has not in the least altered the typical helpless and authoritarian character structure of the masses of people".[21] Fascism as a meta-ideological concept and sexual repression would be the fundamental pair through which Reich viewed the recurrence of possible illiberal scenarios, considering that "fascist mysticism is orgastic longing under the conditions of mystification and inhibition of natural sexuality".[22] Thus, for Reich, fascism was an outcome not politically reducible to a single political polarity, presenting itself instead as a cross-cutting form—both as right-wing and left-wing fascism—when its essence facilitated the reemergence of a deep psychic layer (a second characterological layer). Any revolution intending to achieve lasting success would therefore need to be accompanied by

20 E. Fromm, *Psychoanalytic Characterology and Its Application to the Understanding of Culture*, [1932] 1949, p. 207 ff.

21 W. Reich, *The Mass Psychology of Fascism*, [1933] 1980, p. XXIII.

22 Ibid., p. XVII.

a form of social reorganization capable of facilitating liberation from sexual frustrations. Fascism, however, presented itself precisely as the expression of such a state of drive repression, having made the concealment of those primordial violent instincts politically usable under the presentable guise of bourgeois character. It also contained within itself the "conflict between pauperization and conservative thinking"[23] in the absence of revolutionary forces to counteract it. Fromm, from his perspective, would explore social characterology from the 1930s onward, presenting it as a medium between base and superstructure.[24] This reflected Reich's idea that characterology answered the question of social reproduction (replacing the role of the Freudian superego), while the problem of production remained the domain of economics and sociology.[25] Social character was defined by the structure of the world of work in the same society and the role the individual occupied within it. Social character shaped individuals' behaviour, leading them to act in conformity with a particular social model. Individuals were seen as deriving pleasure from conforming to preordained social patterns, having abandoned any pretense of critical and autonomous choice legitimized by a given social normative standard. Ideals (and ideas), while rooted in an economic base, maintained their own independent value. For example, the idea of freedom as free initiative established itself in the bourgeoisie in opposition to the restrictive dominance of the market by the feudal class. If the ideal of freedom had been exhausted within economic production relations, then the critique and consequent exit from a feudal-medieval form of social organization would not have been explainable. The ideal of freedom, while articulated on a material basis of definition, was not exhausted by it, presenting itself instead as a value "deeply rooted in the nature of man".[26] Thus, there was a mediating relationship between base and superstructure, enacted by social character. For Fromm, this mediation was bidirectional: "from the economic basis to the ideas and from the ideas to the economic basis".[27] A second element of mediation concerned the idea of the *social unconscious* as a counterpart to social character. The social unconscious was defined by the thoughts that society allowed to become conscious or contained within the unconscious. The social unconscious was realized through collective mechanisms of repression. Man conformed to society's character by repressing certain feelings and thoughts, fearing social isolation and ostracism, which were virtually equivalent to death.[28] Nevertheless, the emptying of awareness of pieces of reality selectively placed in the unconscious led to the necessity of filling and coherently organizing the facts of experience. As

23 Ibid., p. 62.
24 E. Fromm, *Psychoanalytic Characterology and Its Relevance for Social Psychology*, [1932] 1949.
25 W. Reich, *Character Analysis*, [1933] 1972, p. 210 ff.
26 E. Fromm, *Beyond the Chains of Illusion: My Encounter with Marx and Freud*, [1962] 1990, p. 67.
27 Ibid., p. 68.
28 Ibid., p. 82.

Fromm would say, "The repression of the awareness of facts is, and must be, supplemented by the acceptance of many fictions".[29] In this sense, ideologies would come to the rescue as surrogates for ideas made subject to repressive mechanisms. As Fromm clarified in 1941:

> To understand the dynamics of the social process we must understand the dynamics of the psychological processes operating within the individual, just as to understand the individual we must see him in the context of the culture which molds him.
>
> (E. Fromm, *Escape from Freedom*, [1941] 1965, p. VIII)

If Hitler embodied the symbol of such individual sadism, the German people, fleeing from their own freedom, threw themselves into the hands of the one who would lead them to ruin. In this respect, the continuation of critical theory research, while remaining faithful to a certain interpretative line of Marxism, integrated structural elements of political economy critique with superstructural profiles of ego analysis and cultural production. However, the possibility of the passage from structure to superstructure remained to be justified; the connection between psychoanalysis and Marxism became the junction that allowed the synthesis between Marx and the internal psychic structures of social groups. These were considered by Fromm as forms of introjection of authoritarian powers.

In general, the overall development of a triangulation between economic-political structure, ideological superstructure and mass psychoanalysis within authoritarian society (along with cultural critique) was recognized. These polarities together would contribute in a uniquely semi-independent way to tracing the trajectory of Frankfurt School reflection on fascism and the endogenous illiberal tendencies of democratic societies. Löwenthal, in a 1946 essay entitled "Terror's Atomization of Man",[30] insisted precisely on the persistent nature of "totalitarian terror"[31] and its perpetuation within the post-Nazi German economic-productive structure. He identified various parameters for verifying an authoritarian regime—chief among them the collapse of the subjects' personality and the replacement of moral conscience with impulsive-imitative acts under an external authority defined as "Hitler-Ego".[32] Material conditions of indigence would lead to the resurgence of the feelings "fear, hunger and thirst"[33] that fascism would exploit to its advantage in a rational and systematic way.[34]

29 Ibid., p. 93.
30 L. Löwenthal, "Terror's Atomization of Man", [1946].
31 Ibid., p. 2.
32 Ibid., p. 3.
33 Ibid., p. 4.
34 Ibid., p. 7.

Critical theory, between the 1940s and 1950s, would introduce autonomous research programs distinct from Marxist debate, elaborating on the basis of a reinterpretation of the cultural *zeitgeist* the transition to a philosophy of history of Western civilization as a series of temporal concatenations of the domination of instrumental rationality and its aporias. Horkheimer and Adorno, in *Dialectic of Enlightenment* [1947], embarked on a path of reading the aporias of instrumental reason in Western civilization that would lay the theoretical groundwork for understanding contemporary society on levels different from those strictly related to the critique of political economy of the earliest phase. The analysis of civilization as the history of man's domination over man would come to be articulated through psychoanalytic categories of identification of deep instinctual structures and dynamics of cultural production. These would be sublimated to the point of oppressing the impulses of destruction and creation of the new, also providing a path for understanding fascism articulated on the level of superstructure and centred on the critique of instrumental reason.

The theoretical predecessor from which they would draw inspiration was precisely Freud's *Civilization and Its Discontent* [1930].[35] In this text, Freudian reflection considered the relationship between civilization and discontent. Freud's man was fundamentally antisocial, and only civilization could tame him to group life. This asociality was the source of his own unhappiness: the suppression of impulses corresponded with an increase in civilization [*Kultur*], but this also brought with it a progressive burden of neurosis. A paradox thus emerged: the protection expected from institutions in fact contributed to an increase in unbearable frustrations. Freud had drawn an analogy between the process of civilization and the libidinal evolution of the individual. Drive sublimation came to define a certain degree of civilization: art, science and all higher psychic activities constituted sublimations aimed at advancing the degree of civilization. In Freudian terms, drive sublimation was understood as a mechanism intended to redirect sexual or aggressive drives toward non-sexual or non-aggressive goals, as in the case of science or the arts. In this redirection, there was an intermediate phase of desexualization of the sexual (or aggressive) drive and its introjection into the ego. According to Freud, "Sublimation of instinct is an especially conspicuous feature of cultural evolution".[36]

However, in this context, civilization and its own artistic and social institutions became the receptacle for these very drives. Thus, the neuroses associated with modern societal life and, ultimately, the narcissistic aberrations of mass politics could be traced back to long-term processes of introjecting sexual drives into the ego. Furthermore, the renunciation of aggressive tendencies imposed by civilization also led to a state of discontent. Since civilization imposed limits not only on sexuality but also on aggression, it became clear

35 S. Freud, *Civilization and Its Discontents*, [1930] 1961.
36 Ibid., p. 49.

why individuals struggled to find any form of happiness within it: "In actual fact, primitive man was better off in this respect, for he knew nothing of any restrictions on his instincts. . . . Civilized man has exchanged some part of his chances of happiness for a measure of security".[37] These were the psychoanalytic premises for the development of a research program on the authoritarian personality and, as we shall see, for understanding the psychological implications of the cultural industry in mass society.

3.1 Reich: mass psychology and fascism

According to Reich, fascism is the emblem of the repressive society par excellence. It produced a social system that repressed deep primary biological drives through the use of ideology. Reich's Freudo-Marxist approach to psychoanalysis views the revolution against National Socialism as the ultimate and necessary outcome for the liberation of the masses from the most brutal repression of the unconscious. Only in this way can we hope to allow the emergence of the most basic and socially cohesive structure of humanity, which Freud failed to fully grasp. This form of liberation from the cruellest lustful and sadistic impulses was never realized in history; instead, history witnessed a succession of organized forms of individual oppression, along with a heavily intensified process of industrialization of production: the factory. The narcotization of primary impulses in industrialized societies did not eliminate these impulses but rather redirected them toward other social targets, such as identifying groups seen as enemies of society—Jews, communists and so on. These groups were the targets identified by Hitler as part of the policy to purify the German race.

However, it would be mistaken to think that fascism, according to Reich, is reducible to specific historical and economic conditions, such as those that arose in Europe after the end of World War I. For Reich—and this marks a fundamental departure from the purely Marxist view of the history of power—fascism represents an inherent characteristic of the human psyche itself. Thus, it can manifest in various historical forms and is certainly not limited to specific dynamics like those of Italian Fascism, Japanese fascism, or German National Socialism. The psychic structures upon which the expressions of authoritarian power are based are therefore independent of material conditions in the strict sense, although their activation depends, in one way or another, on specific social contexts.

In *Character Analysis* (1933), Reich examined the biopsychic character structure according to three levels.[38] Each of these levels, while functioning autonomously, was seen as a sedimentation of social relationships. The most superficial level involved a cooperative and friendly plane of intersubjective relationships. However, between this level and the third level, which related

37 Ibid., p. 62.
38 W. Reich, *Character Analysis*, [1933] 1972.

to the fundamental biological core where the primary instincts of love and sexuality were located, lay the Freudian unconscious, which Reich saw as represented by impulses of violence and domination. To reach the deepest stage of primary biological drives, it was necessary first to recognize that the intermediate level represented something imposed by socio-institutional structures (family, church, military etc.). Freud had already analyzed the structure of artificial masses and the love relationship that the supreme leader of the church or military had with the members of his group.[39] Overcoming this level was possible, and indeed necessary, to create a non-frustrated and non-repressive society. Reich's psychoanalysis was directed toward this goal. For Reich, the character structure, which represents the intermediate level, was what reproduced the social structure in the form of ideology. Only if the third level were not equivalent to a natural predisposition toward others would the liberal view of rules limiting social behaviour be acceptable as the only bridge between the first and third levels. However, for Reich, this was not the case. The third level, on the contrary, dealt with a perpetually frustrated psycho-biological core where individuals remained victims of systematic forms of oppressive power. Fascism, like other authoritarian ideologies throughout human history, was an expression of the second psychological level. For Reich, fascism has specific characteristics, such as being a mass movement. However, this does not mean it ceases to be a potentially international phenomenon. Fascism, in fact, represents a psychic and social attitude. Consequently, while Wilhelmine Germany was militaristic but not fascist, only National Socialist Germany became truly fascist.[40] As a movement based on the exaltation of irrationalism, fascism does not qualify as a genuinely revolutionary movement. Instead, it is based on an impulsive reaction to existing phobias but lacks a rational analysis of the causes that produced the present social conditions. The very function of prejudice in National Socialist ideology underscores the irrational nature of fascism. However, it is not fascism that generated the theory of race; rather, fascism is the result of the pathological character of the man orgastically impotent. It represents the inhibition of natural sexuality (the third level), which generates a form of mysticism, such as religiosity born from sexual perversion (not at all from paganism). Fascism thus represents a form of mystical-religious sublimation that no longer manifests in salvific suffering placed in the beyond. Instead, it is expressed in the realization of a murderous drive situated in the present and within clearly definable spatial boundaries. Reich's theory is not a belated renunciation of Marx. Rather, it is a rejection of a certain mechanistic Marxism. In the vulgarized version of the much-maligned Soviet Marxism, the economic base was opposed to the ideological superstructure, and it was presumed to establish laws of determination of the former over the latter. Nonetheless, for Reich, the truth is that the economic base itself receives

39 In S. Freud, *Group Psychology and the Analysis of the Ego*, [1921] 1949.
40 W. Reich, *Character Analysis*, [1933] 1972.

impulse and development from an ideological superstructure. It has already been noted that Marx left open the problem of the relationship between the material brain-based base and its cognitive transformation: that is, the problem of consciousness and how the psychic structure could act on the economic process itself. Therefore, if Marx identified underlying structural dynamics in the 19th-century economy, almost 70 years later, those tools required updating. Reich's sex-economic (or analytical-characterological) approach aimed to reconstruct the subjective point of view absent in Marx. Indeed, if mechanistic Marxism (but not Marx himself) saw man as an instrument of the history of class struggle, as a worker or a cog in the production of surplus value in a production process, Reich emphasized the character of the human living being. For Reich, communism failed in its proposal for a just and livable society for modern man. However, this did not preclude the possibility that some of its concepts could be reinterpreted within a broader framework, one that abandoned the vision of social classes (bourgeoisie/proletariat opposition) in favour of a sex-economic analysis of fundamental psychic structures where the characterological structure of the masses transformed into a theory-practice of politics. The break with vulgar Marxism lay in understanding the relative autonomy of the ideological superstructure from the economic one. On this point, Marcuse responded when, in a lecture given in Frankfurt titled "Progress and Freud Theory of Instincts" [1956], he specified that "pansexualism . . . rather belongs to the image of repressive society"[41] while true erotic liberation, finally free from the repressive dominance of reality, would tap into the principle of happiness and self-satisfaction. Referring to data on the socio-economic structure obtained from the 1925 German population census and the distribution of votes with the corresponding rise of the nationalist right in the period 1929–1933, Reich demonstrated how the essence of the problem of totalitarianism lay in understanding the psychological structure of the masses and its relationship with the economic base of society. Understanding the origins of war required not merely accepting underlying economic motives but also defining the ideological structure of mass psychology that had developed within a particular social system. Even more crucially for understanding fascism, it became essential to resort to explaining the deep irrationalism of ideology—the mysticism of the *Führer*'s leadership fascination—in its disconnect from the underlying economic base. The sex-economy had discovered, beyond Freud, the role of the non-procreative sexuality of the child: that is, libido as vital energy that drives psychic structures from childhood. The control of this energy historically articulated with the creation of a series of political and religious institutions aimed precisely at repressing individuals' free sexual expression, such as the condemnation of masturbation, premarital sex and so on.

As a result of sexual prohibition, these institutions generated an inhibition of critical thought while favouring the formation of a subject subordinate to

41 H. Marcuse, "Progress and Freud Theory of Instincts", [1956] 1970, p. 40.

an authoritarian order. The institutions of contemporary society thus became centres of control for the submission of individuals and the masses to dominant thought. These institutions represented, in miniature, the authoritarianism of the state in general. The subordination of man to such powers was realized through the instillation of sexual fears, guilt and humiliation toward the life thoughts generated by sexual impulses. Sexual limitation thus became, in the hands of authoritarian institutions, a sanctioning tool of power aimed at manipulating the masses. In this way, the ideology of leadership represented by the *Führer*, the party or the church intercepted an irrational psychological need because it was detached from the actual material needs of the masses. The promise of libidinal fulfilment formulated through sexually appealing symbols helped build a regime propaganda system. Sexual inhibition became a means of directing the masses toward supposed libidinal liberation goals. In this way, people forgot the economic conditions of oppression and instead turned to ideological satisfaction. Sexual and material needs unfulfilled by the family and the authoritarian society found satisfaction in the fascination with images, discourse and authoritarian political personalities. In this way, seemingly distant figures such as father/authority, mother/homeland and honor/lineage merged.

National Socialism capitalized on such psycho-cognitive assimilations in its nationalist and anti-Semitic propaganda. It was precisely from the mother-father dynamic that National Socialism constructed a national identity and established criteria for excluding individuals not considered part of this collective, primarily Jews. For Reich, the identification of the masses with the leader and the nation was a symptom of national narcissism, where members of various social classes, despite different experiences, became increasingly identified with the father/*führer* as they fell into material and sexual misery. This 'I-we' identity relationship was foundational to the theory of race, which was the only true theoretical-ideological development of National Socialism. Here, the mixing of blood between superior and inferior races was believed to inevitably lead to the decline of the stronger civilization. For this reason, Jews had to be prevented from establishing themselves in German society. The purity of the race and pan-Germanic narcissism underpinned Hitler's expansionist and criminal policies. The ideology revealed the material base from which it originated: indirectly, the economic base on which it rested, and directly, the interrelation of discursive worlds. If ideologies were irrational, then men were organized in an irrational manner. This was the process enacted by fascism and its mystical beliefs about Aryan superiority, the purity of the Germanic people and the invincibility of the *Führer*. Horkheimer would later expand on the Freudian and Reichian theme of instinctual repression, placing it within the familial context. In the essay "Authoritarianism and the Family" [1949],[42] he reflected on the connection between familial emotions and social bonds as a necessary narrative for creating a coherent world. The authority of the family was seen as the foundation

42 M. Horkheimer, "Authoritarianism and the Family", [1949] 1959, pp. 381–398.

of national authority,[43] where the Jacobinism of the Third Reich attempted to establish a direct connection between the individual and the nation.[44]

The legacy of this experience was, from this perspective, the isolation of the modern individual. Even the abstract conception of the individual as a subject of universal rights was a product of modernity aimed at breaking familial and social bonds, as well as realizing productive interests: "[I]n this era of mass society man is alone".[45] It is here that Horkheimer saw the danger of a resurgence of authoritarianism. The current economic crisis affecting the family would lay the groundwork for "the attitudes which predispose men for blind submission",[46] while the emotional detachment from the maternal figure, which occurs in the atomization of individuals, would generate that "coldness" as a prelude to "the potential fascist of our time".[47] Thus, there is a continuity between the economic crises that accompanied the rise of the authoritarian family and its decline in contemporary societies. While the advent of National Socialism absorbed paternal authority into the concept of *Volk*, the decline of the family as a realm of mediation between the individual and cultural belonging appears as a global phenomenon in post-war liberal societies.[48]

3.2 The authoritarian society: sexual repression and social institutions

Horkheimer's revisions were made possible by Fromm's pioneering work, which, starting in 1929, addressed issues related to German workers,[49] providing a comprehensive examination of the relationship between society, authoritarian character and sadomasochistic tendencies.[50] Fromm's work was influenced by Reich's rethinking of historical materialism and its relationship with ideology from a subjectivistic perspective. Reich revisited the issue of voluntary servitude of the masses that Fromm had explored in his 1929 text, attempting to answer why post-Weimar German workers were inclined toward subordination and passive acceptance of domination and slavery.[51] In

43 Ibid., p. 384.
44 Ibid.
45 Ibid., p. 386.
46 Ibid., p. 388.
47 Ibid., p. 391.
48 Ibid., p. 398.
49 E. Fromm, *The Working Class in Weimar Germany: A Psychological and Sociological Study*, [1929] 1980. This psychological-qualitative investigation by Fromm, focused on the characterological analysis of workers and white-collar employees, also made use of over 1,000 questionnaires, about half of which were lost during the escape from Nazi Germany. The text was published posthumously in 1980, while part of the results appeared in Fromm's contribution to the volume edited by Horkheimer, *Studien über Autorität und Familie*, [1936] 1987.
50 H. Fromm, *Der autoritär-masoschistische Charakter*, [1936].
51 Cfr. W. Reich, *The Mass Psychology of Fascism*, [1933] 1980; E. Fromm, *Arbeiter und Angestellte am Vorabend des Dritten Reiches: Eine sozialpsychologische Untersuchung*, [1929] 1980. For a critical and reconstructive analysis of this point, see L. Scuccimarra, "Assoggettamento, repressione, emancipazione. Alle origini della psico-politica francofortese", 2022, pp. 49–68.

other words, it was a matter of explaining the irrationality of the working class's behaviour in the face of increasingly engulfing mechanisms of capitalist domination. This required a reconsideration of the sociological perspective of Marxism in terms of ideological-consciousness perspectives. Psychic forces would integrate economic-political analyses of the production structure, and libidinal drives would accompany the definition of social processes.[52] Fromm found an answer to this dilemma in the idea of translating unconscious libidinal content into organizational and productive structures of the economy. Workers' consciousness grappled not only with the blatant and objective asymmetries of power and wealth but also, on a subjective level, with the unconscious drives that shaped their self-understanding as social actors. Society was seen as being held together by such libidinal flows, which operated as both ideological and infrastructural glue. According to this schema of rethinking the structure-superstructure relationship, Marcuse would suggest a path toward a psychoanalytic synthesis of historical materialism. The role of drives in psychoanalytic characterology would offer a key to understanding ideology based on mechanisms of systemic reproduction and the push toward social action not brought to consciousness. These would be linked to sadomasochistic attitudes related to the exaltation of the anal character, which, in turn, would be functional to the assertion of authoritarian regimes. The weakening of the ego and its narcissistic counterpart would allow for a closer alignment between psychic satisfaction and sadomasochistic obedience to authoritarian powers. The increase in one would accompany the increase in the other. In this context, the narcissistic reconstruction of the subject would be realized through a substitutive projection of the self into the leader, who, in his uniqueness, would fulfil the sadomasochistic drives of his subjects.

Fromm then initiated a program to revise Freud's theory of instincts in "*Die gesellschaftliche Bedingtheit der psychoanalytischen Therapie*" ["The Social Conditioning of Psychoanalytic Therapy"] [1935][53]—a choice that led to his break with Horkheimer, Adorno and Marcuse, as well as his departure from the IfS. Nevertheless, Fromm's intellectual influence would be decisive in the development of sociological and psychoanalytic programs subsequently undertaken by the IfS, such as Horkheimer's analysis of *Studien über Autorität und Familie*[54] and Adorno's *F-scale*.[55] Fromm's hierarchical structure of the authoritarian society aimed to define degrees of masochistic satisfaction related to obedience to the chain of command: the stricter the authority exercised, the more pleasure it produced for the one who obeyed. Even the worldviews of individual social members reflected a masochistic element of

52 E. Fromm, "The Method and Function of an Analytic Social Psychology", [1932] 1970.

53 E. Fromm, "Die gesellschaftliche Bedingtheit der psychoanalytischen Therapie", 1935, pp. 365–397.

54 M. Horkheimer, "Allgemeiner Teil", in M. Horkheimer (ed.), *Studien über Autorität und Familie*, [1936] 1963.

55 On this see N. McLaughlin, "Origin Myths in the Social Sciences: Fromm, the Frankfurt School and the Emergence of Critical Theory", 1999, pp. 109–139.

inevitability of fate: the soldier follows the dictates of his country's politics, the merchant follows the laws of the economy and so on. The regimentation of psychic life into a complex network of subordinating relationships highlighted the impotence of the men involved, generating feelings of masochistic endurance of the inevitable. The masochistic-authoritarian society thus shaped individuals aligned with command structures who found pleasure in the very self-limitation of freedom. This allowed the individual to alleviate the sense of anxiety that permeated his self-perception of precariousness and powerlessness when "faced with a world that he is unable to understand or control".[56] In the subject's submission to the authority of the leader, a narcissistic aspect was hidden: there was no possibility of identifying with a superior, only participating in his authority, thereby replacing several denied narcissistic satisfactions. Psychically, this was a regressive condition that was fully manifested in the case of fascist authoritarianism, which Fromm described as exhibiting pregenital characteristics in a broad sense and certainly from a psychological perspective.

This point marked an important fracture between authoritarian and democratic societies. In the latter, indeed, the individual would be given the opportunity to identify with commanding figures. The function of the imperative model would thus facilitate a process of potential identification between the subordinate and the superior through the fulfilment of socially imposed requirements: work, competition and so forth. However, Fromm also identified forms of democratic authoritarian discipline in which, despite a potential for identification between leader and subordinate, there was enough distance to psychologically discourage the idea that such identification was actually possible. Fromm's reflection on the relationship between masochism and authority would be systematically expanded in *Escape from Freedom* [1941],[57] a text rich with critical insights into Freudian psychoanalysis but also a proponent of a precise thesis on the sadomasochistic nature of fascist authority. Unlike authoritarian societies per se, authoritarian democracies replaced the figure of the supreme leader with more abstract mechanisms of domination aimed at fulfilling economic, societal and political-strategic needs. Here too the citizen would experience the "strength to act through his leaning on superior power",[58] thus, through the disciplinary power of the state. Fromm reproached Freud for developing a static view of the subject as merely a tool in a market of needs and their satisfaction. Fromm therefore aimed to develop a theory of dynamic psychology as an alternative methodology for understanding not only the adaptation of the psyche to various social contexts, but also for explaining the genesis of the frustrations they generate. If capitalism had achieved the subordination of subjects by transforming not only profit accumulation

56 E. Fromm, "Der autoritär-masochistische Charakter", [1936] 1987, p. 123.
57 E. Fromm, *Escape from Freedom*, [1941] 1965.
58 Ibid., p. 194.

but also market competition and social success into ends in themselves, the consequence would be the loss of the individual and his spontaneous attachment to the world (primary bond), leading to a loss of dignity and a sense of inadequacy. In reality, even Luther's and Calvin's Protestantism had prepared the ground for this technical and psychological transformation of the modern economic man by emphasizing the negative externalities resulting from the realization of his own goals.

The humiliation of man on Earth was followed by that in heaven: man had become a mere instrument for the glory of a God who, in turn, no longer empathized with him but instead positioned him as subordinate. Even secondary bonds were redefined: the other entered into a logic of similarity or complete otherness and submission. The long preparation that accompanied the acceptance of this condition of subordination to the divine was, for Fromm, essential in legitimizing the subjugation that would follow with the advent of a totalizing *Führer*. Thus, the authoritarianism of the new post-bourgeois and post-liberal society was able to express sadomasochistic tendencies of domination as collective mass neuroses. It was on this pre-existing basis that Hitler's speculations on the struggle and dominance of the strong would find fertile ground. Sadistic and masochistic impulses would help the modern individual temporarily escape from a sense of loneliness, existential insignificance and detachment from reality. The sadomasochistic character, with its blind complacency toward authority, would merge with fascist ideology. For Fromm, understanding the origins of fascism would not concern socio-economic reasons considered in isolation but rather the presence of psychological mechanisms within the economic production structure and its labour relations. The point, therefore, would be to recognize that "Nazism is an economic and political problem, but the hold it has over a whole people has to be understood on psychological grounds".[59] Once again, the relationship between base and superstructure would be treated by the Frankfurt School as a synthetic concept analytically partitionable only for expository purposes.

3.3 The *Studien* on authority and the family (1936)

The psychology of Nazism emerged from the historical traumas of the post-1929 period, which saw not only economic factors and military defeat but also the fall of the monarchy. Hitler, therefore, was able to take the place of these symbols by assuming the mantle of an authoritarian, sadomasochistic personality. The destructive impulse of sadism was accompanied by a form of humiliating gratification derived from participation in his power. For Fromm, the solitary cry of the German man defeated in the Great War was pacified by the figure of the omnipotent leader, with whom one connected through the acceptance of total submission. To escape social and psychological isolation,

59 Ibid., p. 232.

Germans had to surrender to the will of an absolute leader. Having lost every primary link to their natural condition, they could not rely on new guiding principles, resulting in movement toward a new slavery. In this only seemingly secure form, primary bonds were shattered, and the ego numbed any form of critical self-awareness. The fear of remaining socially and psychologically isolated was averted. However, this "escape from freedom" did not lead to a renewed form of self-liberation. Fromm had anticipated these considerations, later elaborated in 1941,[60] during the already-mentioned collective work directed by Horkheimer in the 1934–1935 period: the *Studien über Autorität und Familie*. The text was published in Paris in 1936 and developed with the intent of understanding the internal forces supporting Nazi-Fascist tendencies a year after the publication of Reich's work on fascism and mass psychology. Fromm's contribution to the *Studien* consisted of an essay titled "*Sozialpsychologischer Teil*", which followed Horkheimer's more general essay and elaborated on reflections already developed in Fromm's earlier studies on the relationship between sadomasochism and authoritarianism.[61] Horkheimer, in turn, was tasked with providing the overarching framework for the *Studien*, as reflected in the title of his chapter, "*Allgemeiner Teil*". He began his essay with what would come to be defined as a meta-perspective of the philosophy of history, establishing a dialectical relationship between culture, ideology and the economic-productive structure.[62] It is significant that Horkheimer felt the need to incorporate psychoanalysis into the typically Marxian relationship between economic and social dynamics on the one hand and the superstructural level on the other. While Hegel viewed the movement of history as the development of spirit, critical theory understood transformations in culture and psychic nature as effects of the material and productive life of society. However, the relationship between these two levels was not seen as a mere unidirectional deterministic causation. Horkheimer instead referred to dialectical short circuits between material spheres and psycho-cultural structures. The material domain of socio-productive organization certainly retained structural priority over all other dimensions of cultural life. Nevertheless, each level operated under its own specific laws, while the transformation of psychic and cultural structures inevitably involved changes in the relationship between the forces, needs and forms of life in a given society.[63] Such transformation, whether mere adaptation or substantial change, presupposed a binary structure of dominant/subordinate. Authority, therefore, was embedded in

60 Ibid.

61 E. Fromm, "Sozialpsychologischer Teil", [1936] 1987, pp. 77–135.

62 That Horkheimer intended to develop a project on dialectics is evident from both his letter to Adorno dated March 15, 1935, and his letter to Mme Favez, secretary of the Geneva branch of the Institute, in February 1939. On this, see R. Wiggershaus, *The Frankfurt School: Its History, Theories, and Political Significance*, [1986] 2007, p. 150 ff. and p. 177 ff.

63 Cfr. M. Horkheimer, "Allgemeiner Teil", in M. Horkheimer (ed.), *Studien über Autorität und Familie*, [1936] 1963.

cultural systems themselves, functioning as both a driving and a restraining force in social life. Materially adverse conditions for the majority alongside an elite in command were seen as an ineliminable aspect of the movement of human history. Authority thus came to be defined as a meta-structural category accompanying the historical process. The relationship of individuals to authority would thus unfold not only through dynamics specific to work, institutions, church, school, university, press and theatre but also, and particularly, within those social formations that shape character types: the family. For this reason, Horkheimer, as early as the 1930s, understood the analysis of the family as an exercise in authority or a place of structuring the conscious and unconscious psychic processes of the individual. In the child's developmental process, the family would serve as a mediation between external societal conditions and the processes of internalization of authoritarian psychic structures. The authoritarian family would thus be the precursor to the fascist society. For Horkheimer, fascism constantly maintained an ambiguous attitude toward the family. While recognizing the family as the sacred foundation of national life, it attempted from the outset to appropriate it ideologically.[64] The fundamental conflict that fascism saw as a bridgehead for its assertion was the consideration of a particular family model and the view of nature in its instinctual and immediate character. It was this latter dimension that, for Horkheimer, would lead Hitler to exalt the unconscious instinctual aspects of his people, offering the illusion of a power "in whose name the ban on repressed nature would be lifted".[65] But the trick, so to speak, of National Socialist propaganda would be to incorporate the rebellious instincts of the German people, which remained unconscious, into a new model of totalitarian rationality. By doing so, National Socialism could turn the repressed desires of its own people to its advantage. So what would be the way out of this social and ideological impasse? Here, Horkheimer's pessimism about the tools offered by reason itself would emerge clearly in the assertion that "rational persuasion can never be as effective, because it is not congenial to the repressed primitive urges of a superficially civilized people".[66] Democracy and its means would be powerless against fascist propaganda. Democracy could resist such manipulation only by appealing to primitive instincts, paradoxically leading "to compromise the democratic way of life by stimulating destructive unconscious forces".[67] As the third author of the *Studien*, Fromm addressed the issue of the dialectical connection between class domination, psychic internalization and the legitimization of political-philosophical and religious ideology. He had already developed, in previous studies, a form of revision of Freud's conception of the relationship between the ego, the superego and the father figure. For Fromm,

64 M. Horkheimer, *Eclipse of Reason*, [1947] 2004, p. 84.
65 Ibid., p. 81.
66 Ibid., pp. 81–82.
67 Ibid., p. 81.

the father was no longer a model but a reflection of social authority, of which he himself was a mediator for the child. The ego thus developed in relation to the progress of social production. Repressive forms of authority (paternal or societal) generated sadomasochistic tendencies in the individual, who, in turn, found in the authoritarian society the opportunity to realize these same original impulses. The authoritarian society, therefore, realized the individual's sadomasochistic drive through a hierarchical economic structure.

The fascist psyche was the result of such remodelling in which, however, the external reality (moral rules, social norms etc.) lacked internalization into the superego, while the ego, for its part, remained prey to the unconscious fears of the id. Consequently, the ego projected the destructive fears of the id onto specific groups and individuals. The fascist ego, unable to internalize moral imperatives and externally given rules as structures of common living, ended up expelling the destructive impulses of the id and thus targeting particularity and difference. Such morbid projections were receptacles of unconscious fears, prohibitions of the id related to the desire/shame of castration and, in turn, linked to the paternal figure, as well as to unresolved homosexual impulses. In this framework, the Jew became the quintessential sacrificial victim of a lack of movement in the ego. He became the necessary target of the fascist psyche: today the Jew, tomorrow other groups: intellectuals, the elderly, migrants. In *Dialectic of Enlightenment* [1947], as Horkheimer and Adorno will extensively acknowledge Fromm's influence on this point, the real problem will not reside in psychic projections as such but in the inability of the fascist mind to engage in reflection: "[I]t no longer reflects on itself, and thereby loses the ability to differentiate".[68] Marcuse contributed to the *Studien* as a third author, concluding the first section with a contribution on "*Ideengeschichtlicher Teil*" ["History of Ideas Part"]: that is, on the history of the idea of authority and family. Despite the limited selection of discussed contributions, Marcuse adopted a line functional to the reconstruction of the Christian-bourgeois root of the family and, thus, a certain anti-authoritarian attitude. However, the assertion of such freedom would already contain in embryo the development of an anti-libertarian attitude related to metaphysical authorities of faith, which hold inscrutable authoritarian relationships. Luther, Calvin, Kant and Hegel are the modern progenitors of this tradition, but Marcuse's reconstruction would also continue with Marx and the bourgeois view of Sorel and Pareto on the totalitarian state. Finally, it is interesting to refer to a theory of authority based on the binary opposition between freedom and unfreedom. For Marcuse, every authoritarian form ensures the spontaneous recognition of a free and subjective power (or relative to an individual or group) by subordinate subjects: "In the relationship of authority, freedom and bondage, autonomy and heteronomy are thought

68 M. Horkheimer, T. W. Adorno, *Dialectic of Enlightenment*, [1947] 2002, p. 156.

together and united in the one person of the authority object".[69] Nevertheless, as will be clarified, this does not present itself in terms of coexistence but of foundation, where free power constitutes the unfreedom of another power. The Christian-bourgeois reason would thus contain within itself such ambivalence: from the *deus absconditus* of Calvin to the split in Kantian morality between the pure form of universal law and its sensible realization, the reversal into the irrational of socially sanctioned authoritarian relationships would play out. Already, from these early reflections, it is evident that even in Marcuse, the Freudian ambivalence of the civilization process inevitably contains the paradox that shapes its own destiny of self-destruction.

3.4 Fascism and propaganda

Between 1936 and 1938, alongside his interests in mass psychology, Kracauer developed a pioneering study aimed at analyzing the relationship between totalitarianism and propaganda, titled *Totalitäre Propaganda*. The study focused on the role of propaganda in fascist totalitarian regimes. While the author acknowledged that propaganda also played a role in democratic institutions, he noted that "the methods of political propaganda that developed in fascist countries were a novelty".[70] Kracauer's essay was never published in *ZfS* and only appeared in 2013, published by Suhrkamp.[71] The reasons for the lack of publication were attributed to Adorno's negative assessment considering it theoretically inadequate, particularly with regard to its treatment of Marxism, psychoanalysis and, not least, the use of Horkheimer's thought.[72] The work was influenced by Fromm's studies of the time, but Adorno felt this did not ensure a rigorous elaboration, especially regarding the theme of mass psychology. However, Adorno was more lenient in his evaluation of the phenomenological and empirical aspects of the essay, as well as the quotations of statements made by Hitler, which, however, lacked adequate theoretical elaboration by the author.

In Section A of the text, Kracauer examined the historical, economic and social factors that favoured the rise of National Socialism. These reflections were in continuity with another work by Kracauer written in 1930 on the

69 H. Marcuse, "Ideengeschichtlicher Teil", [1936] 1987, pp. 136.

70 S. Kracauer, *Totalitäre Propaganda*, [1936/8] 2013, p. 231. Kracauer's text is today an important and insightful testament to the Frankfurt School's 1930s interest in the socio-political role of Nazi propaganda. However, it does not seem plausible to interpret the totalitarian propaganda analyzed by Kracauer as an expression of a more generic "right-wing populism" (p. 397) without distorting the text. See J. Abromeit, "Siegfried Kracauer and the Early Frankfurt School's Analysis of Fascism as Right-Wing Populism", 2022, pp. 395–422.

71 S. Kracauer, *Totalitäre Propaganda*, [1936/8] 2013.

72 The critical texts by Adorno are published in T. W. Adorno, "I. Gutachten über die Arbeit 'Die totalitäre Propaganda Deutschlands und Italiens', S.I bis S.106, von Siegfried Kracauer", [1938] 2013, pp. 262–265.

situation of wage workers: *Die Angestellten* [*The Employees*].[73] White-collar workers constituted an emerging mass category. This was certainly accompanied by the traumatic experience of the Great War, which also generated an interclass solidarity [*Schutzenkamaradschaf*] (*Guardian companion sheep*) among surviving soldiers, accompanied by disaffection toward state institutions. This helped lay the groundwork for an authoritarian inclination among the population, a fertile ground for propaganda and mobilization actions, first by the *Freikorps* and later by the special units of the SA and SS. Despite numerous criticisms, Adorno acknowledged a significant merit of the essay: the idea that fascism resorted to the fetishization of the authoritarian personality to generate the idealization of the people as a mass—a consideration contrary to the idea that the masses were the result of the development of a political ideology. On one hand, the authoritarian leadership eliminated class social differences by unifying the people into a mass against which was posed the image of a parasitic enemy (rather than one with differing economic interests). On the other hand, the cult of personality emerged as an idealized outcome of mass desires. Thus, the relationship between the authoritarian leader and the mass was a pseudo-opposition, which Adorno even deemed "illuminating" in its broader applicability. Considering the "dilemma" of the reintegration of the masses within the "capitalist system", Kracauer saw "fascism" as a "pseudo-solution"[74] operating on the basis of "terror" and "propaganda".[75]

Fascism could not survive without propaganda. The latter became the principal tool for influencing the psyche of the individual, modifying self-perception in line with the mass. Despite references to concepts of psychic regression and ressentiment typical of Fromm's and Horkheimer's reflections, Kracauer's focus on fascist propaganda shifted the axis of reflection from the formation of the self in the family to the authoritarian and regimented organization of citizens' lives. The use of speech took precedence over written text. As Kracauer himself noted, National Socialism had strongly promoted the dissemination of regime radio devices (*Volksempfänger*). The use of radio communication not only created a public space around the subject but also facilitated total identification with the surrounding environment. The repetition of the message, rhythm, voice pauses and crescendo in tone were clever techniques useful for the homogenization of personality and the elimination of subjective critical viewpoints.[76] Kracauer would cite Benjamin and the 1936 thesis, according to which, while fascism proceeded with an aestheticization of politics, communism would conversely provide a politicization of art.[77] It is indeed true

73 S. Kracauer, "Soziologie als Wissenschaft. Der Detektiv-Roman: Die Angestellten", [1930] 2004–2012.

74 S. Kracauer, *Totalitäre Propaganda*, [1936/8] 2013, p. 233.

75 Ibid.

76 Ibid., p. 40 ff.

77 See also W. Benjamin, *The Work of Art in the Age of Mechanical Reproduction*, [1946] 2008.

that communism also utilized the proletarian masses as subjects of political propaganda. But while the socialist revolution considered their temporariness in view of collective liberation through the abolition of classes and alienation from labour, fascism required the mass to remain permanently unchanged so that the interests of the few in command could continue to be realized.

For Kracauer, the ideology of National Socialism was characterized by a "will toward the unknown" [*Wille zum Ungewissen*],[78] a nihilistic "will to power" [*Wille zur Macht*].[79] This was articulated in seven points, clarifying how fascism had generated a relationship between leader and followers not based solely on the exercise of violence. This was a theme already addressed by Horkheimer in the 1936 *Studien*. However, Kracauer contextualized the issue historically, referring to figures such as Hitler, Strasser, Goebbels and central figures of Italian Fascism starting with Mussolini, the latter portrayed through continuous references to Silone's observations. It was emphasized how these figures introduced irrationalistic and emotional elements into politics, creating a fictitious idea of a people-mass that wholly identified with the values of its leader. The violence exercised by the regime, both internal and external to the people, had an instrumental function, which was to separate enemies from friends based on the idea of "productive work" [*schaffende Arbeit*] as distinguished from parasitic work. The anti-Semitic consequences of this policy are well known.[80]

3.5 Toward a research program on anti-Semitism

On February 28, 1941, Horkheimer presented a research program on anti-Semitism to the Rockefeller Foundation which was never funded. This was an initial development of a theme that highlighted the changed priorities in the research focus of the IfS. This was the "Research Project on Antisemitism" [1941],[81] which aimed to outline the lines of what was perceived as a general trend "in all more recent culture".[82] Anti-Semitism developed along two lines of thought: the "rationalist"[83] one—focused on denying the existence of a direct psychological determination and instead seeing it as the result of a social construction—and the other distinctly an "anti-Semitic" one.[84] Although ultimately abandoned, as was the case with the never-published text "Theory of Fascism", mentioned among the IfS activities of 1939, Horkheimer's research program gave rise to individual initiatives that culminated in the analyses of anti-Semitism in *Eclipse of Reason* [1947] by Horkheimer himself, and later

78 S. Kracauer, *Totalitäre Propaganda*, [1936/8] 2013, p. 24.
79 Ibid.
80 Ibid., p. 87 ff.
81 M. Horkheimer, T. W. Adorno, "Research Project on Anti-Semitism", 1941, pp. 124–133.
82 Ibid., p. 124.
83 Ibid., p. 125.
84 Ibid.

in *Minima moralia* [1951] by Adorno, just to mention two of the most significant works on the subject.[85] The issue was also revisited in the collective work *Studies in Prejudice* [1949], for which Horkheimer sought financial support from both the American Jewish Committee (AJC) and the Jewish Labor Committee (JLC). There were many reasons that led Horkheimer to develop a large-scale program on the topic. These regarded not only the evident concern for the situation in Germany but also the widespread anti-Semitic sentiment prevalent in American society, in both workplaces and universities during the 1920s and 1930s.[86] As Adorno would later observe regarding American preachers, influential figures such as Father Coughlin were still broadcasting anti-Semitic proclamations over the radio in 1941, engaging in a veritable apology for Nazism and its spread among countless American radio listeners. The primary task was to understand the phenomenon in light of qualitative studies that highlighted the psychological mechanisms underlying such behaviours. This is addressed in the already-mentioned study by Adorno and collaborators, *The Authoritarian Personality* [1950]. Arendt's interpretation, which developed in parallel to Adorno's, provided a counterpart. Arendt, who had emigrated to America in the meantime, argued in *The Origins of Totalitarianism* [1951][87] that the anti-Semitism of National Socialism was the reactionary result of a long historical process that paralleled the rise of the modern bourgeois state with the introduction of the principle of equality.

3.6 Authoritarianism and anti-Semitism

In two writings, "*Plan des Forschungsprojekts über Antisemitismus*" ["Plan of the Research Project on Anti-Semitism] [1943][88] and, even more, "*Zur Psychologie des Antisemitismus*" ["On the Psychology of Anti-Semitism"] [1943],[89] Horkheimer summarized what had been partially achieved and what was still

85 M. Horkheimer, *Eclipse of Reason*, [1947] 2004; T. W. Adorno, *Minima Moralia. Reflections on a Damaged Life*, [1951] 2005. See also R. Stackelberg, "Cultural Aspects of National Socialism: An Unfinished Project of the Frankfurt School", 1988, pp. 253–260.

86 On this, see J. Jackobs (quoting from L. Dinnerstein): "'From 1920 to 1940' that is to say in a period during a portion of which members of the Horkheimer circle were living in New York, and during which the IfS was affiliated with Columbia University, 'the percentage of Jews in Columbia University's College of Physicians and Surgeons fell from 46.94 to 6.45; the percentage of City College of New York graduates admitted to any medical school dropped from 58 to 15; and not one graduate of either Hunter or Brooklyn College in New York City entered an American medical school. . . . A similar decline occurred in law schools. . . .' 133 Jews in the United States also encountered discrimination in employment in the period between the two world wars". In J. Jackobs, *The Frankfurt School: Jewish Lives and Antisemitism*, 2015, p. 62.

87 H. Arendt, *The Origins of Totalitarianism*, [1951] 1976.

88 M. Horkheimer, "Plan des Forschungsprojekts über Antisemitismus", [1931–1949] 1985, pp. 165–171.

89 M. Horkheimer, "Zur Psychologie des Antisemitismus", [1931–1949] 1985, pp. 172–183.

to be completed regarding a program for the critique of anti-Semitism. From this perspective, the programmatic indication of an investigation that started from European fascist anti-Semitism, and extended to the identification of antidemocratic and racist propaganda tendencies in the American context is particularly interesting.[90] This expanded the semantic scope of anti-Semitism to include religious forms and discriminatory political propaganda.[91] This line of research would indeed be pursued by Adorno in the following years. In truth, a large-scale study of German anti-Semitism had been proposed by Weil himself (and Pollock) to his father in order to obtain additional funds for the creation of a social research institute, which would later become the IfS. The novelty was, therefore, the addition of a psycho-social approach to the theme of anti-Semitic discrimination. Although Adorno, in a 1936 letter to Horkheimer,[92] had announced his desire to address the topic of fascism and the sociopsychological mediations connected to it, it was only from 1944 to 1950, through the collaboration of Frenkel-Brunswik, Levinson and Nevitt Sanford, that the extensive study *The Authoritarian Personality* [1950] came to light. Here, the unconscious propensity for the expression of discriminatory judgments among educated, middle-class American citizens was analyzed. In line with the stated objectives, Adorno carried out a comprehensive theoretical-empirical research on the character of the anti-Semitic subject, defined without the explicit formulation of questions on anti-Semitism and in a context unrelated to the Nazi state's anti-Jewish propaganda. It is clear that these authoritarian syndromes were not directly linked to the specifically Nazi desire for the annihilation of the Jewish race. However, such tendencies were evidence of a rejection of democratic rules and the principles that should have underpinned them.

The absence of a class willing to govern in place of the recently deposed monarchies at the end of the 18th century had favoured the rise of a "non-state", according to Neumann's interpretation, situated above society and its classes but driven by competing interest groups.[93] This transformation of the state allowed Jews not only to be placed on the same level as other citizens, but also to emancipate themselves from the status of second-class citizens. It was only at the end of the 19th century, with the rise of imperialism (1884–1914), that the wealthier classes began to see the colonial expansions of nation-states as an opportunity to expand their commercial interests. From that moment on,

90 "The fifth study must address the question of how European experiences could be transferred to the American situation", in M. Horkheimer, "Plan des Forschungsprojekts über Antisemitismus", [1931–1949] 1985, p. 169.

91 "Then we have the philosophical-religious antisemite . . .", in M. Horkheimer, "Zur Psychologie des Antisemitismus", [1931–1949] 1985, p. 179.

92 Letter from T. W. Adorno to M. Horkheimer, June 25, 1936. In T. W. Adorno, M. Horkheimer, *Briefwechsel (1927–1969)*, 2003–2004, pp. 165–166.

93 On the influence of Neumann's theory on Arendt, see V. Iakovou, "Totalitarianism as Non-State. On Hannah Arendt's Debt to Franz Neumann", 2009, pp. 429–447.

the public perception of Jews changed, and their distinctiveness as a socially separated group fueled the political development of anti-Semitism. Certainly, with the outbreak of the Great War and the dismantling of the system which had guaranteed fundamental rights, international security, unemployment and inflation, it happened that the stateless and the minorities, rightly termed "cousins-germane",[94] had no governments to represent and to protect them and therefore were forced to live either under the law of exception of the Minority Treaties, which all governments (except Czechoslovakia) had signed under protest and never recognized as law or under conditions of absolute lawlessness. Totalitarian politics were born through the gradual stripping away of the rights of belonging to a state or a political, ethnic or religious community. As Arendt effectively summarized, the loss of the "right to have rights"[95] (that is, to be considered worthy members of a community of subjects of law, to "live in a framework where one is judged by one's actions and opinion"[96]) would be the final step before the descent into the abyss of totalitarianism and the Holocaust.

Totalitarianism was indeed a new and aberrant phenomenon, unlike anything humanity had previously developed, whether in despotic, dictatorial or even illiberal forms of power. Fascist and Bolshevik totalitarianism shared the nullification of social classes in favour of an indistinct mass of individuals. The dismantling of political parties, propaganda, psychological terror and espionage and the elimination of political dissidents were just a few of the most brutal methods employed by totalitarian state powers for the organization and management of society. To this, the "final solution" [*Endlösung*] was added—the planned total destruction of the Jews, the scum of the earth, the ultimate enemy of Nazi Germany.

3.7 Psychoanalytic and structural aspects of anti-Semitism

Anti-Semitism represents the tragic peak of the dialectic of self-negation between base and superstructure, the merging of being and thinking in a tragic game of absolute mimetic-identitarian reflections. Jews, like gays, the disabled and communists, represent the abstract negation of the regime's identity in line with Nazi ideology. In the chapter "Elements of Anti-Semitism" in *Dialectic of Enlightenment* [1947], Horkheimer and Adorno argue that "for the fascists the Jews are not a minority but the antirace, the negative principle as such".[97] Thus, the elimination of the negation, the different, from the Nazi state's identity system appeared as a task of purifying ascension for the regime. Within the Frankfurt School tradition, the question of the origin of

94 H. Arendt, *The Origins of Totalitarianism*, [1951] 1976, p. 269.
95 Ibid.
96 Ibid., p. 297.
97 M. Horkheimer, T. W. Adorno, *Dialectic of Enlightenment*, [1947] 2002, p. 137.

anti-Semitism coincides with the effects of capitalist crises, war and its transposition into the German collective psyche. The implosion movement of pre-war capitalism projected onto Jews the responsibilities for redistributive inefficiencies in German society. The reconstruction of the transitions that accompanied the transfer from structure to superstructure would thus reveal the essence of the madness of the Third Reich and the horrific outcomes that the reorganization of economic production led to.

Certainly, the rational formulation and political resolution of a "final solution" to the Jewish problem took shape first with encouragement of migration as early as 1933 and then continued with increasingly restrictive anti-Jewish measures that led to forced deportations in the late 1940s, culminating in the extermination elaborated in the Wannsee Conference protocol of January 1942. The outcome to which this led, the Shoah, remains a unique event in history. Never before had man conceived, discussed and systematically organized an industry of death as in the case of the genocide of the Jews. As stated in the first introduction footnote of this work, explaining National Socialism, as Horkheimer said at the beginning of his essay "*Die Juden und Europa*" [1939], meant revealing the mystery of anti-Semitism, but this required grasping the essence of capitalism: "Whoever wants to explain antisemitism must speak of National Socialism. . . . Whoever does not want to speak of capitalism should also remain silent about fascism".[98] German anti-Semitism fully reflected the dual root of a fascist mentality characterized by projective mechanisms and a productive structure in which Jews occupied only the sphere of circulation but not that of production.[99] Thus, the Jews were identified as the true obstacle to the happiness of the German people. The structural-productive level thus came to be intimately connected with the psychic-superstructural order. In this regard, Horkheimer and Adorno inform us of the externalizing mechanism of a psyche oppressed by socio-economic distress that objectifies its death instincts in an unreflective domain: "Anti-Semitism is based on false projection. It is the reverse of genuine mimesis and has deep affinities with the repressed; in fact, it may itself be the pathic character trait in which the latter is precipitated".[100] It is the reverse process of true mimesis. In fact, while the latter projects outward to imitate externality, the former can be said to "resemble its surroundings".[101] This involves the transference of socially unacceptable id impulses. Since the ego cannot coexist with violent impulses, the superego distances them by constructing the image of malignant dangers in the world

98 This is the synthesis between the crisis of capitalism and its ideological reflections in National Socialism articulated by Horkheimer and quoted as an epigraph at the beginning of this essay. See M. Horkheimer, "Die Juden und Europa", 1939, p. 115.

99 "The banker and the intellectual, money and mind, the exponents of circulation, are the disowned wishful image of those mutilated by power, an image which power uses to perpetuate itself". M. Horkheimer, T. W. Adorno, *Dialectic of Enlightenment*, [1947] 2002, p. 141.

100 Ibid., p. 154.

101 Ibid.

and selecting Jews as the corresponding factual entities. For Horkheimer and Adorno, this process concealed latent homosexual tendencies. The fear of castration by the father transforms, from infancy, into hatred and resentment, with the objects of fixation changing over time.[102] One might hypothesize that the fascist man is one who failed to resolve the Oedipus complex and, in the task of internalizing the structure of the superego, not wanting to revert to primitive forms of impulse satisfaction, realizes a coexistence between the superego, the ego and the id through projective forms of destructive instincts.[103]

In attempting to understand the dual origin of the link between Nazism and anti-Semitism, it becomes necessary to turn to the concept of instrumental rationality as the key feature of modernity. This is the broader root to which to ascribe the aberrations of modern anti-Semitism. The totalitarian extremization of the rational-instrumental paradigm turns into irrational and oppressive forms in the fascist totalitarian society. The theory of rackets previously analyzed and the view of the Nazi state as a "non-state" are characteristics of a society that has lost the references through which to realize the dynamics of social recognition and redistribution of produced wealth. We have already addressed the implications at the productive level of the crises of the circulation of goods in the capitalism of the 1930s–1940s. These had led not only to economic planning but also to the regimentation of social relations into new hierarchies of power. While explaining the objectifying attitude of reduction to means-ends logic, instrumental rationality cannot, however, provide the ultimate reason for understanding the suppression of Jews. It is necessary to understand how the most extreme manifestation of fascist racial hatred finds a domain of explanation capable of considering the socio-psychological level.

For the Frankfurt School, the reification of totalitarian consciousness is the result of an objectification process of social relations within a pyramidal ideological framework of which the *Führer* occupies the top. The same process of total identification of the German people with their leader renders it impossible for the subject to critically escape the established order. In this way, subjective thought is expelled from the process of objectifying social relations and thus from the constitution of a new political order. The principle of identity inhibits any internal differentiation within the system. Therefore, any real or ideological entity conceived as divergent from the dominant system has no right to exist, let alone express itself. The consideration of Jews as an obstacle to Germany's free economic development must be traced back to popular resentment that, in placing them at the top of world capitalism, ends up seeing

102 Ibid., p. 160.

103 Rensmann states that "damaged narcissism and feelings of inferiority, intimately linked to the deflation of the (masculine) armored self, promote aggression that continually breaks through and a striving for dominion that itself is an unmediated expression of the destruction drive". In L. Rensmann, *The Politics of Unreason: The Frankfurt School and the Origins of Modern Antisemitism*, 2017, p. 46.

them as manipulators of the economic and political fortunes of nations. The belief in a permanent Jewish conspiracy has deep roots in the stereotyping of Jews as a cunning, greedy people accumulating wealth not produced by their own labour. According to Nazi ideology, Jews represent the very essence of capitalism and its unjust voracity. Therefore, the elimination of Jews becomes part of a reconversion of the economy into state capitalism. The Frankfurt School's thematization of anti-Semitism as the "Jewish question" mirrored, in many respects, a classic topos of German philosophy. To fully appreciate the historical and theoretical scope of this treatment, one has to place studies ranging from the analysis of the authoritarian personality to those on social agitators and the lunatic fringe (the extremist fringe) analyzed by Adorno on a continuum.[104] Adorno had already anticipated, in his 1938 essay on Richard Wagner,[105] the idiosyncratic processes of assimilation-repulsion toward Jews by the German composer who, like him, displayed behavioural traits characterized by verbosity and gesticulation.[106] Yet Wagner's disgust for Jews was not simply a personal inclination but a form of cultural regression that could be generalized.

Considering these premises, it was possible to appreciate the broad range of discriminatory cases that Western societies had produced from the 1930s to the 1960s on both the European and American continents. More specifically, the theme of anti-Semitism was situated within the Frankfurt School's reflection on the psycho-social regressions developed during the civilizing process. To understand the phenomenon of anti-Semitism in a profound sense, one had to once again turn to Freud's theory of instincts, this time under the guidance of a new interpretation.

On the basis of this methodological premise, Horkheimer's 1936 studies on the authoritarian family were the precursors to extensive research on German anti-Semitism.[107] Paternal authoritarianism within the family, the matrix of a primary form of socialization, constituted the foundation for the formation of subjects already predisposed to command subordination, thus facilitating the task of gaining authoritarian power over citizens as a form of secondary socialization. The distinction between the primary and secondary levels would later collapse with the advent of large-scale industry and the loss of the father's economic and authoritative autonomy. Familial mediation would be replaced by the direct and immediate relationship of the fascist authoritarian

104 T. W. Adorno, *Aspects of the New Right-Wing Extremism*, [1967] 2020.

105 T. W. Adorno, *Fragmente über Wagner*, 1939, pp. 1–49. Subsequently in T. W. Adorno, *Versuch über Wagner*, 1952.

106 Ibid., p. 15 ff.

107 Not according to this continuity axis, as seen by Jay, who instead establishes a differentiation between an initial phase (approximately until 1943), in which Horkheimer understood the Jewish question as a class struggle in line with the Marxist perspective, and a second phase related to the anti-Semitic outcome of Nazism. See M. Jay, "The Jews and the Frankfurt School: Critical Theory's Analysis of Anti-Semitism", 1980, particularly p. 149.

state with the individual. This bond would, in turn, be all the more binding as it became free from mediations. In 1944, the IfS report concluding the prejudice project funded by the AJC was delivered.[108] Here, the results obtained from 1941 to 1944 concerning two aspects—the nature and operation of anti-Semitism—were summarized.[109] Regarding the first theme, it was a matter of tracing psychological and cultural attitudes within the European and American traditions, while the second aspect involved identifying a declared "politically militant antisemitism".[110] The report's sections ranged from the analysis of psychology and cultural trends to the development of a scale measuring anti-Semitism. Next, sections two and three dealt with case studies of anti-Semitism in America and Europe, respectively. Lastly, in the fourth part, measures to combat anti-Semitism were proposed.[111] Underlying all the themes at play was the idea that manifestations of anti-Semitism expressed forms of anti-democratic opposition.[112]

A few months later, in May 1944, thanks again to the financial support of the AJC, Horkheimer and his collaborators organized a conference in New York that would lend its name to the collection of texts: Studies in Prejudice.[113] This marked the conclusion of the first phase of research on anti-Semitism under the sponsorship of the AJC. From 1945 to 1950, the members of the Frankfurt School expanded their research project on anti-Semitism through initiatives aimed at deepening the analysis of fascism. As early as March 1945, the IfS organized a series of public presentations at Columbia University under the title The Aftermath of National Socialism: Cultural Aspects of the Collapse of National Socialism. On this occasion, Horkheimer presented a paper titled "Totalitarianism and the Crisis of European Culture", while Adorno discussed "The Fate of the Arts", Pollock addressed "Prejudice and the Social Classes" and, finally, Löwenthal spoke on "The Aftermath of Totalitarian Terror". In 1946, Horkheimer published an essay titled "Sociological Background of the Psychoanalytic Approach",[114] which was included in a collective study on the issue of anti-Semitism. In this work, he stated: "[D]espite the importance of the problem of anti-Semitism as a social phenomenon, not much has as yet been achieved toward its solution by sociology or philosophy".[115] In 1947, Horkheimer wrote *Fortune Polls on Antisemitism*,[116] in which he established that while polls inform us about the preferential psychological tendencies of a given subject, they cannot tell us about the "measure of the amount of

108 IfS, *Studies in Antisemitism. A Report*, 1944, pp. 1–144.
109 Ibid., pp. 3–4.
110 Ibid., p. 5.
111 Ibid., pp. 1–2.
112 Ibid., p. 10.
113 M. Horkheimer, S. H. Flowerman (eds.), *Studies in Prejudice*, 1949.
114 M. Horkheimer, "Sociological Background of the Psychoanalytic Approach", 1946, pp. 1–10.
115 Ibid., p. 1.
116 M. Horkheimer, "Fortune Polls on Antisemitism", *Nachlass Max Horkheimer*, 1947, pp. 1–18.

prejudice or race hatred"[117] of the interviewee. That same year, Gurland's typescript "Fight against Antisemitism within the Framework of Germany's Education for Democracy, Draft Program" (1947)[118] was produced, in which the author, in line with the IfS's interpretive framework, defended the idea that the eradication of anti-Semitism in Germany was crucial for the cause of global democracy and that education fostering the rejection of anti-Semitic intolerance was a prerequisite for the stabilization of democracy. In 1948, Horkheimer presented a lecture on fascism at the Paris UNESCO workshop. His address would be published in *Tensions That Cause Wars*, which will be discussed later.[119]

The second phase of research on anti-Semitism culminated in the 1950 publication of the five volumes of *Studies in Prejudice*, which offered a systematic treatment of the topic of anti-Semitism. The published works included Bettelheim and Janowitz's *Dynamics of Prejudice: A Psychological and Sociological Study of Veterans*; Ackerman and Jahoda's *Anti-Semitism and Emotional Disorder: A Psychoanalytic Interpretation* and Adorno, Frenkel-Brunswik, Levinson and Nevitt Sanford's *The Authoritarian Personality*.[120] A fourth study, Löwenthal and Guterman's *Prophets of Deceit*,[121] examined the propaganda techniques of fascism while a fifth—Massing's *Rehearsal for Destruction*—addressed the historical issue of anti-Semitism in Germany.[122] Horkheimer opened the introduction to this collection of studies by providing an overarching indication of the significance of the research conducted on the topic of anti-Semitism in the years '49–'50. Although no longer manifesting with the destructive force previously displayed, anti-Semitism will reveal itself as a pathology of society that must be contained with appropriate means in order to prevent the generation of new and further outbreaks. The intellectual influence of the IfS director had already appeared in Löwenthal and Guterman's text *Prophets of Deceit*,[123] in which they referenced Horkheimer's article "Egoism and the Freedom Movement" [1936][124] as a general guide for their study. Löwenthal and Guterman examined those American agitators who replicated the attitudes of both small and large authoritarian European leaders.

117 Ibid., p. 1.

118 A. R. L. Gurland, "Fight against Antisemitism within the Framework of Germany's Education for Democracy, Draft Program", *Horkheimer Archiv*, 1947, pp. 1–62.

119 M. Horkheimer, "The Lessons of Fascism", 1950, pp. 209–242.

120 B. Bettelheim, M. Janowitz, *Dynamics of Prejudice: A Psychological and Sociological Study of Veterans*, 1950; N. W. Ackerman, M. Jahoda, *Anti-Semitism and Emotional Disorder: A Psychoanalytic Interpretation*, 1950; and finally, T. W. Adorno, E. Frenkel-Brunswik, D. J. Levinson, R. Nevitt Sanford, *The Authoritarian Personality*, [1950] 2016.

121 L. Löwenthal, N. Guterman, *Prophets of Deceits*, [1949] 2021.

122 P. W. Massing, *Rehearsal for Destruction: A Study of Political Anti-Semitism in Imperial Germany*, 1949.

123 L. Löwenthal, N. Guterman, *Prophets of Deceits*, [1949] 2021.

124 Ibid., p. xlvi; M. Horkheimer, "Egoism and Freedom Movements: On the Anthropology of the Bourgeois Era", [1936] 1993, pp. 49–111.

These agitators, stigmatizing the undue influence of alleged "alien enemies of America",[125] referred to communists, Jews and refugees as "parasitic insects" of society,[126] echoing some of Kracauer's earlier considerations. In this case too, the enemy exhibited "functional" characteristics such that "communists, plutocrats, refugees"[127] will eventually incorporate the Jews among themselves, and the latter brings us back to the former. The agitators had nothing in common with reformers or revolutionaries. Unlike these, they appealed to irrational and subconscious feelings to amplify the listener's indignation and intolerance toward subjects identified as enemies of the nation.

3.8 Adorno and *The Authoritarian Personality* (1950)

The aforementioned volume by Adorno, Frenkel-Brunswik, Levinson and Nevitt Sanford, titled *The Authoritarian Personality*, proposed a political psychology study aimed at operationalizing Fromm's 1936 concepts on the sadomasochistic character of the authoritarian subject.[128] As stated by the authors themselves, the goal was to integrate deep psychology with statistical generalization. The structure of the study included three opinion-attitude scales related to the tendency toward anti-Semitism (A-S scale), ethnocentrism (E scale) and political-economic conservatism (PEC scale). These scales were supplemented by a fourth index measuring susceptibility to fascist propaganda themes (F scale). While the first three scales included ideologically explicit questions, the F scale aimed to reveal the implicit potential for anti-democratic closure inherent in the authoritarian personality.[129] In a strict sense, it was thus a marker of implicit pre-fascist tendencies intended to measure the degree of prejudice, without specifying the minority group in question. The sample of interviewees consisted of students from Berkeley University, who generally represented the American middle class and were thus fully embedded in a democratic socio-political context. It goes without saying that statistically significant evidence of a propensity toward anti-Semitism or, more generally, toward fascism would have fundamentally undermined the ideological

125 L. Löwenthal, N. Guterman, *Prophets of Deceits*, [1949] 2021, p. 1.
126 Ibid.
127 Ibid., p. 65.
128 T. W. Adorno, E. Frenkel-Brunswik, D. J. Levinson, R. Nevitt Sanford, *The Authoritarian Personality*, [1950] 1969.
129 The measurement indices of the F-scale examined the following inclinations: conventionalism (adherence to middle-class values), authoritarian submission (submission to the moral authorities within the group), authoritarian aggression (tendency to condemn group members who rebel against adopted conventions), anti-intraception (rejection of subjective and creative expressions), superstition and stereotypy (inclination toward magical beliefs to interpret reality and the use of rigid categories), power and "toughness" (interest in forces of power/domination and submission, as well as physical strength), destructiveness and cynicism (hostility and detachment from humanity) and projectivity (external projection of unconscious impulses that define the world as a wild and dangerous territory).

premises of equal respect in American liberal democracy and beyond. The authors sought to address this concern by constructing measurement scales. The scales defined two ideal types, Mack and Larry: the first exhibiting a high degree of prejudice while the second exhibited a low level. The objective was not to analyze the fascist tendencies of a generation that had emerged from the war in Europe, but rather to assess the vulnerability of individuals raised in post-war America to totalitarian temptations. As noted by Jay,[130] rather than focusing on an authoritarian personality akin to that of Wilhelmine society, Adorno and his collaborators were actually analyzing a general psychological propensity in a society in which the role of the family—especially the mother's role in relation to her children—had undergone profound changes. Certainly, susceptibility to fascist allure had to be clearly distinguished from susceptibility to anti-Semitism, which was understood as a multifactorial tendency: hence, the different scale indicators. The theoretical premise of this new perspective was based on the acceptance of the monopolistic state model theorized by Pollock in *State Capitalism: Its Possibilities and Limitations* [1941],[131] which identified, as discussed extensively, two forms of state capitalism—authoritarian and democratic—that signalled the transformation of the monopoly state. For his part, Horkheimer in *Die Juden und Europa* [*The Jews and Europe*] [1939] had partly anticipated Pollock's analyses, particularly the idea that the economic crises of capitalism had produced a radical transformation of the state and the social structures connected to it.[132] Once again, the Frankfurt School's reflection revealed the inseparable link between structural changes and psycho-superstructural and ideological effects, synthesized in the assumption that there are economic foundations to anti-Semitism.

Phenomena such as alienation, reification and so on were acknowledged as products of an economic structure that shaped both social and individual-psychic relationships, transforming humans from subjects into consumers and producers in a market society.[133] From this perspective, envy of Jews and anti-Semitism in general were not merely expressions of direct antipathy toward this group. Rather, they represented an ideology, a stereotypical way of thinking or the result of a failure to integrate the systemic-economic level with the level of subjectivity. In other words, the breakdowns of economic life—crises—turned into closures of opportunities for social realization and only then into feelings of resentment toward other social groups. As Horkheimer and Adorno had already stated in *Dialectic of Enlightenment* [1947]: "Anti-Semitic behaviour is unleashed in situations in which blinded people, deprived of subjectivity, are let loose as subjects".[134] The fascist ego,

130 M. Jay, *The Dialectical Imagination: A History of the Frankfurt School and the Institute of Social Research, 1923–1950*, 1973.
131 F. Pollock, "State Capitalism: Its Possibilities and Limitations", 1941, pp. 200–225.
132 M. Horkheimer, "Die Juden und Europa", 1939, pp. 115–137.
133 Ibid.
134 M. Horkheimer, T. W. Adorno, *Dialectic of Enlightenment*, [1947] 2002, p. 140.

unable to internalize moral imperatives and externally imposed rules as structures of communal living, resorted to externalizing destructive impulses of the id, which targeted particularity and difference. These projections contained unconscious fears and prohibitions tied to castration anxiety connected to the paternal figure, as well as unresolved homosexual impulses. This explains why, in *The Authoritarian Personality* [1950], the authors, when citing Sartre on anti-Semitism, highlighted his thesis regarding the subject's inability to experience and, thus, the need to resort to ideological substitutes like anti-Semitism or pseudo-conservatism. While avoiding a psychological reductionism in explaining anti-Semitism, they clarified that this experiential incapacity was, more precisely, a failure of the ego to internalize the superego in terms of constructing a coherent system of values capable of coexisting within a unified personality: hence, the recourse to an external authority.

In this regard, some personality differences between Mack and Larry, according to the F scale, were noted. These included Mack's high scoring and Larry's low scoring on efficiency and diligence as values in themselves, as well as the minimization of psychological determinants in social relationships and the inclination toward anti-interceptive attitudes of rejecting subjective and imaginative impulses. However, there were some convergences between the two ideal types that prohibited placing them at opposite poles. The text concluded with a question and a certainty: how could the personality structure inclined toward ideological fascist temptations be altered? One thing was certain: for the authors, the illusion of achieving transformation through psychological tools alone could not be entertained. Personality traits were indebted to the intersection of three dimensions that Fromm had already defined in relation to the authoritarian character: psychic structure, social belonging and political inclination.[135] The authoritarian personality was thus the result of an education that found fertile ground in the family's formative environment as well as the surrounding culture—as Horkheimer had recognized in *Autorität und Familie*.[136]

Much later, in the 1950 essay "The Lessons of Fascism", Horkheimer would once again underscore the importance of family education in breaking the link between social conditions and their psychological determination, according to the well-known equation between frustration and aggression.[137] It will also happen that the introjection of social dynamics under pressing conditions will be realized just as had happened to the inmates in their attempts to secure in the camps. Four years later, in the final section of an article that appeared in *Das Parlament* on March 25, 1955,[138] Horkheimer, referring to efforts

135 E. Fromm, *The Working Class in Weimar Germany: A Psychological and Sociological Study*, [1929] 1980.

136 M. Horkheimer, "Allgemeiner Teil", in M. Horkheimer (ed.), *Studien über Autorität und Familie*, [1936] 1963, pp. 3–76.

137 M. Horkheimer, "The Lessons of Fascism", 1950, pp. 209–242.

138 M. Horkheimer, "Zur Psychologie des Totalitären", *Nachlass Max Horkheimer*, 1955 p. 10.

to counter the totalitarian mentality and politics, asked, paraphrasing Lenin: "What must we do?" [*Was ist zu tun?*] to distance "the totalitarian type" [*Die Totalitäre Typus*][139] from our society? His answer was that only through the education of the young would it be possible to defuse this disease, which had not ended with the defeat of National Socialism.

3.9 Cultural regressions in liberal democracies

During the 1941 research program titled Cultural Aspects of National Socialism. A Research Project,[140] the IfS established an inseparable connection between cultural regression and fascism, based on the historical experience of National Socialism. The text opens with the assertion that the decisive trends in Nazi Germany could not be understood without addressing the related cultural problems, which had not yet been investigated on the basis of an integrated methodology. In *Art and Mass Culture* [1941],[141] Horkheimer observed how the lie of fascist propaganda also reflected in artistic production in general. The sense of vitality was no longer nurtured even in aesthetic experience, as had occurred in classical periods. The distinction between communication and artistic experience was now disappearing. If, as Horkheimer, reading Dewey, argued, art once broke down barriers, today "radio and cinema in no way yield the palm to airplane and gun".[142] What hope could stand in the face of such political and cultural disintegration? Horkheimer, at the conclusion of the essay, found a possibility in the idea that "the deaf ears in Europe imply an opposition to the lies that are being hammered at men from all sides and that . . . the masses, even in fascist countries, secretly knew the truth".[143] This attitude would give strength to the resistance to the discourse still perceived as "senseless"[144] in the face of the senseless tyranny of fascism. Adorno would revisit the theme of cultural and moral rebirth much later in *Education after Auschwitz* [1966].[145] How can we prevent Auschwitz from happening again? If there is one task that education must fulfil in every time and place, it is to ensure that such an atrocity never occurs again. Nevertheless, the possibility of its recurrence cannot be excluded, not only because what has already happened can happen again, but also because there seems to be an internal movement in the history of civilization that constantly reappears in the form of an anti-civilization principle, as Freud had intuited.[146]

139 Ibid.
140 IfS, "Cultural Aspects of National Socialism. A Research Project", *Horkheimer Archiv*, 1941, pp. 1–117.
141 M. Horkheimer, "Art and Mass Culture", 1941, pp. 290–304.
142 Ibid., p. 295.
143 Ibid., p. 304.
144 Ibid.
145 T. W. Adorno, "Education after Auschwitz", [1966] 1998, pp. 191–204.
146 Adorno's reference is to S. Freud, *Civilization and Its Discontents*, [1930] 1999, pp. 1169–1252. See also T. W. Adorno, "Education After Auschwitz", [1966] 1998, p. 191.

Nationalistic tendencies, mass movements, authoritarian cultures—these and other forms jeopardize the moral autonomy of the Kantian subject, the only one who can protect us from the obscuring of reason.[147] The loss of the ability for rational self-determination based on universalizable principles renders individuals slaves to the arbitrary will of a few or to the emotional states of barbaric hordes and masses. It is precisely the massification of individual wills that serves as the warning sign of a society moving toward authoritarianism. This potential drift is connected to forms of democratic regression built on the close link between anxiety and political regression. The analysis of social pathologies aimed at preventing free collective democratic deliberation is the focus of Neumann's last work, *Anxiety and Politics* [1957], published after his premature death in 1954.[148] Neumann maintained an ambivalent position on Freudian psychoanalysis. He attributed populist regressions to states of anxiety caused by repressive actions—from propaganda to oppression—designed to provoke instinctual repression. From this, diverse forms of anxiety would emerge, in which identification with the leader's power would eliminate the critical-negative distance of thought. Anxiety, as Neumann wrote, in a "totally repressive system institutionalizes depressive and persecutory anxiety".[149] In the case of Nazism and fascism, the anxieties of the bourgeoisie were aimed at destruction through the "identification by the oppressed people with its rulers".[150]

Neumann broke with the traditional psychoanalytic tradition, considering, in the wake of Reich and Fromm, the importance of social elements in favouring regressive impulses in the psyche, as opposed to the naturalistic-anthropological vision of instinct theory. In the latter, there appeared to be a more direct relationship between the structures of the psyche and historical-social regressions, in which *Kultur* was no longer able to function as an inhibitor. Neumann, while not adopting Fromm's reformist project, did consider that overcoming the individualistic view was the means of resolving regressive social phenomena that, in Freud, remained tied to archetypal structures of the psyche. As Adorno would later observe, the "manipulative character"[151] of the authoritarian personality leverages the erasure of the individual's will for self-determination as part of the mass. The absence of empathy, obsession with efficient organization and fetishization of technology—these are the traits of the Nazi psyche as a "reified consciousness"[152] or, simply, the way of experiencing life typical of "people who cannot love"[153] and who simultaneously feel the weight of indifference toward themselves. It is in this context of generalized emotional

147 T. W. Adorno, "Education After Auschwitz", [1966] 1998, p. 196.
148 F. Neumann, "Anxiety and Politics", [1957] 2017, pp. 612–636.
149 Ibid., p. 627.
150 F. Neumann, *The Democratic and the Authoritarian State*, [1957] 1964, p. 245.
151 T. W. Adorno, "Education After Auschwitz", [1966] 1998, p. 198.
152 Ibid., p. 199.
153 Ibid., p. 200.

detachment that indifference to the lives of others would produce the horrors of Auschwitz, thanks to the silent support of a vast bureaucratic-administrative as well as military apparatus. To educate after Auschwitz, therefore, would mean to educate people from childhood in the ideals of the Enlightenment" i.e., to continually question the reasons that led to the barbarism of the Holocaust.[154] In the face of the cultural and moral ruins of Germany:

> To write poetry after Auschwitz is barbaric. And this corrodes even the knowledge of why it has become impossible to write poetry today. Absolute reification, which presupposed intellectual progress as one of its elements, is now preparing to absorb the mind entirely. Critical intelligence cannot be equal to this challenge as long as it confines itself to self-satisfied contemplation.
>
> (T. W. Adorno, *Prisms*, [1967] 1983, p. 34)

Adorno later revised this thought, opening up to the legitimacy of expressing the pain born from the tragedy of such an event.[155] Nevertheless, fascism and its mad figures, which Adorno, with an Anglophone expression, already referred to in a 1960s lecture as the "lunatic fringe",[156] did not end with the extinction of the dictatorial systems of the 1930s. Authoritarian tendencies would once again take shape within democratic systems, where these systems would prove to be organizations not yet having "lived up to [their] own concept".[157] It is the far-right radicals, as well as citizens and parents—along with the youth—who must be re-educated to the values of love for others. This is because the madness of fascism, in the form of anti-Semitism, will still manage to live beneath the surface, keeping alive that sense of revenge toward and envy of groups perceived as undeservedly advantaged. The madness of this psychological process lies in the failure to understand the source of one's economic marginalization within the structure produced by monopoly capitalism itself. Adorno had already recognized this in 1941, during the drafting of the *Research Project on Anti-Semitism*.[158] Confusing cause and effect is what fascist myopia, devoid of a true political theory, has done, even though anti-Semitism as a phenomenon preceded fascism. As Adorno stated, "During the so-called enlightened era of the last 200 years, no stratum of

154 Ibid., p. 195.

155 "It may have been wrong to say that after Auschwitz you could no longer write poems. But it is not wrong to raise the less cultural question whether after Auschwitz you can go on living". In T. W. Adorno, *Negative Dialectics*, [1966] 1973, p. 362.

156 This refers to the lecture Adorno delivered on April 6, 1967, at the University of Vienna, coinciding with the political success of Germany's right-wing NPD (the National Democratic Party of Germany, founded in 1964). The text remained unpublished until 2019. See T. W. Adorno, *Aspects of the New Right-Wing Radicalism*, [1967] 2020.

157 Ibid., p. 7.

158 M. Horkheimer, T. W. Adorno, "Research Project on Anti-Semitism", 1941, pp. 124–143.

the population has been free from anti-semitism".[159] Why did all this happen? Because, according to Adorno, there was a disconnection between the formalism of law and democratic institutions on the one hand and the absence of real power that the constituting people could assert against the government of the state and the organization of society on the other. When this occurred, economic disparities between classes also increased, as did the possibility of the weaker groups being able to claim their full bourgeois rights, thus increasing social inequalities. Therefore, as Adorno would affirm in a 1962 report for the German Coordinating Council of Societies for Christian-Jewish Cooperation, the danger of National Socialism would be far more threatening from within democracies than from outside.[160] But if the education of new generations can eventually curb the extremist tendencies of an incomplete democracy, it is unclear what socio-political reform program should be pursued to implement these changes. This element of political praxis seemed to fall outside the scope of Adorno's reflection. As we will see, for Marcuse, things will be different. He would identify the possibility of neutralizing illiberal structural residues in both authoritarian fascist societies and (quasi)democratic societies through a cultural revolution.

3.10 Critique of culture as critique of capitalism

It must be acknowledged that Walter Benjamin's role in the theoretical developments of the Frankfurt School became progressively central after his premature death, although, during his lifetime, he remained at the margins of the IfS's inner circle. In his 1936 essay "The Work of Art in the Age of Mechanical Reproduction",[161] Benjamin focused on the concept of "aura", understood as the originality, genius and uniqueness of a work of art. He argued that this aura had been reduced to a fetish, and the ritualistic context of artistic consumption was transferred into a continually replicable time-space. In doing so, Benjamin opened the door to the problem of the relationship between the crisis of aesthetic experience and its repercussions on the understanding of history and its salvific possibilities. Mechanized art would no longer be able to guarantee such an expectation. This outcome would easily become the tool of totalitarian regimes and their expressive translation into the demands of transforming "property relations"[162] among increasingly proletarianized masses. The concessions offered by fascism were coupled with the preservation of

159 Ibid., p. 129.

160 T. W. Adorno, *Fighting Antisemitism Today: A Lecture*, [1962] 2025.

161 W. Benjamin, *The Work of Art in the Age of Mechanical Reproduction*, [1946] 2008. The third version of the text will be followed, as this, though shorter than the second, was the one published by Adorno in 1955 and most widely circulated at the time. It was likely composed between 1936 and 1937.

162 Ibid.

social imbalances. In this sense, therefore, "fascism is an aestheticizing of political life"[163] (which paralleled the politicization of art in Soviet communism) and the fascist attempts to pursue this direction: "All efforts to aestheticize politics culminate in one point. That one point is war".[164]

The artistic and cultural superstructure thus became expressively linked to the structural base of totalitarianism. In Italy, Marinetti and futurism made war aesthetically appealing, even asserting that: "War is beautiful because thanks to its gas masks, its terrifying megaphones, its flame throwers, and light tanks—it establishes man's dominion over the subjugated machine".[165] Among the eminent figures of the Frankfurt School, Adorno was certainly the one who found the deepest intellectual affinity with Benjamin's thought. This affinity was first expressed in one of his early reflections on the fetishist character of music. In his 1938 essay "On the Fetish-Character in Music and the Regression of Listening",[166] Adorno highlighted the transformation of both the production and the consumptive enjoyment of cultural products, especially music, in all its forms. The use of media tools like radio had taken on a "totalitarian [connotation, as it] was assigned to the task, on the one hand, of providing good entertainment and diversion, and on the other, of fostering the so-called cultural goods".[167] However, this artificial care for culture was itself an illiberal form of regimentation of society. This became even more evident with the phenomenon of the entertainment stars, leading Adorno to claim that "the star principle has become totalitarian".[168] Here, the listeners were more interested in the figure of the performer than in listening to the music itself. For example, the authority of the conductor came to be seen as equivalent to that of "a totalitarian *Führer*".[169] But why did such a reversal occur? What caused modern society to so profoundly transform the consumption of its own artistic products? For Adorno, the underlying discourse of this reversal has an explicitly Marxist foundation: consumer society has inverted the relationship between the use-value and exchange-value of commodities. Cultural products as commodities have been transformed into fetishes: "The consumer is really worshipping the money that he himself has paid for the ticket to the Toscanini

163 Ibid., p. 41.
164 Ibid.
165 Ibid.
166 T. W. Adorno, "On the Fetish-Character in Music and the Regression of Listening", [1938]. For a comprehensive introduction to the relationship between the Frankfurt School and cultural criticism, see A. Demirović, *Der nonkonformistische Intellektuelle. Die Entwicklung der Kritischen Theorie zur Frankfurter Schule*, 1999, p. 556 ff.
167 T. W. Adorno, "On the Fetish-Character in Music and the Regression of Listening", [1938] 2002, p. 292.
168 Ibid., p. 293.
169 Ibid., p. 301. On the sociocultural implications of Adorno's collaboration with Paul Lazarsfeld and the Princeton Radio Project, see B. Babich, "Adorno's Radio Phenomenology: Technical Reproduction, Physiognomy, and Music", 2014, pp. 957–996.

concert".[170] This fetishization of "success"[171] subjectivizes a product of the spirit, turning it into a *sui generis* exchange product. Cultural products, unlike ordinary commodities, have only an appearance of exchange value as they were originally conceived in terms of use-value. It is capitalist consumer society that deceptively elevates exchange value to the level of use-value, enabling the transformation of cultural products into commodity-fetishes. This introduces a great deception into society. Not only does the bourgeois pretence of attending theatres and cinemas serve to display one's social ability to afford a front-row seat, but, more broadly, it deceptively satisfies the immediate enjoyment of a cultural experience. Herein lies the problem. To conceive of cultural products as commodity-fetishes that provide immediate gratification places them within a circuit of exchange, removing them from their primary vocation: the satisfaction of a spiritual need, which is far removed from being a means of gratification within a process of circulation. If the fetishism of commodities as cultural products is characteristic of a social system that redefines interpersonal relations through this new currency, the result will be that "The new fetish is the flawlessly functioning, metallically brilliant apparatus as such, in which all the cogwheels mesh so perfectly that not the slightest hole remains open for the meaning of the whole".[172] The comprehensive view and self-distancing from society as a whole will trap humanity in what Marcuse defines as the one-dimensional man.[173]

The fetish character of music is also linked to another trend: the regression in listening. Adorno traces a precise connection between the repetitiveness of certain musical uses, of "infantile instruments"[174] like the ukulele and banjo and the regression in listening, extending to the fixation on an "infantile stage".[175] This insidious trend toward psychological and communicative regression is only seemingly harmless from a social standpoint as it produces intellectually ensnared individuals incapable of fully conscious action. The social implication that Adorno will take care to highlight will consist of two dangerously connected points: on one hand, the infantile, regressive escape from the problems of lived reality will return to assert its claims to social duties. On the other hand, the regressive slide in listening will lead to a passive acceptance of unexamined forms of authority proposed by advertising messages or the media more generally.

These two trends, in turn, are linked to two socially relevant effects from the perspective of a critique of authoritarian society: "Regressive listening is

170 T. W. Adorno, "On the Fetish-Character in Music and the Regression of Listening", [1938] 2002, p. 296.
171 Ibid.
172 Ibid., p. 301.
173 H. Marcuse, *One-Dimensional Man*, [1964] 2002.
174 T. W. Adorno, "On the Fetish-Character in Music and the Regression of Listening", [1938] 2002, p. 307.
175 Ibid., p. 303.

always ready to degenerate into rage",[176] since the illusion of immediate satisfaction of needs throws us back into the condition of the society that hosts us, bending the individual's consciousness before advertised commodities and uncritically accepting what is offered. The "advertising turns into terror"[177] assumes a "compulsory character".[178] Horkheimer warns that the immanent logic of technological society and state capitalism will eventually render cultural criticism devoid of an object of inquiry.[179] Adorno, in his radio adaptation of the arguments developed with Horkheimer in the chapter on "The Culture Industry Reconsidered" [1963],[180] emphasizes that the culture industry, as a form of "[integration] of its consumers from above",[181] no longer treats the consumer as a "sovereign"[182] but as its "object".[183] The order established by the culture industry is an a-dialectical one, aimed at legitimizing a status quo devoid of critical-negative oppositions. For Adorno, the categorical imperative governing this condition of reification in social relations is the imperative of "you must bend" with no specification regarding in front of whom, thus alluding that it refers to those immediately present. This irrational rationality of brute authority supporting the pseudo-industrial mechanism of cultural production will not lead to regained happiness. Rather, the culture industry will facilitate the advancement of regressive processes of the psyche, which will find comfort in intellectually simplified objects and the illusion of mastering and judging the cultural quality of products fed to it.

Paradoxically, however, the diabolic alliance between the culture industry and the masses reveals its most insidious side here. For Adorno, the same culture industry, the true enemy of the masses, will "obstruct . . . the emancipation for which human beings are as ripe as"[184] in our time. Mass culture thus imposes an objectification of social relations, ultimately imprisoning them within a predetermined, uniform scheme. In the posthumously published essay "*Das Schema der Massenkultur*" ["The Scheme of Mass Culture] [1942],[185] Adorno reiterates that breaking free from the mechanical repetition of conventional mass formulas exposes the author to the risk of being considered either an idiot or an intellectual.[186] The reign of mass culture and the culture industry will become one of mere conformity to dominant thought, where time itself will be reduced to a single dimension—a supposed eternal

176 Ibid., p. 311.
177 Ibid., p. 304.
178 Ibid.
179 M. Horkheimer, "Philosophie als Kulturkritik", 2014, pp. 81–103.
180 The reference is to T. W. Adorno, "Culture Industry Reconsidered", [1963] 1975, pp. 12–19.
181 Ibid., p. 12.
182 Ibid.
183 Ibid.
184 Ibid., p. 19.
185 T. W. Adorno, "The Schema of Mass Culture", [1942] 2001, pp. 61–97.
186 Ibid.

return of the same—aimed at erasing contrasts and, consequently, the chronological progression that accompanies the mediations determined by the existent. This ahistorical consideration of the existing will translate into abstract and a-dialectical thought.[187] Given this condition, the necessity of a persistent critique of culture as a superstructure of social mechanisms arises so that the processes of reification initiated by forms of totalitarian domination may be dissolved through the transcendence of the entire system-society. However, two obstacles present themselves along the way: for Adorno, cultural criticism is unable to address "absolute reification"[188] since, after Auschwitz, the Enlightenment hope for spiritual progress is unfulfilled to the point of making it "impossible to write poetry today".[189] On the other hand, for Horkheimer, philosophy finds itself in a paradoxical situation, one in which the critique of culture has lost its object. The reasons for this intellectual decline in grasping reality lie in the irreversible post-war regression of industrial society, which led to the degradation of critical-dialectical thought. Here, culture becomes a mere "cultural good", and its forms are emptied. For the Horkheimer of the 1960s, Freud's thesis remains valid: the expansion of civilization (*Kultur*) corresponds to a progressive accumulation of destructive psychic forces. It is clear that neither the reification of culture nor even its loss of object is the incidental result of accidental historical factors. Rather, this devolution began before mass society, with the rise of fascism in Europe. Fascist ideology itself was presented as a form of reified consciousness, an intellect entangled in a way that allowed the Nazi regime to implement strategies of manipulation over consciousness. Horkheimer and Adorno, in the section titled "Propaganda" in *Dialectic of Enlightenment* [1947], defined such manipulation as turning "language into an instrument, a lever, a machine".[190] By shifting social injustices from one point to another, "It counts [manipulations] on their [human beings] ability to be counted on".[191] For both thinkers, fascist culture is essentially a "half-culture"[192] in which the inability to experience reality is pathologically filled by the exaltation of some singular aspect of cultural-cognitive neurosis. These neuroses fully emerge in Adorno's 1951 study on the role of Freudian theory in fascist propaganda.[193] Here, the projection mechanism of ego narcissism onto the authoritarian leader is reconstructed. As a manipulative mechanism of the psyche, fascism made irrational goals appear as natural outcomes for the masses. For this reason, according to Adorno, fascism could only utilize propaganda, not rational discourse, to emotionally convince the

187 Ibid.
188 T. W. Adorno, *Prisms*, [1967] 1983, p. 34.
189 Ibid.
190 M. Horkheimer, T. W. Adorno, *Dialectic of Enlightenment*, [1947] 1997, p. 212.
191 Ibid.
192 Ibid.
193 T. W. Adorno, "Freudian Theory and the Pattern of Fascist Propaganda", [1951] 2007, pp. 118–137.

masses into action. Only the mobilization of unconscious regressive processes could take hold of minds already weakened by the exercise of brutal power that divided those inside the group from those outside it. The figure of the "little great man" continues the idea of the bourgeois as a mass leader, thus connecting to the populist character that defines part of fascist ideology.[194] Everyone could be like him; he would ultimately be a representation of the father of the primal horde, embodying the narcissistic drives of the masses made up of individual egos. Adorno addressed the theme of fascist propaganda (with particular reference to anti-Semitism) in a study that revisited part of a work published posthumously in 1975 (though dating back to 1943) concerning the psychological technique used in the propaganda radio broadcasts of Martin Luther Thomas, a militant Christian preacher. He focused on the radio as a medium capable of disguising the true demagogic-fascist intentions of messages seemingly tailored for a religious audience. Radio communication techniques can maintain an appearance of accuracy and plausibility in the transmitted message, even when conveying racial hatred. However, radio speakers, in executing mass domination techniques, never operate in isolation. Their success depends on their ability to exploit the masses to the aims of the strongest.[195] Despite the necessary differences, both Nazism and Luther Thomas fulfilled a task of racial and anti-Semitic propaganda. For Adorno, Luther Thomas carried out this strategy through "the unification of the horrible and the wonderful, the drunkenness of annihilation that pretends to be salvation".[196] The original development of such reflections, albeit related to a different historical context, is part of Adorno's 1951 essay "Anti-Semitism and Fascist Propaganda",[197] which explicitly refers to material gathered in the three essays published separately in the *Research Project on Anti-Semitism* a decade earlier.[198]

In the essay on anti-Semitism and fascist propaganda, Adorno explicitly focuses on the psychological character of militant propaganda in the United States of America. The way the message is delivered by political-religious agitators, generally radio speakers, appears not only illogical but also pseudo-emotional. For Adorno, the American agitators' propaganda is aimed entirely at personalizing the message, presenting themselves as tireless men with an unwavering commitment to others. In this form of propaganda, means are mistaken for ends, emphasizing mobilization as a form of patriotism toward the Christian God.[199] Consequently, since the aim of the propaganda is self-promotion, it

194 Ibid.
195 Cfr. M. Horkheimer, T. W. Adorno (eds.), Institut für Sozialforschung, *Soziologische Exkurse*, [1956] 2013.
196 T. W. Adorno, *The Psychological Technique of Martin Luther Thomas's Radio Addresses*, [1975] 2000, pp. 130–131.
197 T. W. Adorno, "Anti-Semitism and Fascist Propaganda", [1946] 2002.
198 M. Horkheimer, T. W. Adorno, "Research Project on Anti-Semitism", 1941, pp. 124–143.
199 T. W. Adorno, "Anti-Semitism and Fascist Propaganda", [1946] 2002.

ends up becoming self-fulfilling. Certainly, for Adorno, the American religious preacher cannot explicitly declare his authoritarian aims. In the United States of America, rules—both written and unwritten—limit the spread of overtly fascist invectives. However, in Adorno's view, the secret of American fascist propaganda lies in presenting an empty and irrational discourse within the context of mere commercial selling. Thus, the masking of true intentions becomes possible thanks to an eminently capitalistic social apparatus. In this way, even "anti-Semitic merchandise" can be communicated as just another product, with the crucifixion becoming a symbol of the pogrom.[200] The fascist agitators will present themselves as hysterical figures, violating the taboos meant to restrain behaviour and pushing the public's emotions beyond socially acceptable norms and general rational self-control. This mechanism realizes the process of the collectivization of the ego and its psychic regression, which Adorno continued to emphasize.

In 1967, Adorno revisited the theme of fascist propaganda as a new authoritarian trend within German democracy,[201] noting how it serves, even more than to disseminate an ideology, to subordinate the masses. As already recognized in 1962, even in post-totalitarian democratic contexts, the tension between massified productive bases and superstructural manipulation persists.[202] Propaganda thus becomes a "psychological technique of masses".[203] As a pure instrument of command—and therefore not communicative—propaganda conveys the falsehood of facts that are often unverifiable, serving only to legitimize the regime in power (as seen in Hitler's well-known technique of using the big lie, which he outlined in *Mein Kampf* [*My Struggle*] [1925–1926] as a distorted revision of Le Bon's ideas from 1895). Ultimately, despite changes in places, times and characters, the reifying effects of fascist propaganda on society, though expressed in smaller proportions, remain the same as those of the Third Reich. For Adorno, the winning card of the new German right-wing parties or extremist American preachers is their political apology for the status quo: that is, the fetishization of existing power relations. An element of inauthenticity pervades the modern man's sense of self, to the point that for Horkheimer, from birth, one has become accustomed to a single lesson: namely, that "there is only one way of getting along in this world—that of giving up his hope of ultimate self-realization".[204] A form of mimicry and cultural flattening of the individual emerges, where "[success] can [be achieved] solely by imitation".[205] Receiving an education means replicating a series of behaviours acquired within society: playing in a certain way, giving

200 Ibid.
201 T. W. Adorno, *Aspects of the New Right-Wing Extremism*, [1967] 2020.
202 T. W. Adorno, *Prisms*, [1967] 1983.
203 Ibid.
204 M. Horkheimer, *Eclipse of Reason*, [1947] 2004, p. 96.
205 Ibid.

up certain eccentricities. In short, it means becoming a normalized individual, fully functionally aligned with the needs of the organizational context. Mimicry, as Horkheimer tells us,[206] as a more archaic survival mechanism, will prove crucial even in modern capitalist conditions. Everything remains as it is. The culture that once served as a counterpoint to mere existence, in its decline into mass culture, will turn to an apology for reality: "Motion pictures, the radio, popular biographies and novels have the same refrain: This is our groove, this is the rut of the great and the would-be great—this is reality as it is and should be and will be".[207] But this instrumental shift in the function of culture in its massified version will only weaken the individual's role in society: "the working class has been impaired by the general dissolution of individuality".[208] Despite what Horkheimer calls "rhetoric of individualism",[209] the slogans and advertising techniques, with their communicative prominence, will negate precisely what they claim to promote. The trivialization of media content and the apparent democratization of cultural products will reduce individual taste to a shared fashion that also concerns being part of a social group. The individual as such will no longer have any value in the mass society of the cultural industry. The entirety of the Frankfurt School's cultural critique also reorients Marxian political economy toward a critique of the alienation within the cultural industry. Although Marx once undertook a critique of society through the tools of political economy,[210] the Frankfurt School, lacking the historical possibility of relying on a defined collective subject—the proletariat—turned instead to a "culturalist critique"[211] as the privileged locus of alienation in liberal societies born from the ashes of World War II.

3.11 'The totalitarian man': technology and fascism in liberal society

From the 1950s onward, with the reestablishment of democracies in Europe, members of the Frankfurt School became increasingly interested in new trends of domination within society. The political and economic framework now resembled that of liberal democracies that had emerged from totalitarian experiences. This setting was vastly different from what Marcuse had identified in 1934 as the "heroic-popular vision"[212] of National Socialism. However, this new context remained consistent with the broader hypothesis that certain

206 Ibid.
207 Ibid.
208 Ibid., p. 97.
209 Ibid., p. 107.
210 H. F. Dahms, "Chapter 1 The Early Frankfurt School Critique of Capitalism: Critical Theory between Pollock's 'State Capitalism' and the Critique of Instrumental Reason", 2011, p. 8.
211 Ibid., p. 34.
212 H. Marcuse, "The Struggle against Liberalism in the Totalitarian View of the State", [1934] 1968.

liberal distortions were taking on an authoritarian turn. Consequently, cultural and intellectual production became an essential component of a society fundamentally trapped within the pernicious mesh of forms of instrumental rationality. It is thus unsurprising that the Frankfurt critique of culture and its products drew upon Marx's critique of the fetishism of commodities. The totalizing dominance of commodities, in which language itself disappeared and only the appearance of finished products occupied the collective consciousness, constituted an artificial world made natural by liberal capitalism. The loss of a critical perspective coincided with the loss of the historicity of thought and, thus, the dialectical opposition between nature and culture. The totalizing dominance of commodities, especially cultural ones, closed off the options for critical reflection and conscious choice concerning production relations and societal organization. Subjects themselves lost critical consciousness, becoming merged with a naturalized externality. From this perspective, the manipulation of organic and cultural nature by mass media paralleled the propaganda typical of fascism. Both forms of thought control enacted manipulative mechanisms of submission and pseudo-happiness. In his 1950 work *The Lessons of Fascism*, Horkheimer introduced a series of themes that characterize the condition of modern man: the fusion of individualism into an authoritarian group identity, the increasingly dominant role of technology and mass communication and a comprehensive manipulation of ideas.[213] In this essay, Horkheimer traces the historical steps that led Mussolini and Hitler to power and the consequent transformation of the market economy into a war economy. Above all, he warns the reader of the new totalitarian tendencies and their potential resurgence in various parts of the world. In this context, Horkheimer's 1954 reflections on the emergence of a new anthropological subject born of fascism and not yet neutralized focused on the figure of the "totalitarian man" [*totalitäre Typus*].[214] Horkheimer defines the totalitarian man as one who "controls his emotions, his inner self",[215] neutralizing emotions in response to what is socially codified. The totalitarian type thinks in "black and white",[216] dividing humanity between those who belong to his group and those who do not: the enemies. He shows no compassion and sees others merely as instruments for his own purposes. The totalitarian man "thinks in stereotypes"[217] and in hierarchies. In reality, he is a "pseudo-conservative" because he does not recognize the restorative dimension of past values.[218] Paradoxically, for Horkheimer, one of the real problems post-war modernity will have to face is the lack of true political conservatives. For this reason, Horkheimer argued

213 M. Horkheimer, *The Lessons of Fascism*, 1950.
214 Ibid.
215 M. Horkheimer, "Zur Psychologie des Totalitären", [1954] 1985, p. 80.
216 Ibid., p. 81.
217 Ibid.
218 Ibid., p. 82.

that more resources must be invested in the education of young people and in strengthening education overall.[219] The overcoming of the fascist figure of the totalitarian man will only be possible through a profound political education, one that not only presents young people with a series of political facts but also encourages them to reflect on "what lies behind politics".[220] Thus, although reality has changed, authoritarianism and the repression of self-realization instincts will not end with the fall of fascism. The advent of post-war technological society and, more generally, the capitalist system that supports it forms the backbone of a system of domination perpetuated even within democratic societies. Löwenthal, in his 1946 essay "Terror's Atomization of Man",[221] had already warned of the superfluity that humanity had reached during the development of machine society: "[A]nd mass employment is increasingly a manipulated product of the state and state-like powers which channelize surplus mankind into public works, including armies and official or semi-official political organizations, in order to keep it at once alive and under control".[222] These, in turn, have been placed under strict disciplinary control. As a result, there is a continuity between the totalitarian authoritarianism of technological society and emerging fascist tendencies within such societies.

The examination of the relationship between technology and illiberal trends in capitalist society was undoubtedly one of the primary research areas developed by Marcuse. He initiated a philosophical research project, based on a Hegelian-Marxist framework, aimed at critically rethinking the dialectical-negative element and transcending socio-historical reality. Hegelian idealism, stripped of its metaphysics, was for Marcuse a pathway toward an immanent critique of society.[223] As mentioned earlier, the society to which Marcuse directed his critique was different from the one that accompanied the outbreak of World War II. Marcuse acknowledged this while defining the philosophical transition from ontology to technological society, in which a fundamental dimension of human experience had been suppressed: the ability to transcend society through the exercise of determinate negation.[224] This is Marcuse's one-dimensional man, who experiences the reduction of the subject/object dichotomy into a single entity. The dominance of technology

219 Ibid.

220 Ibid.

221 L. Löwenthal, "The Crisis of the Individual: II. Terror's Atomization of Man", [1946], available online.

222 Ibid.

223 Marcuse's study on Hegel not only had the merit of rehabilitating idealism but also laid the groundwork for a new methodology in the social sciences, defined through the historicization of principles. See, in this regard, H. Marcuse, *Reason and Revolution: Hegel and the Rise of Social Theory*, [1941/1954] 1955.

224 Originally published in French in 1960 as a text for lectures delivered at the École Pratique des Hautes Études, the essay was more recently translated into English in H. Marcuse, "From Ontology to Technology: Fundamental Tendencies of Industrial Society", [1960] 2011, pp. 132–140.

forces humanity into pre-given options, in which pure instrumentality deprived of finality becomes a universal instrument of domination. Thus, the exit from fascism today appears only as an apparent victory, limited to the realm of subjective freedoms that cannot find objective realization. Technological society reintroduces mechanisms of oppression within a fictitious regime of freedom: "A comfortable, smooth, reasonable, democratic unfreedom prevails in advanced industrial civilization".[225] This can occur precisely because the type of instrumental rationality characteristic of technological society has not allowed for the transcendence of society itself, trapping humanity within the mechanisms of a purposeless mechanistic order. In this context, it is irrelevant for Marcuse to ask whether the satisfaction of needs in such a society is achieved through authoritarian power. Technological rationality organized its base in such a way that "contemporary industrial society tends to be totalitarian".[226] Here, the adjective "totalitarian" does not refer to a terrorist-type organization but rather to an economic-technical society. There is a certain rationality within the overall irrationality of technological society: productive efficiency, the transformation of goods into surplus necessary goods. The individual identifies with the society to which he belongs as in a form of totalizing mimesis. This immediate identification with existing reality is accompanied by the absorption of false ideological consciousness, as if it were a form of authentic consciousness. Technological society, assuming the ideology that characterizes it, manipulates individuals in its defense, establishing a properly totalitarian system. Horkheimer had addressed the concept of ideology extensively. The starting point was always an interpretation of Marx's philosophy of praxis in which ideology no longer appeared as a mere external causal expression of a productive structure. Instead, it was to be understood as part of a critical-dialectical relationship, raising self-awareness through an examination of reality.

In *A New Concept of Ideology?* [1930],[227] Horkheimer had already discussed Mannheim's writings, especially his text *Ideology and Utopia*,[228] at times polemically. The goal was to defend, drawing on Marx, a certain definition of ideology as a sociologically useful concept for understanding the *zeitgeist*. Mannheim had erroneously reduced this idea to a metaphysical transcendent and, once universalized, deprived it of its ability to explain social reality. Thus, while Marx sought to ensure that the abstractions of German idealism found a historicized economic-political base for an adequate definition of ideology (thereby providing the tools for the proletariat to break free from it),

225 H. Marcuse, *One-Dimensional Man*, [1964] 2002, p. 3.

226 Ibid., p. 5.

227 H. Horkheimer, "A New Concept of Ideology?", [1930] 1993, pp. 3–27.

228 K. Mannheim, *Ideology and Utopia*, [1929] 1991. For a reconstruction of the debate, see M. Jay, "The Frankfurt School's Critique of Karl Mannheim and the Sociology of Knowledge", 1974, pp. 72–89.

Mannheim, on the other hand, had ended up legitimizing any social concretion, abandoning any critical ambition or connection to reality.[229]

In *Ideologie und Wertgebung* ["*Ideology and Values*"] [1951],[230] Horkheimer asserted that

> [Although] the word ideology today is a vague term and is used in a universal sense, it still contains an element that stands in contrast to the claim of the spirit to be considered unconditional in terms of its existence or content.[231]

It was thus maintained that the dominant ideology would be able to influence only the surface of the psyche, as at its deeper levels, it would be contaminated by "constant experience of contradictory reality".[232] In fascist ideology, the different becomes the forbidden, and what opposes the social norm must be suppressed. The Jew becomes the ultimate symbol of this erotic impulse to be repressed.[233] Racial hatred serves as the psychic mechanism through which the admission of instinctual attraction toward the other—toward the different—is rejected, feared for shaking the certainties of the fascist psyche. This desire is thus inverted into "erotic resentment".[234]

If these were the conclusions reached by Horkheimer, it would be Marcuse who systematically traced the relationship between ideology and propaganda. The latter would be presented as a typical practice not only of authoritarian regimes but also of more truly totalitarian and fascist societies.[235] Although the theme of ideology would constitute the central focus of reflection on technological society, Marcuse would identify, alongside the destructive forces at work in society, countervailing emancipatory tendencies aimed both at containing the former and at liberating creative and integrative energies. Marcuse had already addressed this issue in *Eros and Civilization* [1955].[236] Here, in the second part of the text, the author provides a utopian framework for a non-repressive society. Marcuse transforms Freud's vision expressed in *Civilization and Its Discontents* [1930][237]—which synthesized the view that civilization begins with the inhibition of primary sexual instincts (which lead to stable

229 "If the transformation of the concept of ideology from the particular to the total shifts our attention from real events upward to the misty regions of contending 'world postulates', its further development takes the ground out from under our feet". In M. Horkheimer, "A New Concept of Ideology?", [1930] 1993, p. 15.
230 M. Horkheimer, "Ideologie und Wertgebung", 1951, pp. 220–227.
231 Ibid., p. 220.
232 M. Horkheimer, "Egoism and Freedom Movements: On the Anthropology of the Bourgeois Era", [1936] 1993, p. 97.
233 Ibid., p. 100.
234 Ibid.
235 H. Marcuse, *One-Dimensional Man*, [1964] 2002, p. 3.
236 H. Marcuse, *Eros and Civilization*, [1955] 2023.
237 S. Freud, *Civilization and Its Discontents*, [1930] 2002.

social relations) and destructive instincts (with respect to domination over man and nature)—into a theory of social emancipation. Marcuse's reinterpretations would follow two main directions: on one hand, Freud's archetypes of the ego, id and superego would be historicized within processes of cultural accumulation, production and functional integration of society; on the other hand, and consequently, the destructive force of Thanatos would be seen as counterbalanced by the emancipatory force of Eros. Marcuse's revolutionary utopia, unlike Freud's hypothesis, would argue that man is not doomed to inevitably increase his neuroses with the progressive sublimation of instincts. Instead, he can proceed toward the liberation of primordial destructive instincts through an internal process within culture and civilization. Marcuse had previously tackled the affirmative character of bourgeois culture, which he judged to have caused an act of "segregation from civilization of the mental and spiritual world as an independent realm of value that is also considered superior to civilization".[238] However, in a post-bourgeois society, by limiting the amounts of energy necessary to meet needs, the intensity of repressive forces is also reduced. Through the substitution of Freud's principle of reality with that of performance, Marcuse could envision a fundamental transformation of society. It is based on this transition that the premise for a non-repressive society becomes possible. This, however, would require a subversion of the established order: that is, of technological society and its principle of reality/performance. In the repressive desublimation of technological society, Marcuse sees the "replacing mediated by immediate gratification".[239] While in forms of sublimation, such as in artistic activity, the alienation produced is irreconcilable with the existing principle of reality that "sustains the organism in the external world",[240] in repressive desublimation, the principle of pleasure is absorbed by that of reality. The paradox of this process lies in the fact that the more society moves toward providing immediate pleasures, creating the false image of greater accessibility to freedom, the more it enacts repressive forms of dominance. It is on this point that Marcuse critiques Reich's pseudo-solution of the liberation of sexual instincts. For Marcuse, uncontrolled liberation of instincts represents a regressive step, lacking an appropriate analysis of society. Marcuse's liberation would be rather a form of "erotization of the entire personality"[241] that sees an expansion of libido in the formation of social bonds: the constitution of a stable order. If one considers the social change in the use of instinctual energy, it becomes clear how Marcuse conceives the relationship between "desublimation and technological society".[242] The difference between pre-technological and technological society lies in a progressive

238 H. Marcuse, "The Affirmative Character of Culture", [1937] 2007, p. 87.
239 H. Marcuse, *One-Dimensional Man*, [1964] 2002, p. 75.
240 H. Marcuse, *Eros and Civilization*, [1955] 2023, p. 25.
241 Ibid., p. 156.
242 H. Marcuse, *One-Dimensional Man*, [1964] 2002, p. 76.

decrease of erotic energy through the mechanization of labour and an intensification of immediate sexual impulse. The world surrounding the individual no longer demands the renunciation of immediate need satisfaction, nor does it push toward the sublimation of such impulses. However, the apparent increase in the freedom to satisfy these impulses is the result of institutionalized desublimation: that is, a societal apparatus supported by authoritarian forms of power. It is thus necessary to implement a strategy for liberation from uncontrolled instinctual and aggressive impulses generated by the unhappiness produced by repressive powers. In this regard, Marcuse specifies that "this unhappiness lends itself easily to political mobilization"[243] so that it can easily "become the instinctual reservoir for a new fascist way of life and death".[244] Technological society thus seems destined to replicate the destructive experience of National Socialism or at least reproduce a variant of it. In this regard, Marcuse identifies a way out in the act of the "Great Refusal": the intellectual rejection and act of resistance against all those unnecessarily repressive and authoritarian mechanisms both in production and in the organization of family and social relations.[245] If one were to read Marcuse's texts *Eros and Civilization* [1955] and *One-Dimensional Man* [1964] as complementary, one could reconstruct all the historicized psychic structures and the basis for the critique of society on which to base such an act of rebellion. More fundamentally, for Marcuse, the repressive organization of instincts will be functional to the idea of an irreconcilability between the pleasure principle and the reality principle (or performance in its specific historical form). Freud had placed this unyielding struggle at the origin of the transition from the patriarchal domination of the primitive horde to its internalization in the process of historical realization. However, Freud's theory was based on a prejudice that viewed universal historical development as a biologistic externalization of history. Freud thus developed the idea of the "release of repressed" as a form of cyclical reappearance of individual neuroses in history. However, it was precisely this transition from individual to group psyche that presented one of the scientifically weakest forms of Freud's theory. Marcuse addressed this and the overcoming of a biologistic view of Freudian group psychology through the adoption of new analytical tools. Thus, the fundamental shift in Marcuse's research consists of viewing the structures of the psyche in relation to those of material production and political organization.

In the 1965 essay "Repressive Tolerance",[246] he highlights what would come to be defined as "an objective contradiction between the economic and political structure on the one side, and the theory and practice of toleration on

243 Ibid., p. 80.
244 Ibid.
245 Ibid.
246 H. Marcuse, "Repressive Tolerance", [1965] 1969, p. 115.

the other".[247] The latter would ultimately legitimize forms of tolerance of already predetermined options by dominant structures in relation to the control of advanced liberal societies. The tolerance of the multiple forms of expressive freedom of thought and religious belief—an asset of classical liberalism since Mill—would thus turn into forms of repressive tolerance. Summarizing the interpretive path proposed so far, one might observe how the Frankfurt School's analyses of the superstructure converge with the conclusions drawn in the analysis of the structure. While the Frankfurt School scholars certainly took individual, autonomous paths regarding the reworking of Freudian categories and, more generally, the reconsideration of the relationship between psychoanalysis and society,[248] the shared framework that emerges reveals a progressive increase in the processes of automatization concerning the placement of the subject within increasingly objectifying productive, social and cultural dynamics. The contemporary individual is seen as incapable of genuine experience. The libidinal drives of the id dethrone the self-censoring power of the superego. The very Freudian structures of the psychic apparatus become obsolete in a world of production that has absorbed the subject's capacity to remove the very negative events of existence. Thus, the subject's ability to place thought and self-analysis as a noetic (thus non-identitarian) excess irreducible to the homogenizing form of capitalist production vanishes. Instead, the subject is replaced by an unstoppable flood of commodities that assume a primary and almost, one might say, totalizing role in social agency. While fascism as a historical form of state and economic power organization ended with the conclusion of the Second World War, the fascist mentality as a propensity towards the annulment of critical and self-reflective thought of the self continues to persist within societies organized according to forms of mass capitalism. In these, totalizing forms of world organization built on abstract identitarian criteria will be reintroduced: the equal to itself.

Identitarian fascism will thus reappear under new guises: from ways of organizing labour relations aimed at stripping the role of the worker and their claims to false options of liberal political choice that will ultimately flounder in the face of the dictates of large global economic monopolies and their supporting institutions. It is with respect to the attempt to overcome such conditions of annihilation of critical subjectivity that the utopia of a finally emancipated society must take its cue to finally demonstrate readiness for radical renewal.

247 Ibid., p. 115.

248 It is worth noting that in 1970, Fromm published a collection of essays titled *The Crisis of Psychoanalysis*. In the first essay—"The Crisis of Psychoanalysis"—written in 1969, he asserts that "the creative renewal of psychoanalysis is possible only if it manages to overcome its positivist conformism and returns to being a critical and provocative theory, in the spirit of radical humanism", in E. Fromm, *The Crisis of Psychoanalysis*, [1970] 1976, p. 45. For a comprehensive analysis of the topic, see L. Micaloni, *Inconscio e critica: Psicoanalisi, società e politica nella Scuola di Francoforte*, 2023, particularly, chapters VI and VII.

3.12 Beyond fascism: utopia and social transformation

Marcuse's stance regarding the revolutionary subject or, more precisely, the man in revolt is deeply rooted in his overall philosophical vision of advanced capitalist society.[249] In this regard, as suggested, Marcuse can be read recursively through the exploration of themes present in his works *One-Dimensional Man* (1964) and, prior to that, *Eros and Civilization* (1955). In the former, Marcuse reinterprets the themes of reification and alienation as instances of the loss of critical subjectivity due to an economic power that becomes political. *One-Dimensional Man* describes the man objectified within administrative mechanisms of social control in advanced industrial society. This phenomenon found full realization in the United States, through industrial automation and the welfare state as expressions of total administration. The one-dimensionality of mass man leads to a condition of desublimation of the ego's drives, meaning the frustration of the fulfilment of desires and needs induced by a particular form of industrial production. Therefore, Marcuse's reworking of Freudian thought in the 1950s must be understood as a psychic counterpart to the historical-social condition later exposed in the 1960s. The individual in technological society is not free because the organization of the production world, labour relations and especially the market imprison him in functions aimed at achieving productive goals oriented toward increasing capital, not happiness. Contemporary industrial society is thus "totalitarian" due to the manipulation of interests and the definition of needs. The choices available in such societies are merely apparent forms of freedom in which even free elections in formal democracies do not eliminate the power asymmetry between slaves and masters. Regarding the political alternatives in the current scenario, Marcuse considers two contradictory possibilities: a) that advanced industrial society is capable of halting the future qualitative change and b) that tendencies capable of breaking the constraints of the status quo will prevail.

Marcuse historicizes the Freudian metaphysical link between libidinal repression, social stabilization and cultural production, seeing emancipation as the socially definable possibility of new associative forms. He also considers the current situation as a phase of stagnation preceding the possibility of transforming society in a socialist direction. The Freudian principle of reality thus overcomes the pleasure principle, transforming it into a principle of performance—i.e., a principle functional to the unlimited growth of capital. Marcuse's concept of revolt thus takes shape from these analytical premises, in which the political option of socialism emerges as a determined negation of the status quo, a true and proper virtuous dialectical moment. It is from sexual liberation that the libido regimented by the governing system finds new forms of expression, thus reopening the path for Eros's dominance over Thanatos. In *An Essay on Liberation* [1969], Marcuse acknowledges that the

249 In fact, Marcuse, albeit in a limited historical-philosophical context, had addressed the theme of revolution with reference to the critical recovery of Hegel's thought. See H. Marcuse, *Reason and Revolution: Hegel and the Rise of Social Theory*, [1941/1954] 1955.

"working class",[250] once "historical agent",[251] has now become a "counter-revolutionary" force.[252] Nevertheless, there is a formation of a "new working class",[253] the "intelligentsia"[254] in the broader sense, including not only professors and students but also white-collar workers and technicians with the power to "reorganize and redirect the mode and relationships of production".[255] In *Counterrevolution and Revolt* [1972], Marcuse refers directly to the repressive and counter-revolutionary tendencies of advanced monopolistic capitalism, in which "the full weight of suppression falls on the two centers of the radical opposition: the colleges and the black and brown militants".[256] The Nixon administration had institutionalized this trend. For Marcuse, this was not yet an explicitly fascist society. The question was whether this phase of preventive counter-revolution would be functional and preparatory to a subsequent "fascist phase".[257] In "Re-examination of the Concept of Revolution" [1968],[258] a text written in the wake of the Paris events of May 1968, the reference is to Marx's theory of revolution as the ultimate and unavoidable outcome of capitalism. Marx's revolution:

1 Is a socialist revolution, overthrowing the capitalist system, introducing collective ownership of the means of production, and control by the "immediate producers".
2 Initiates in the advanced industrial society (because of the magnitude of the internal contradictions) at this stage of capitalism and because of the possible realization of the socialist principle "to each according to his needs"; the shortening of the first phase is essential, otherwise repression would be perpetuated.
3 Is to occur in an economic crisis, which weakens the established state apparatus.
4 Is to be carried out by large-scale (organized) mass action of the working class, leading to the dictatorship of the proletariat as a transitory stage.

(H. Marcuse, "Re-examination of the Concept of Revolution", [1968], p. 18)

For Marcuse, revolution expresses the democratic viewpoint of the "majority of population",[259] emphasizing "the importance of the "subjective factor": awareness of the facts of exploitation".[260] In Marx, revolution ensures a form

250 H. Marcuse, *An Essay on Liberation*, 1969, p. 16.
251 Ibid.
252 Ibid.
253 Ibid., p. 55.
254 Ibid.
255 Ibid.
256 H. Marcuse, *Counterrevolution and Revolt*, 1972, p. 24.
257 Ibid.
258 H. Marcuse, "Re-examination of the Concept of Revolution", [1968].
259 Ibid., p. 21.
260 Ibid., p. 18.

of "continuity in change",[261] in which the same technological and productive apparatus remains unchanged. What changes are the holders of such powers. This view is teleological and needs to be transcended. However, Marx did not consider the possibility of the "socialism or barbarism"[262] alternative: i.e., the eventuality of a revolution's failure. It is this uncertainty of the outcome of political action that Marcuse seeks to address, tackling the issue of the reification of man concerning technological society and the general indoctrination of consciousnesses. Thus, the overcoming of Marx's view hinges on this point. It means reconsidering Marx's theory of revolution based on the possibility of a structural transformation of capitalism into socialism or their possible coexistence in light of new associative forms compared to those existing in Marx's time. A continuity line remains between Marx, who celebrated the first experiment in direct democracy in the Paris Commune of 1871,[263] and the forms of self-government of factory councils that Marcuse identified as alternatives to the failure of mass parties. Councils would only serve as revolutionary tools when they "represent the people in revolt".[264] For this purpose, a reversal of the dominant power of hegemonic classes is necessary, and thus a direct takeover of the organs of society (e.g., universities) and the state. The "base"[265] must be able to exercise direct control over authority: i.e., realize a form of direct democracy. If socialism and direct democracy proceed together, monopolist capitalism will instead align with the advancement of bourgeois interests opposed to broadening political participation. Therefore, monopolist capitalism has an intrinsic "authoritarian tendency",[266] whose containment does not result from an automatic production of social contradictions that inevitably rebound against it. For Marcuse, the subjective element in favour of socialism must overcome the objective authoritarian tendency of the economy and society. While it is true that "capitalism produces its own gravediggers", for Marcuse, "their faces may be very different from those of the wretched of the earth from those of misery and want".[267]

There is thus a historical necessity for the formation of a collective subject capable of actively pursuing a radical reform of society. From 1968, Marcuse reaffirms the uniqueness of the student protests in Paris, emphasizing that a radical movement can originate outside the working classes. Therefore, it will not be the national liberation movements of the so-called Third World that will bring about a radical change in society (since these are "expressive of the internal contradictions of the global capitalist system"),[268] but American

261 Ibid.
262 Ibid., p. 25.
263 K. Marx, *The Civil War in France*, [1871] 2014.
264 H. Marcuse, *Counterrevolution and Revolt*, 1972, p. 45.
265 Ibid.
266 Ibid., p. 47.
267 Ibid., p. 57.
268 H. Marcuse, "Re-examination of the Concept of Revolution", [1968], p. 22.

and European students from bourgeois families who can grasp the orientation of the themes and the need for social change. Marcuse will also call for the liberation of the working class from the apparatuses of bureaucracy and the party, lest it transform into a support force for a neofascist regime. The social redefinition of the Marxian revolutionary class will also need to sever its relationship with technology for a redefinition of its needs. This would not imply a regression in technological development toward the reformulation of more basic needs, but rather the upholding of the freedom of individuals who have achieved self-awareness. In this context, "the role of this opposition is a strictly preparatory one: their task is radical enlightenment, in theory and by practice, and the development of cadres and nuclei for the struggle against the global structure of capitalism".[269] Marcuse also addresses the issue of the revolutionary subject in *USA: Questions of Organization and the Revolutionary Subject: A Conversation with Hans Magnus Enzenberg* [1970].[270] Here, it is hypothesized that "Marx never maintained that the contradictions of the capitalist system are concentrated exclusively in the class of industrial laborers".[271] On the contrary, it is argued that these contradictions encompass society as a whole, in both its base and its superstructure, including all social classes. One should not "make a fetish"[272] of the concept of class: being Marxist means overcoming a reifying view of society limited to the working class alone. In advanced capitalist societies, we no longer face workers as the most numerous class. Marcuse cites the case of numerous employees in the advertising industry who are also part of the productive mechanism of surplus value and, likewise, victims of it.[273] The transversality and fluidity of capitalist exploitation led Marcuse to prophetically anticipate that the type of social war that will emerge in the United States will not be a popular but a racial war, thus not grounded in a form of class struggle. This will result in state repression against minorities, blacks and unconventional or mainstream subjects, so to speak. The contradictions of capitalism will increasingly show their most brutal reflection on society. Regarding this framework, "the only real opposition . . . is that of the radical youth and the ghetto militants".[274]

These are the radicals of the new left, as Marcuse writes in "On the New Left" [1967],[275] a typescript prepared for a lecture at the University of San Diego and kept closed until a few years ago in the *Marcuse Archiv* (HMA 317.01). In this text, reference is made to students, civil rights activists, writers, professors and artists as the revolutionary subjects of the present. For

269 Ibid., p. 25.
270 H. Marcuse, *USA: Questions of Organization and the Revolutionary Subject: A Conversation with Hans Magnus Enzenberg*, [1970] 2005.
271 Ibid., p. 139.
272 Ibid.
273 Ibid., p. 139 ff.
274 Ibid., p. 141.
275 H. Marcuse, "On the New Left", [1967] 2005, pp. 122–127.

Marcuse, the new left radicalism is characterized by a clear tendency toward moral protest that highlights the hypocrisy and cynicism of previous generations, those who fomented the Vietnam War policy cloaked in a false ideology known as the struggle for freedom and democracy. However, it is only by recovering a visionary sense of socialism that Marcuse believes the possibility of a "concrete utopia"[276] as a tool for analyzing and transforming reality can be played out, leading to the "Great Refusal".[277] For Marcuse, utopia is not an absence of occurrence or "that which has 'no place'" but "that which is blocked from coming about by the power of the established societies".[278] In light of this, however, it will no longer be a matter of pressing for an "abolition of private ownership and control of the means of production",[279] but of redefining the ways in which productive forces are utilized.

276 H. Marcuse, "Protosocialism and Late Capitalism: Toward a Theoretical Synthesis Based on Bahro's Analysis", 1980, p. 25.
277 H. Marcuse, *One-Dimensional Man*, [1964] 2002.
278 H. Marcuse, *An Essay on Liberation*, 1969, p. 4.
279 Ibid., p. 85.

Conclusion

In "Grand Hotel Abgrund" [abyss] [1933],[1] an essay published posthumously in 1977, Lukács launches an accusatory indictment of the inability of German Marxist intellectuals to foresee and resist the rise of National Socialism. It is an analysis of great political lucidity but, above all, a warning against sterile intellectual postures that ultimately end up passively legitimizing dominant powers. Many years later, in the 1962 preface to *The Theory of the Novel*,[2] Lukács revisits the issue by criticizing Adorno for having settled into the "Grand Hotel Abyss" as "a beautiful hotel, equipped with every comfort, on the edge of an abyss, of nothingness, of absurdity".[3] The Hungarian philosopher reproaches Adorno for falling into "conformism disguised as non-conformism",[4] meaning that Adorno had retained only the semblance of a critical approach, devoid of any transformative capacity. Why? Because the bourgeois intelligentsia that Adorno embodies had stopped at the edge of the abyss without making the required jump into the revolutionary class. The Frankfurt intellectuals ultimately adhered to the capitalist system of production, unknowingly becoming complicit with the fascist ideology that accompanies it. Surrendering to the contradictions generated by this system, they relaxed into a position of privilege: the luxurious halls of the Grand Hotel Abyss, sublimating the horrors of history while savouring refined foods. This surrender, in reality, revealed a form of narcissistic self-satisfaction cloaked in religious and pseudo-revolutionary mythology.

According to Lukács, the Frankfurt intellectuals thus failed to develop analytical tools capable of exerting a critical hold on reality, as, having abandoned the intellectual project of a philosophy of praxis and the political project of revolutionary transformation, they sought refuge in an ideological superstructure of self-pity. The self-satisfaction with a culture that had become a mechanized replica of reality culminated in distancing critical spirit from the

1 G. Lukács, "Grand Hotel Abgrund", [1933] 1977, pp. 572–579.
2 G. Lukács, *The Theory of the Novel*, [1916] 1971.
3 Ibid., p. 22.
4 Ibid.

DOI: 10.4324/9781003630340-5

task most congenial to it: the formulation of a civilized utopia for society. Thus, there was a need to develop a new critical theory of political economy capable of illuminating and overcoming the contradictions of contemporary capitalism. The critique of ideology must engage with the critique of social ontology to avoid remaining a mere rhetorical exercise of self-entangled thought. Although Lukács's judgment offers inescapable points of discussion, the Frankfurt project to renew reflection on the state and politics embraced the rethinking of the psychoanalytic paradigm of the Freudian left, rejecting Lukács' rationalistic hypothesis of forming a proletarian "class consciousness" as the mechanism for historically overcoming the reification of the self and its false consciousness under capitalism. As discussed, Fromm had already responded in 1929 as to why the exploited German working masses tended to replicate social impoverishment schemes rather than turning against the prevailing order to reform society to their advantage. Fromm used the tools of social psychoanalysis: identifying the superstructural libidinal flow within the structural unfolding of production relations allowed understanding of the reconfiguration of social relations without falling into their psychologization or causal definition as certainly vulgar Marxism would have done. Horkheimer expressed approval of this perspective starting with his 1932 essay "History and Psychology". Here, the causes of social reproduction were traced back to impulses that falsify the conscience rather than to generalized structural forms of domination to be brought to consciousness through the role of a political vanguard. Domination was instead confined to historically successive elites in command roles, replicating intergenerational social control drives through organization into rackets. If this was the downward trajectory of capitalist society, then the Frankfurt School simply saw that the very subject of a possible revolution—the proletariat and its class consciousness as a premise for action—had disappeared.

Finally, there was Horkheimer and Adorno's general disenchantment with the emancipatory possibilities of Western civilization. In *Dialectic of Enlightenment* [1947], they stated: "[T]he history of civilization is the history of the introversion of sacrifice—in other words, the history of renunciation".[5] Moreover, it cannot be denied that Adorno was already fully aware of the identity drifts in the automated reorganization of post-war society. This is evident from his 1968 essay "Late Capitalism or Industrial Society?",[6] in which the philosopher drew a parallel between the erasure of social classes, the automation of industrial production and the fully administered society. Repression was seen as a pervasive element of society, encompassing every aspect of private life. From all this, it is evident that the main figures of critical theory were far from unaware of the transformations maturing in post-war European society. The Frankfurt School grasped this tendency through Horkheimer's reference

5 M. Horkheimer, T. W. Adorno, *Dialectic of Enlightenment*, [1947] 2002, p. 43.
6 T. W. Adorno, "Late Capitalism or Industrial Society?", [1968] 1987.

to the theory of rackets and the parallel consolidation of authoritarianism. Lukács's accusation against the Frankfurt School must therefore be directed only at those within the Frankfurt circle who allowed the flattening of being and experience, the result of the unchallenged dominance of commodity-ness and its replicability to reverberate in thought.

If Grünberg's warning, recalled at the beginning of this study, that critical theory cannot admit mandarins [*Mandarinanstalten*][7] but only intellectuals inorganically confronting consolidated power systems (rejecting any apology for the real on pain of a performative contradiction) still holds valid, then a renewed critical theory should follow the path of rethinking today's forms of work and industrial production organization. The falsification of Marx's theory of the impoverishment of classes results in a social levelling of economic interest groups in which everyone, from the worker to the freelance professional, thanks to consumer credit and other forms of indebtedness, lives the illusion of free access to most goods once reserved for socially privileged strata. The consumer society will also turn "car drivers, cinema goers, and comrades" into subjects gripped by the anguish of a "gnawing fear for one's job and one's life"[8] nullifying the revolutionary class self-awareness of the proletariat. If, in the past, "[s]hared poverty turns proletarians into a class", today

> Shorter working hours, better food, housing, and clothing, protection for family members and for the worker in his old age, an average increase in life expectancy—all these things have come to workers with the development of the technical forces of production.[9]

Therefore, it no longer makes sense to hypothesize a revolutionary alliance. As Adorno will observe, despite the non-fulfilment of the theory of impoverishment in the forms defined by Marx, one cannot exclude that social poverty may take the form of "unfreedom" or "dependence upon a social apparatus no longer controlled by its operators".[10] It is from a concern for individual and natural survival that groups oriented toward self-preservation of sectional interests—"conspiratorial cliques"[11]—will form again. A new rackets society will take shape within a pseudo-democratic framework, regenerating union, party and trade association monopolies, where the entire social organization will turn toward "the form of open fascism".[12] Adorno fully acknowledges the progressive fusion between the base and superstructure of modern (post-)industrial society: the exploitation of production and labour

7 C. Grünberg, "Festrede gehalten zur Einweihung des IfSs für Sozialforschung an der Universität Frankfurt a. M. am 22 Juni 1924", 1924, p. 4.
8 T. W. Adorno, "Reflections on Class Theory", [1942] 2003.
9 Ibid., p. 103.
10 T. W. Adorno, "Late Capitalism or Industrial Society?", [1968] 1987, p. 237.
11 T. W. Adorno, "Reflections on Class Theory", [1942] 2003, p. 100.
12 Ibid.

is no longer perceived as such on the ideological self-consciousness front, while an objectifying identity between productive forces and their consciousness will be realized. In other words, more than ever today, it is necessary to consider what Adorno had already defined as a nullification of differences in the identity of the masses. Yet this same internal tendency of advanced industrial society had already been intercepted by Marcuse in reference to the process of repressive desublimation, in which the reality principle (not simply mass culture) has triumphed over the sublimations of high culture, becoming capable of realizing those truths that art projected only into the sphere of utopian alienation.[13]

The question that arises, then, concerns whether human and collective emancipation can still be conceived in a new productive and societal configuration. *Kultur* and *Zivilisation*, knowledge and technique, as instrumental processes of production, cannot be separated. They travel together. Consumerist overproduction reveals something evil—namely, the reduction of human beings to cogs in a process of *Zivilisation*. The outcome of this retreat of *Zivilisation* into *Kultur* determines a vicious cycle between knowledge and technique, positioning the latter and the production that ensues as ends in themselves. This also manifests in the progressive coincidence between ideology and structure, where in which former concludes by proposing self-legitimizing forms of the existing. The mass consumer society will produce its own staunchest self-defense, expunging from itself any form of immanent critique. The identity relationship between the status quo and ideological legitimation will realize identity-driven, non-dialectical forms of social justification, eliminating that critical counterbalance which, instead, could have questioned the existing through the noetic act of determinate negation.

Neither Horkheimer nor Adorno can be held responsible for failing to grasp Lukács's interpretation of the "Grand Hotel Abyss". In reality, this responsibility falls solely on those who misuse political utopia by retreating into the comfort of the Hegelian figure of the 'beautiful soul'—and therefore uncritical—acceptance of the existing order. This misuse will primarily manifest in Habermas's attempt to transcend models of technical-productive rationality (structure) by replacing them with discursive and recognition-based rationality. However, the loss of a critical-immanent approach to the organizational structures of society will result in the development of an argumentative

13 See H. Marcuse, *One-Dimensional Man*, [1964] 2002, Chapter 3. In his 1968 address in memory of his friend Hans Meyerhoff, titled "Beyond One-Dimensional Man" [1968] 2005, Marcuse revisits the concept of the "desublimation" of high culture, linking it positively to the Paris student protests aimed at emancipating themselves from archaic forms of oppression. While Freud argued that civilization could not permit the desublimation of culture without risking a return to pre-civilized forms, late Marcuse, in contrast, appears to view this as a necessary step toward self-liberation from the constraints of the authoritarian patriarchal society that preceded the student revolt.

rationality paradigm that ultimately serves productive forms of domination (because it is generated by them).[14]

If capitalism is, in the Marxian sense, a comprehensive vision of society, then the philosophical challenge for post-Habermasian critical theory must involve a rethinking of politics starting from the relationship between the world of production and the superstructure— i.e., the theoretical nexus between materialism and the world of ideas—as a space for the critical self-transcendence of the political. This requires, in turn, rejecting the hypothesis that post-metaphysical contingency can offer a solution.[15] If metaphysics as utopia is to function as a counterbalance to demystifying historical ideologies,[16] it must also rediscover the emancipatory potential of "what is", thus reconfiguring itself in terms of a philosophy of praxis in the present, rather than as a non-place. Only in this way will it be possible to critically rethink reality and overcome the rigidifications that inhibit the dialectical flow of history, in which the crystallization of circular and tautological mechanisms becomes a replicative form of social dominance. Therefore, it does not seem desirable to abandon dialectical opposition, which would lead to the resurgence of an identity-based dynamic of rationality that inevitably excludes confrontation with alterity and negation, thus becoming a covert ideological banner. Critical theory must liberate itself once and for all from this surreptitious legitimization of the status quo and turn toward a renewed understanding of the forms of the self and its associative life.

14 As M. Thompson argued, "[T]he power of language to constitute the world for any subject is not prior to the powers of institutional forms to organize the context of meaning that shapes the very intentional states that serve as the very content of thought itself". In M. Thomspon, "The Base-Superstructure Hypothesis and the Foundations of Critical Theory", 2014, p. 187.

15 The recent critical debate has not failed to reflect on this point. For an overview of the positions at stake, see L. Cortella (ed.), *Teoria critica e metafisica*, 2009. On the need to reconnect the function of critique with that of metaphysics, S. Kouvélakis states: " 'Critique' is no longer the name of a theory that breaks with the traditional forms of intellectual activity, advancing an interdisciplinary research program aimed at historically grasping the totality of social relations from the standpoint of an immanent transformative praxis. Nor is it in service of pursuing a rational goal set as an ideal to be achieved or as a categorical imperative. If the word 'critique' has any meaning, it can only signify an ethical core that reclaims the truth-content of ancient religious beliefs. What we should remember from Kant is precisely what remains problematic for the program of Critical Theory, namely, his dualism, which posited an a priori limit to human knowledge—thereby allowing space to be preserved for transcendence". See S. Kouvélakis, *La critique défaite. Émergence et domestication de la Théorie critique. Horkheimer—Habermas—Honneth*, 2019, p. 247.

16 M. Horkheimer, *Anfänge der bürgerlichen Geschichtsphilosophie*, [1930] 1971.

Appendix

The Frankfurt School or Critical Theory

The Frankfurt School, known more appropriately as Critical Theory,[1] is a philosophical and sociological movement spread across many universities around the world. It was originally located at the Institute for Social Research (IfS), an attached institute at the Goethe University in Frankfurt, Germany. The Institute was founded in 1923 thanks to a donation by Felix Weil with the aim of developing Marxist studies in Germany. After 1933, the Nazis forced its closure, and the Institute was moved to the United States, where it found hospitality at Columbia University in New York City. The academic influence of the critical method is far reaching. Some of the key issues and philosophical preoccupations of the school involve the critique of modernity and capitalist society and the definition of social emancipation, as well as the detection of the pathologies of society. Critical Theory provides a specific interpretation of Marxist philosophy in regard to some of its central economic and political notions like commodification, reification, fetishization and critique of mass culture.

Some of the most prominent figures of the first generation of Critical Theorists were Max Horkheimer (1895–1973), Walter Benjamin (1892–1940), Friedrich Pollock (1894–1970), Theodor Adorno (1903–1969), Herbert Marcuse (1898–1979), Leo Löwenthal (1900–1993) and Eric Fromm (1900–1980). Since the 1970s, a second generation began, guided by Jürgen Habermas, who, among other merits, contributed to the opening of a dialogue between the so-called continental and analytic traditions. With Habermas, the Frankfurt School turned global, influencing methodological approaches in other European academic contexts and disciplines. It was during this phase

1 The expression "critical theory of society" was proposed by Horkheimer and Marcuse in two different essays from 1937 to describe the interdisciplinary methodological synthesis between philosophy and social sciences, as well as the dialectical nature of the critique of political economy. M. Horkheimer, "Traditional and Critical Theory", in *Critical Theory. Selected Essays*, [1937] 2002, pp. 188–243; H. Marcuse, *Philosophy and Critical Theory*, in Horkheimer and Marcuse, *Philosophy and Critical Theory*, [1937], in *Critical Theory and Society*, 1990, pp. 58–77. This term also refers to the distinctive interpretation of Hegelian-Marxist philosophy promoted by the IfS under Horkheimer's direction.

that Richard Bernstein, a philosopher and contemporary of Habermas, embraced the research agenda of Critical Theory and significantly helped its development in American universities. The third generation of critical theorists, therefore, arose either from Habermas' research students in the United States and in Europe (1971–1982) or from a spontaneous convergence of independently educated scholars. Therefore, the third generation of Critical Theory scholars consists of two groups. The first group spans a broad timespan—denying the possibility of establishing any sharp boundaries. It can be said to also include scholars such as Andrew Feenberg, even if he was a direct student of Marcuse, or people such as Albrecht Wellmer, initially an assistant of Adorno and later, following Adorno's premature death in 1969, of Habermas. Klaus Offe, Josef Früchtl, Hauke Brunkhorst, Klaus Günther, Axel Honneth and, significantly younger in age, James Bohman, William Scheuerman, Cristina Lafont and Rainer Forst, among others, are also members of this group. The second group of the third generation, in contrast, is composed mostly of American scholars who were influenced by Habermas's philosophy during his visits to the United States. Some of these include Seyla Benhabib, Thomas McCarthy, Richard J. Bernstein, Gerald Allan Cohen, Andrew Arato, Nancy Fraser, David Ingram, Eduardo Mendieta, Amy Allen and Hayden White. Finally, it is worth noting that the impact of Critical Theory on the international academic landscape has extended beyond the Anglo-American sphere, encompassing Latin America, Italy, Francophone regions and Scandinavia. The influence of Critical Theory in the Balkans and South Africa is equally noteworthy.

1.1 Critical Theory: historical and philosophical background

Felix Weil's father, Herman, made his fortune by exporting grain from Argentina to Europe. In 1923, Felix decided to use his father's money to found an institute specifically devoted to the study of German society in light of a Marxist approach. The initial idea of an independently founded institute was conceived to provide for studies on the labour movement and the origins of anti-Semitism, which, at the time, were being ignored in German intellectual and academic life. Not long after its inception, the IfS was formally recognized by the Ministry of Education as an entity attached to Goethe University Frankfurt. Felix could not imagine that in the 1960s, Goethe University Frankfurt would receive the epithet of Karl Marx University. After a brief period under the direction of the sociologist Kurt Albert Gerlach, who prematurely passed away in 1922, the first officially appointed director was Carl Grünberg (1923–1929), a Marxist professor at the University of Vienna. His contribution to the IfS was the creation of a historical archive mainly oriented to the study of the labour movement (also known as the Grünberg Archive).

In 1930, Max Horkheimer succeeded Grünberg. While continuing under a Marxist inspiration, Horkheimer interpreted the Institute's mission to be more directed toward an interdisciplinary integration of the social sciences. Additionally, the *Grünberg Archiv* ceased publishing, and an official organ was instead launched with a much greater impact: the ***Zeitschrift für Sozialforschung***, later published in English following emigration to the United States under the title ***Studies in Philosophy and Social Science***. While never officially supporting any party, the IfS entertained intensive research exchanges with the Soviet Union. It was under Horkheimer's leadership that members of the IfS were able to address a wide variety of economic, social, political and aesthetic topics, ranging from empirical analysis to philosophical theorization. Different interpretations of Marxism and its historical applications explain some of the hardest confrontations on economic themes within the Institute, such as the case of Pollock's criticism of Grossman's standard view on the pauperization of capitalism. This particular confrontation led Grossman to leave the Institute. Pollock's critical reinterpretation of Marx also received support from intellectuals who greatly contributed to later developments of the school such as, for instance, in the case of Leo Löwenthal, Theodor Wiesengrund-Adorno and Erich Fromm. In particular, with Fromm's development of a psychoanalytic trend at the IfS and with an influential philosophical contribution by Horkheimer, it became clear how, under his directorship, the IfS faced a drastic turning point which characterized all of its future endeavours.

The following sections, therefore, briefly introduce some of the main research patterns introduced by Fromm and Horkheimer, respectively. Since the beginning, psychoanalysis in the Frankfurt School was conceived in terms of a reinterpretation of Freud and Marx, under what came to be known as the Freudo-Marxist approach. The consideration of psychoanalysis by the Frankfurt School was certainly due to Horkheimer's encouragement. It was Fromm, nevertheless, who achieved a significant advancement of the discipline; his central aim was to provide, through a synthesis of Marxism and psychoanalysis, the missing link between ideological superstructure and socio-economic base. A radical shift occurred in the late 1930s, however, when Adorno joined the school, and Fromm decided to leave due to academic disagreements. The school's interest in psychoanalysis coincided with a marginalization of Marxism and a growing interest in the interrelation between psychoanalysis and social change, as well as with Fromm's insight into the psychic (or even psychotic) role of the family. This interest became crucial in empirical studies of the '40s that led, eventually, to Adorno's co-authored work *The Authoritarian Personality* [1950].[2] The goal of this work was to explore—on the basis of empirical research making use of questionnaires, in order to define a "new anthropological type"—the authoritarian personality. Such a character was found to have specific traits, such as such as adherence to conventional values, uncritical thinking and a lack of introspection. Interest in psychoanalysis, particularly Freud's theory of instincts, remained constant. This is evidenced by various writings of Adorno and, notably, Marcuse's essay "Eros

2 T. W. Adorno, E. Frenkel-Brunswik, D. J. Levinson, R. Nevitt Sanford, *The Authoritarian Personality* [1950] 2019.

and Civilization" [1955].[3] Horkheimer's leadership provided a very distinct methodological direction and philosophical grounding to the research interests of the Institute. As an instance of Horkheimer's aversion to so-called *Lebensphilosophie* (philosophy of life), he criticized the fetishism of subjectivity and the lack of consideration for materialist conditions of living. Furthermore, arguing against Cartesian and Kantian philosophy, Horkheimer, by use of dialectical mediation, attempted to rejoin all dichotomies including the divide between consciousness and being and theory and practice, as well as fact and value. Differently from Hegelianism or Marxism, dialectics for Horkheimer amounted to neither a metaphysical principle nor a historical praxis; it was not intended as a methodological instrument. On the contrary, Horkheimer's dialectics functioned as the battleground for overcoming overly rigid categorizations and unhelpful dichotomies and oppositions. It originated from criticism by Horkheimer of orthodox Marxism's dichotomy between productive structures and ideological superstructure, as well as positivism's naïve separation of social facts and social interpretation.

In 1933, due to the Nazi takeover, the IfS was temporarily transferred, first to Geneva and then, in 1935, to Columbia University, New York. Two years later, Horkheimer published the ideological manifesto of the school in his *Traditional and Critical Theory* ([1937] 1976),[4] in which he readdressed some of the previously introduced topics concerning the practical and critical turn of theory. In 1938, Adorno joined the IfS after spending some time as an advanced student at Merton College, Oxford. He was invited by Horkheimer to join the Princeton Radio Research Project. Gradually, Adorno assumed a prominent intellectual leadership in the school, and this led to co-authorship, with Horkheimer, of one of the milestone works of the school: *Dialectic of Enlightenment*, initially developed in 1944 under the title *Philosophical Fragments* and published in 1947.[5] During the time of Germany's Nazi seizure, the IfS remained the only free voice publishing in the German language. The backlash of this choice, though, was a prolonged isolation from American academic life and intellectual debate, a situation described by Adorno with the iconic expression 'message in the bottle' to refer to the lack of a public American audience. Interestingly, and not surprisingly, one of the school's major topics was analyzing the crisis of liberal democracy and the rise of Nazism. Within the school, two distinct lines of research emerged. The first, led by Neumann, Gurland and Kirchheimer, primarily focused on the analysis of legal and political issues related to the effects of economic substructures. The second, led by Horkheimer, concentrated on the notion of psychological irrationalism as a source of obedience and domination.

3 H. Marcuse, *Eros and Civilization*, [1955] 2023.
4 M. Horkheimer, "Traditional and Critical Theory", in *Critical Theory: Selected Essays*, [1937] 2002, pp. 188–243.
5 M. Horkheimer, T. W. Adorno, *Dialectic of Enlightenment*, [1947] 1997.

In 1941, Horkheimer moved to Pacific Palisades, near Los Angeles. He built himself a bungalow near other German intellectuals, among whom were Bertold Brecht and Thomas Mann, as well as other Germans interested in working for the film industry. Other colleagues like Marcuse, Pollock and Adorno followed shortly, whereas some remained in New York. Only Benjamin refused to leave Europe, and in 1940, while attempting to cross the border between France and Spain at Port Bou, he committed suicide. Some months later, Arendt also crossed the same border, passing on Adorno Benjamin's last writing: *Theses on the Philosophy of History*.[6] The division of the school into two different premises, New York and California, was paralleled by the development of two autonomous research programs, one led by Pollock and the other by Horkheimer and Adorno. Pollock directed his research to study anti-Semitism. This research line culminated in an international conference organized in 1944, as well as a five-volume work titled *Studies in Prejudice* [1950], which included, among other works, *The Authoritarian Personality*. Horkheimer and Adorno then developed studies on the reinterpretation of the Hegelian notion of dialectics as well as engaging in the study of anti-Semitic tendencies. After this period, only a few devoted supporters remained faithful to the project of the school. These included Horkheimer himself, Pollock, Adorno, Löwenthal and Weil. In 1946, however, the IfS was officially invited to join Goethe University Frankfurt.

Upon return to West Germany, Horkheimer presented his inaugural speech for the reopening of the IfS on November 14, 1951. One week later, he inaugurated the academic year as the new rector of the university. Horkheimer was involved in the administration of the university, whereas Adorno was constantly occupied with different projects and teaching duties. In addition, in order to keep US citizenship, Adorno had to go back to California, where he earned his living conducting qualitative research analysis. Horkheimer instead attempted to attract his former assistant Marcuse to return when the opportunity arose for a successor to Gadamer's chair in Frankfurt, but neither this initiative nor further occasions were successful. Marcuse remained in the United States and was offered a full position at Brandeis University. Adorno returned to Germany in August 1953 and was soon involved again in empirical research, combining quantitative and qualitative methods in the analysis of industrial relations for the Mannesmann Company.[7]

In 1955, Adorno took over Horkheimer's position as director of the IfS, and on July 1, 1957, he was appointed a full professor in philosophy and sociology. In 1956, Horkheimer retired just when several important publications were appearing, such as Marcuse's *Eros and Civilization*.[8] These events marked the precise intellectual phase of maturity reached at that time by the Frankfurt School.

6 W. Benhamin, "On the Concept of History", [1942/1950].

7 On this passage, see R. Wiggershaus, *The Frankfurt School: Its History, Theories, and Political Significance*, [1986] 2007.

8 H. Marcuse, *Eros and Civilization*, [1955] 2023.

The '60s—which saw famous student protests across Europe—also saw the publication of Adorno's fundamental work *Negative Dialectics* [1966].[9] This study, while far from either materialism or metaphysics, maintained important connections with an "open and non-systemic" notion of dialectics. It appeared only a few years after *One-Dimensional Man* [1964], in which Marcuse introduced the notion of "educational dictatorship"—a strategy intended for the advancement of material conditions aimed at the realization of a higher notion of the good.[10] While Marcuse ostensibly sponsored the student upheavals, Adorno maintained a much more moderate and sceptical profile. In 1956, Habermas joined the IfS as Adorno's assistant. He was soon involved in an empirical study titled *Students and Politics*. The text, however, was rejected by Horkheimer, and it was not published, as it should have been, in the series of the Frankfurt sociological text. Horkheimer's aversion to Habermas was even more evident when he refused to supervise his habilitation. Habermas obtained his habilitation under the supervision of Abendroth at Marburg, where he addressed the topic of the bourgeois formation of the public sphere. This study was published by Habermas in 1962 under the title *The Structural Transformation of the Public Sphere*,[11] just before he handed in his habilitation. With the support of Gadamer, he was then appointed a professor at Heidelberg. Besides his achievements, both in academia and as an activist, the young Habermas contributed to the construction of a critical self-awareness in the socialist student groups around the country, the so-called SDS (*Sozialistischer Deutscher Studentenbund*). It was in this context that Habermas reacted to the extremism of Rudi Dutschke, the radical leader of the students' association who criticized him for defending a non-effective emancipatory view. It was principally against Dutschke's positions that Habermas, during a public assembly, labelled such positions with the epitome of "left-wing fascism". How representative this expression was of Habermas's views on student protests has often been a matter of contention. Discussions of the notion of emancipation had been at the center of the Frankfurt School political debate since the beginning. The concept of emancipation (*Befreiung* in German) covers a wide semantic spectrum. Literarily, it means "liberation from". The notion spans, therefore, from a sense related to action-transformation to also include revolutionary action. After his nomination in 1971 as director of the Max Planck Institute for Research into the Conditions of Life in the Scientific-Technical World at Starnberg, Habermas left Frankfurt. He returned there in 1981 after having completed *The Theory of Communicative Action* (1981, 1984).[12] This decade was crucial for the definition of the school's research objectives.

9 T. W. Adorno, *Negative Dialectics*, [1966] 1973.
10 H. Marcuse, *One-Dimensional Man*, [1964] 2002.
11 J. Habermas, *The Structural Transformation of the Public Sphere*, [1962].
12 J. Habermas, *The Theory of Communicative Action*, 2 vol., 1981, 1984.

In *The Theory of Communicative Action*, Habermas provided a model for social complexities and action coordination based on the original interpretation of classical social theorists as well as the philosophy of Searle's *Speech Acts* [1969] theory.[13] In this work, it also became evident the amount of empirical analysis conducted by Habermas's research team on topics concerning the pathologies of society. Moral development was elevated to a functionalistic model of society oriented to critical and emancipatory purpose. The assumption was that language itself embedded a normative force capable of realizing action co-ordination within society. In this respect, Habermas defined social coordination action as governed by unavoidable pragmatic presuppositions of mutual understanding. Social action, whose coordination-function relies on the same pragmatic presuppositions, was seen as connected to a justification discourse based on the satisfaction of specific validity-claims. Habermas described discourse theory as relying on three types of validity-claims raised by communicative action. He claimed that it was only when the conditions of a) truth, b) rightness and c) sincerity were raised by speech-acts that social coordination could be obtained. As noted in the opening sections, differently from the first generation of Frankfurt School intellectuals, Habermas contributed greatly to bridging the continental and analytical traditions, integrating aspects of American pragmatism, anthropology and semiotics with Marxism and critical social theory.

In 1994, the directorship of the Institut für Sozialforschung was assumed by Honneth. This inaugurated a new phase of research in Critical Theory. Honneth, indeed, revisited the Hegelian notion of "recognition" [*Anerkennung*] in terms of a new prolific paradigm in social and political enquiry. Honneth began his collaboration with Habermas in 1984, when he was hired as an assistant professor. After a period of academic appointments in Berlin and Konstanz, in 1996, he took Habermas's chair in Frankfurt. Honneth's central tenet, the struggle for recognition, represents a leitmotif in his research and preeminently so in one of his most important books, *The Struggle for Recognition: The Moral Grammar of Social Conflicts* [1986].[14] This work represents a mature expansion of what was partially addressed in his dissertation, a work published under the title of *Critique of Power: Reflective Stages in a Critical Social Theory* ([1985] 1991).[15] One of the core themes addressed by Honneth was the claim that, contrary to what Critical Theory initially emphasized, more attention should have been paid to the notion of conflict in society and among societal groups. The issue of conflict represents the internal movement of historical advancement and human emancipation, falling therefore within the core theme of critical social theory. The so-called "struggle for recognition" is what best characterizes the fight for emancipation by social groups. This

13 J. Searle, *Speech Acts: An Essay in the Philosophy of Language*, 1969.

14 A. Honneth, *The Struggle for Recognition: The Moral Grammar of Social Conflicts*, [1986] 1995.

15 A. Honneth, *Critique of Power: Reflective Stages in a Critical Social Theory*, [1985] 1991.

fight represents a subjective negative experience of domination—a form of domination attached to misrecognitions. To come to terms with negations of subjective forms of self-realization means to be able to transform social reality. Normatively, though, acts of social struggle activated by forms of misrecognition point to the role that recognition plays as a crucial criterion for grounding intersubjectivity. Honneth inaugurated a new research phase in Critical Theory. Indeed, his communitarian turn has been paralleled by the work of some of his fellow scholars. Brunkhorst, for instance, in his *Solidarity: From Civic Friendship to a Global Legal Community* ([2002] 2005),[16] canvasses a line of thought springing from the French Revolution of 1789 to contemporary times: the notion of fraternity. By the use of historical conceptual reconstruction and normative speculation, Brunkhorst presents the pathologies of the contemporary globalized world and the function that solidarity plays. The confrontation with American debate, initiated systematically by the work of Habermas, soon became an obsolete issue in the third generation of critical theorists—in part but not only because the group was truly international, merging European and American scholars. Thanks to Habermas's intellectual opening, the third generation of critical theorists engaged in dialogue with French post-modern philosophers like Derrida, Baudrillard, Lyotard and so forth, who, according to Foucault, are the legitimate interpreters of some central aspects of the Frankfurt School.

1.2 What Is Critical Theory?

"What is 'theory'?" asked Horkheimer in the opening of his essay "Traditional and Critical Theory" [1937].[17] The discussion about method has been a constant topic for those critical theorists who have attempted since the beginning to clarify the specificity of what it means to be "critical". A primary broad distinction that Horkheimer drew was that of the difference in method between social theories, scientific theories and critical social theories. While the first two categories had been treated as instances of traditional theories, the latter connoted the methodology the Frankfurt School adopted. Traditional theory, whether deductive or analytical, has always focused on coherency and the strict distinction between theory and praxis. Along Cartesian lines, knowledge has been treated as grounded in self-evident propositions or, at least, in propositions based on self-evident truths. Accordingly, traditional theory has proceeded to explain facts by application of universal laws: that is, by subsumption of a particular to a universal in order to either confirm or disconfirm this. A verification procedure of this kind was what positivism considered to be the best explicatory account for the notion of praxis in scientific investigation. If one were to defend the view according to which scientific truths should pass

16 H. Brunkhorst, *Solidarity: From Civic Friendship to a Global Legal Community*, [2002] 2005.
17 M. Horkheimer, "Traditional and Critical Theory", [1937] 2002, pp. 188–243.

the test of empirical confirmation, then one would commit oneself to the idea of an objective world. Knowledge would be simply a mirror of reality. This view is firmly rejected by critical theorists. Under several aspects, what Critical Theory wants to reject in traditional theory is precisely this "picture theory" of language and knowledge as that defined by "the first" Wittgenstein in his *Tractatus*.[18] According to such a view, later abandoned by "the second" Wittgenstein, the logical form of propositions consists of showing a possible fact and saying whether it is true or false.[19] In order to check whether something is or is not the case, one must verify empirically whether the stated fact occurs or not. This implies that the condition of truth or falsehood presupposes an objective structure of the world.

Horkheimer and his followers rejected the notion of objectivity in knowledge by pointing to, among other things, the fact that the object of knowledge is itself embedded in a historical and social process. Further, with a rather Marxist twist, Horkheimer also noted that phenomenological objectivity is a myth because it is dependent on "technological conditions", and the latter are sensitive to the material conditions of production. Critical Theory thus aims to abandon naïve conceptions of knowledge-impartiality. Since intellectuals themselves are not disembodied entities observing from God's viewpoint, knowledge can be obtained only from the societal-embedded perspective of interdependent individuals. Critical Theory, instead, characterizes itself as a method contrary to the 'fetishization' of knowledge, one which considers knowledge as something rather functional to ideology critique and social emancipation. In light of such finalities, knowledge becomes social criticism, and the latter translates itself into social action and, thus, into the transformation of reality. In addition, Critical Theory has been heavily influenced by the Hegelian notion of dialectics and the aim of reconciling socio-historical oppositions. It has also been shaped by Marx's critique of political economy and society, as well as his critical relationship with the Hegelian tradition, while adopting some of its fundamental analytical perspectives. Indeed, Critical Theory has expanded Marxian criticisms of capitalist society by formulating patterns of social emancipatory strategies. Whereas Hegel found that rationality had finally come to terms with reality with the birth of the modern nation-state (which, in his eyes, was the Prussian state), Marx insisted on the necessity of reading the development of rationality throughout history in terms of a class struggle. The final stage of this struggle would have seen the political and economic empowerment of the proletariat. Critical theorists, in their turn, rejected both the metaphysical apparatus of Hegel and the eschatological aspects connected to Marx's theory. On the contrary, Critical Theory analyses were oriented to the understanding of society and pointed rather to the necessity of establishing open systems based on immanent forms of social criticism. The starting point

18 L. Wittgenstein, *Tractatus Logico-Philosophicus*, [1922] 1994.
19 L. Wittgenstein, *Philosophical Investigations*, [1953] 2009.

was the Marxian view of the relation between a system of production paralleled by a system of beliefs. Ideology, which, according to Marx, was totally explicable through an underlying system of production, for critical theorists had to be analyzed in its own right and as a non-economically reducible form of expression of human rationality. Such a revision of orthodox Marxism, particularly the Soviet variety, became extremely crucial in the reinterpretation of the notion of dialectics for the analysis of capitalism. Dialectics, as a method of social criticism, was interpreted as following from the contradictory nature of capitalism as a system of exploitation. Indeed, it was on the basis of such inherent contradictions that capitalism was seen to open up to a collective form of ownership of the means of production: namely, socialism.

1.3 Traditional and Critical Theory: ideology and critique

From these conceptually rich implications, one can observe some of the constant topics which have characterized critical social theory, including the normativity of social philosophy as something distinct from classical descriptive sociology, the everlasting crux of the theory/practice relation and, finally, ideology critique. These are the primary tasks that a critical social theory must accomplish in order to be defined as "critical". Crucial in this sense is the understanding and criticism of the notion of 'ideology'. In defining the senses to be assigned to the notion of ideology in the descriptive-empirical sense, "one might study the biological and quasi-biological properties of the group"[20] or, alternatively, "the cultural or socio-cultural features of the group".[21] Ideology, in the descriptive sense, incorporates both "discursive" and "non-discursive" elements. That is, in addition to propositional contents or performatives, it includes gestures, ceremonies and so forth;[22] furthermore, it shows a systematic set of beliefs—a worldview—characterized by conceptual schemes. Critical Theory distances itself from scientific theories because, while the latter understands knowledge as an objectified product, the former serves the purpose of human emancipation through consciousness and self-reflection. If the task of critical social theory is to evaluate the degree of rationality of any system of social domination in accordance to standards of justice, then ideological criticism has the function of unmasking wrong rationalizations of present or past injustices—in other words, ideology in the factual and negative sense—such as in the case of the belief that women are inferior to men. Thus, ideological criticism aims at proposing alternative practicable ways for constructing social boundaries. Critical Theory moves precisely in between the contingency of objectified non-critical factual reality and the normativity of utopian

20 R. Geuss, *The Idea of a Critical Theory. Habermas & the Frankfurt School*, 1981, p. 4.
21 Ibid.
22 Ibid., pp. 6–8.

idealizations: therefore, in between the so-called theory/practice problem.[23] Marcuse, for instance, in the essay "*Philosophie und Kritische Theorie*" ["Philosophy and Critical Theory"] [1937], defends the view that Critical Theory characterizes itself as being neither philosophy *tout court* nor pure science; it instead claims to be an overly simplistic approach to Marxism. Critical Theory has the following tasks: to clarify the socio-political determinants that explain the limits of analysis of a certain philosophical view and to transcend the use—the actual limits—of imagination. From all this, two notions of rationality result: the first attached to the dominant form of power and deprived of any normative force, the second characterized by a liberating force based on a yet-to-come scenario. This difference in forms of rationality is what Habermas later presented, *mutatis mutandis*, in terms of the distinction between instrumental and communicative rationality. While the first form of rationality is oriented to a means-ends understanding of human and environmental relations, the second form is oriented to the subordination of human action with respect to certain normative criteria of action validity. This latter point echoes quite distinctively Kant's principle of morality according to which human beings must always be treated as "ends in themselves" and never as mere "means". Critical Theory, Habermas in particular, is no exception to these views on rationality since it sees *Ideologiekritik* not just as a form of "moralizing criticism" but as a form of knowledge and, thus, as a cognitive operation for disclosing the falsity of conscience.[24] This point is strictly connected to another conceptual category which plays a great role in Critical Theory, known as the concept of interest, focusing on the distinction between "true" interests and "false" interests. As Geuss has suggested, there are two possible ways to propose such separation: "the perfect-knowledge approach"[25] and "the optimal conditions approach".[26] Were one to follow the first option, the outcome would be that of aligning with the side of acritical utopianism. On the other hand, the approach based on optimal conditions is reinterpreted, at least for Habermas, in terms of an ideal speech situation that, by virtually granting an all-encompassing exchange of arguments, assumes the function of providing a counterfactual normative check on actual discursive contexts. Within such a model, epistemic knowledge and social critical reflection are attached to unavoidable pragmatic-transcendental conditions that are the same for all. The universality of such epistemological status differs profoundly from Adorno's contextualism, in which individual epistemic principles grounding cultural criticism and self-reflection are recognized to be legitimately different throughout time and history.

23 D. Ingram, *Critical Theory and Philosophy*, 1990, p. xxiii.
24 R. Geuss, *The Idea of a Critical Theory. Habermas & the Frankfurt School*, 1981, p. 26.
25 Ibid., p. 48.
26 Ibid.

Both versions are critical in that they remain faithful to the objective of clearing false consciousness from ignorance and domination, but, whereas Habermas sets a high standard of validity/non-validity for discourse theory, Adorno's historicism remains sensitive to degrees of rationality that are context dependent. For Adorno, Critical Theory, while drawing from Marxism, must avoid hypostatization and closure into a single *Weltanschauung* on the pain of losing its "critical" capacity. By interpreting rationality as a form of self-reflective activity, Critical Theory represents a particular form of rational enquiry that must remain immanently capable of distinguishing ideology from a Hegelian spirit (*Geist*). The mission of Critical Theory, therefore, is not exhausted by a theoretical understanding of social reality; as a matter of fact, there is a strict interconnection between critical understanding and transformative action: theory and practice are interconnected.

1.3.1 The theory/practice problem

During the entire course of its historical development, Critical Theory has always confronted one crucial methodological concern: the "theory/practice" problem. To this puzzle, critical theorists have provided different answers, such that it is not possible to regroup them into a homogeneous set of views. In order to understand the significance of the theory/practice problem, it is useful to refer back to David Hume's "is/ought" question. What Hume demonstrated through the separation of the "is" from the "ought" was the non-derivability of prescriptive statements from descriptive ones. This separation has been the basis of those ethical theories that have not recognized moral statements as a truth-property. In other words, alternative readings of the "is/ought" relation have defended either a cognitivist approach (truth-validity of moral statements) or, alternatively, a non-cognitivist approach (no truth-validity), as in the case of emotivism. Even if characterized by several internal differences, what Critical Theory added to this debate was the consideration of both the anthropological and the psychological dynamics motivating the masses and structuring ideologies. As far as the anthropological determinants in closing up the gap of the theory/practice problem are concerned, it is possible to take into consideration Habermas's *Knowledge and Human Interest* [1968].[27] There, Habermas combined a transcendental argument with an anthropological one by defending the view according to which humans have an interest in knowledge insofar as such interest is attached to the preservation of self-identity. Yet to preserve one's identity is to go beyond mere compliance with biological survival. As Habermas clarifies, human interests derive from both nature and the cultural break with nature.[28] On the other hand, to preserve one's identity means finding in the emancipatory

27 J. Habermas, *Knowledge and Human Interests*, [1968] 1971.
28 Ibid.

force of knowledge the fundamental interest of human beings. Indeed, the grounding of knowledge in the practical domain has far-reaching implications, such as the fact that interest and knowledge find their unity in self-reflection or in knowledge aimed at knowledge itself. The Habermasian answer to the theory/practice problem comes from the criticism of non-cognitivist theories. If it is true, as non-cognitivists claim, that prescriptive claims are grounded in commands and do not have any cognitive content which can be justified through an exchange of public arguments, it follows that they cannot provide an answer to the difference between what is a mere convergent behaviour, established through normative power on the basis, for example, of punishment and what is, instead, the notion of following a valid rule. In the latter case, an extra layer of justification seems to be required: namely, a process through which a norm can be defined as valid. Such a process is for Habermas conceived in terms of a counterfactual procedure for a discursive exchange of arguments. This procedure is aimed at justifying those generalizable interests that ought to be obeyed because they pass the test of moral validity. The Habermasian answer to the is/ought question has several important implications. One implication, perhaps the most important one, is the criticism of positivism and of the epistemic status of knowledge. On the basis of Habermasian premises, indeed, there can be no objective knowledge, as positivists claim, detached from intersubjective forms of understanding. Since knowledge is strictly embedded in serving human interests, it follows that it cannot be considered value neutral and objectively independent. A further line of reflection on the theory/practice problem comes from psychoanalysis, in which a strict separation has been maintained between the "is" and "ought", and false "oughts" have been unmasked through the clarification of the psychological mechanisms constructing desires. Accordingly, critical theorists like Fromm referred to Freud's notions of the unconscious, which contributed defining ideologies in terms of substitute gratifications. Psychoanalysis represented such a strong component of the research of the Frankfurt School that even Adorno in his article "Freudian Theory and the Pattern of Fascist Propaganda" [1951][29] analyzed Fromm's interconnection between sadomasochism and fascism. Adorno noticed how a parallel can be drawn between the loss of self-confidence and estimation in hierarchical domination on the one hand and compensation through self-confidence which can be re-obtained in active forms of dominations on the other. Such mechanisms of sadomasochism, nonetheless, are not only elements of fascism. As Adorno noticed, they reappear in different clothes in modern cultural industry through the consumption of so-called cultural commodities. Notwithstanding the previous discussions, the greatest philosophical role of psychoanalysis within the Frankfurt School was exemplified by Marcuse's thought. In his case, the central problem became

29 T. W. Adorno, "Freudian Theory and the Pattern of Fascist Propaganda", [1951] 2007, pp. 118–137.

that of interpreting the interest in the genealogical roots of capitalist ideology. How can one provide an account of class interests after the collapse of social classes? How can one formulate, on the basis of the insights provided by psychoanalysis, the criteria through which true interests can be distinguished from false interests?

The way adopted by Marcuse was that of a revisitation of Freud's theory of instinctual needs. Differently from Freud's tensions between nature and culture and Fromm's total social shaping of natural instincts, Marcuse defended a third—median—perspective in which instincts were considered only partially shaped by social relations.[30] Through such a solution, Marcuse overcame the strict opposition between biological and historical rationality that was preventing the resolution of the theory/practice problem. He did so by recalling the annihilation of the individual's sexual energy lying at the base of organized society and recalling, in its turn, the archetypical scenario of a total fulfilment of pleasure. Marcuse took imagination as a way to obtain individual reconciliation with social reality: a reconciliation, though, with an underlying unsolved tension. Marcuse conceived of overcoming such tensions through the aestheticization of basic instincts liberated by the work of the imagination. The problem with Marcuse's rationalization of basic instincts was that by relying excessively on human biology, it became impossible to distinguish between the truth and the falsity of socially dependent needs.[31]

1.3.2 The idea of rationality: Critical Theory and its discontents

For Critical Theory, rationality has always been a crucial theme in the analysis of modern society as well as its pathologies. Whereas the early Frankfurt School and Habermas viewed rationality as a historical process whose unity was taken as a precondition for social criticism, later critical philosophies, influenced mainly by post-modernity, privileged a rather more fragmented notion of (ir)rationality manifested by social institutions. In the latter views, social criticism could not act as a self-reflective form of rationality since rationality cannot be conceived of as a process incorporated in history. One point shared by all critical theorists was that forms of social pathology were connected to deficits of rationality which, in their turn, manifested interconnections with the psychological status of the mind.[32] In non-pathological social aggregations, individuals were said to be capable of achieving cooperative forms of self-actualizations only if freed from coercive mechanisms of domination. Accordingly, for the Frankfurt School, modern processes of bureaucratic administration exemplified what Weber considered an all-encompassing domination of formal rationality over substantive values.

30 D. Ingram, *Critical Theory and Philosophy*, 1990, p. 93 ff.
31 Ibid., p. 103.
32 A. Honneth, "The Intellectual Legacy of Critical Theory", 2004, p. 339ff.

In Weber, rationality was to be interpreted as purposive rationality: thus, as a form of instrumental reason. Accordingly, the use of reason did not amount to formulating prescriptive models of society but aimed at achieving goals through the selection of the best possible means of action. If, in Lukács, the proletariat was to represent the only dialectical way out of the total control of formal rationality, Horkheimer and Adorno saw technological domination of human action as the negation of the inspiring purposes of Enlightenment. In *Dialectic of Enlightenment* [1947], Horkheimer and Adorno emphasized the role of knowledge and technology as a "means of exploitation"[33] of labour and viewed the dialectic of reason as the archetypical movement of human self-liberation. Nevertheless, the repression of natural chaos by formal-instrumental rationality pointed to the possible resurgence of natural violence under a different vest so the liberation from nature through instrumental reason opened to the possibility of domination by a totalitarian state. According to this view, reason had been seen essentially as a form of control over nature characterizing humanity since its inception since those attempts aimed at providing a mythological explanation of cosmic forces. The purpose served by instrumental rationality was, in essence, that of promoting self-preservation, even if this goal, paradoxically, turned into the fragmentation of bourgeois individuality that, once deprived of any substantive value, became merely formal and thus determined by external influences of mass-identity in a context of cultural industry. Rationality thus began assuming a double significance: on the one hand, as traditionally recognized by German idealism, it was conceived as the primary source of human emancipation; on the other, it was conceived as the premise of totalitarianism. If, as Weber believed, modern rationalization of society led to a formal reduction of the power of rationality, it followed that hyper-bureaucratization of society resulted in not just a complete separation between facts and values but also a total disinterest in the latter forms. Nevertheless, for Critical Theory, it remained essential to defend the validity of social criticism on the basis of the idea that humanity is embedded in a historical learning process in which clash is due to the actualization of reason re-establishing power balances and struggles for group domination.

Given such a general framework on rationality, it can be said that Critical Theory has undergone several paradigm revolutions, both internally and externally. First of all, Habermas himself has suggested a further pre-linguistic line of enquiry by appealing to the notions of "authenticity" and "imagination". This suggests a radical reformulation of the same notions of "truth" and "reason" in light of their metaphorical capacities of signification.[34] Secondly, the commitment of Critical Theory to validity and universal pragmatics has been widely criticized by post-structuralists and post-modernists, who

33 D. Ingram, *Critical Theory and Philosophy*, 1990, p. 63.
34 J. Habermas, "Questions and Counter-Questions", 1984.

have instead insisted, respectively, on the hyper-contextualism of the forms of linguistic rationality and the substitution of a criticism of ideology with genealogical criticism. While Derrida's deconstructive method has shown how binary opposition collapses when applied to the semantic level so that meaning can only be contextually constructed, Foucault has oriented his criticisms to the supposedly emancipatory power of universal reason by showing how forms of domination permeate micro-levels of power-control such as in sanatoriums, educational and religious bodies and so on. The control of life—known as bio-power—manifests itself in the attempt to normalize and constrain individuals' behaviour and psychic lives. For Foucault, reason is embedded in such practices which display the multiple layers of un-rationalized force. The activity of the analyst in this sense is not far from the same activity of the participant: there is no objective perspective which can be defended and opposed to one's opponent. Derrida, for instance, while pointing to the Habermasian idea of the pragmatic of communication, still maintained a distinct thesis of the restless deconstructive potential of any constructing activity so no unavoidable pragmatic presuppositions or idealizing conditions of communication could survive deconstruction. On the other hand, Habermasian theory of communicative action and discourse ethics, while remaining sensitive to contexts, pretended to defend transcendental conditions of discourse which, if violated, were seen to lead to performative contradictions. Last but not least, to the Habermasian role of consensus or agreement in discursive models, Foucault objected that rather than a regulatory principle, a true critical approach would be rooted in a critique of domination.[35]

The debate between Foucault and Critical Theory—in particular with Habermas—is quite illuminating of the common critical-universalist orientations of the first phase of the Frankfurt School versus the diverging methodologies defended beginning with the Habermasian interpretation of modernity. For Foucault, it was not correct to propose a second-order theory for defining rationality. Rationality is not to be found in abstract forms. On the contrary, what social criticism can only aim to achieve is the unmasking of deeply enmeshed forms of irrationality deposited in contingent and historical institutional embeddings. Genealogical methods, though, do not reject the idea that (ir)rationality is part of history; rather, they pretend to illuminate abstract and procedural rational models by dissecting and analyzing concrete institutional social practices through immanent criticism. To this view, Habermas has objected that any activity of rational criticism presupposes unavoidable conditions in order to justify the pretense of the validity of its same exercise. This rebuttal reopened the demands of transcendental conditions for immanent criticism revealed along the same pragmatic conditions of social criticism. For Habermas, criticism is possible only if universal standards of validity are

35 P. Rabinow (ed.), "Politics and Ethics: An Interview", 1984.

recognized and understanding [*Verständigung*] and agreement [*Einverständnis*] are seen as interconnected practices.

A further line of criticism against Habermas, one which also included the target of Critical Theory as a whole, came from scholars like Chantal Mouffe [2005].[36] What she noticed was that in the notion of consensus nested a surrendering to a genuine engagement in "political agonism". If, as Mouffe claimed, the model of discursive action is bound to the achievement of consensus, then what role can be left to politics once agreement is obtained? The charge of eliminating the consideration of political action from "the political" has also been extended by Mouffe to previous critical theorists such as Horkheimer, Adorno and Marcuse. Criticism concerned the non-availability of context-specific political guidance answering the question "What is to be done?"[37]

What has been noticed is that whereas Critical Theory has aimed at fostering human emancipation, it has remained incapable of specifying a political action-strategy for social change. For the opponents of the Critical Theory paradigm, a clear indication in this sense was exemplified by Marcuse's idea of "the Great Refusal",[38] one predicating abstention from real political engagement and pretenses of transformation of the capitalist economy and democratic institutions. It was, indeed, in view of the theoretical-critical ambitions to present realistic utopias that some representatives of the third generation directed their attention to the themes of intersubjective recognition. Axel Honneth, for instance, starting from a revisitation of the Hegelian notion of (mis) recognition and through a research phase addressing social pathologies, has proposed a revisited version of socialism in one of his latest studies, *The Idea of Socialism: Towards a Renewal* [2017].[39] Nancy Fraser, in contrast, by focusing on the notion of redistribution, has provided key elements to understanding how it is possible to overcome economic inequalities and power imbalances in post-industrial societies where cultural affiliations are no longer significant sources of power. Seyla Benhabib, along similar lines, has aimed to clarify the significance of the Habermasian dual-track model of democracy as one based on the distinction between moral issues that are proper of the institutional level (universalism) and ethical issues characterizing, instead, informal public deliberations (pluralism). Whereas the requirement of a universal consensus pertains only to the institutional sphere, the ethical domain is characterized by a plurality of views confronting each other across different life-systems. Benhabib's views, by making explicit several Habermasian assumptions, aim to countervail post-structuralist worries as well as post-modern charges of the political action ineffectiveness of Critical Theory models.

36 C. Mouffe, *The Democratic Paradox*, 2005.
37 S. Chambers, "The Politics of Critical Theory", 2004, p. 219 ff.
38 H. Marcuse, *One-Dimensional Man*, [1964] 2002.
39 A. Honneth, *The Idea of Socialism: Towards a Renewal*, 2017.

Finally, Forst's philosophical preoccupation has been that of addressing the American philosophical debate with the specific aim of constructing an alternative paradigm to those of liberalism and communitarianism. Forst's attempt has integrated analytic and continental traditions by radicalizing along transcendental lines some core Habermasian intuitions on rights and constitutional democracy. In his collections of essays, *The Right to Justification* [2014],[40] Forst suggests a transformation of the Habermasian co-originality thesis between human rights and democracy according to a reduction ***ad unum*** of the right of justification. This move aims to suggest an alternative and hopefully more coherent route of explanation for the understanding of the liberal constitutional experience.

Reservations about the success of a genuinely critical renewal of the school's developments since Habermas have recently been expressed by Kouvélakis [2019]. The scholar identified a dangerous normalization of social conflicts following the adoption of a transcendental formalism that has embraced the regulative ideal as its guiding criterion.[41] From this perspective arises the "mourning"[42] of society's pathologies, which disturb the normative peace of Honneth's model of recognition but are nonetheless resolved through an inauthentic domestication of the deeper aspirations to political and social justice.

40 R. Forst, *The Right to Justification. Elements of a Constructivist Theory of Justice*, 2014.
41 S. Kouvélakis, *La critique défaite. Émergence et domestication de la Théorie critique. Horkheimer-Habermas-Honneth*, 2019, p. 27.
42 Ibid., p. 28.

References

Abromeit, J., "Siegfried Kracauer and the Early Frankfurt School's Analysis of Fascism as Right-Wing Populism", in Jaeho Kang, Graeme Gilloch, and John Abromeit (eds.), *Siegfried Kracauer. Selected Writings on Media, Propaganda and Political Communication*, Columbia University Press, New York, 2022, pp. 395–422.

Ackerman, N. W., M. Jahoda, *Anti-Semitism and Emotional Disorder: A Psychoanalytic Interpretation*, Harper & Brothers, New York, 1950.

Adorno, T. W., "Anti-Semitism and Fascist Propaganda", S. Crook (ed.), *Theodor W. Adorno, The Stars Down to Earth*, Routledge, London and New York, [1946] 2002, pp. 218–232.

Adorno, T. W., *Aspects of the New Right-Wing Extremism*, Polity Press, Cambridge, [1967] 2020.

Adorno, T. W., "Cultural Criticism and Society", in T. W. Adorno (ed.), *Prisms*, The MIT Press, Boston, MA, [1955] 1999, pp. 17–34.

Adorno, T. W., "Culture Industry Reconsidered", *New German Critique*, 6, [1963] Fall 1975, pp. 12–19.

Adorno, T. W., "Diskussionsbeitrag zu 'Spätkapitalismus oder Industriegesellschaft?'", in T. W. Adorno (ed.), *Gesammelte Schriften*, vol. 8, Suhrkamp, Frankfurt, 1968, pp. 578–587.

Adorno, T. W., "Education after Auschwitz", in *Critical Models: Interventions and Catchwords*, Columbia University Press, New York, [1966] 1998, pp. 191–204.

Adorno, T. W., *Fighting Antisemitism Today. A Lecture*, Polity Press, Cambridge, [1962] 2025.

Adorno, T. W., "Fragmente über Wagner", *Zeitschrift für Sozialforschung*, 8(1/2), 1939, pp. 1–49.

Adorno, T. W., "Freudian Theory and the Pattern of Fascist Propaganda", in A. Arato and E. Gebhardt (eds.), *The Essential Frankfurt School Reader*, Basic Blackwell, Oxford, [1951] 2007, pp. 118–137.

Adorno, T. W., "I. Gutachten über die Arbeit 'Die totalitäre Propaganda Deutschlands und Italiens' S.I bis S.106, von Sigfried Kracauer", in S. Kracauer (ed.), *Totalitäre Propaganda*, Suhrkamp, Berlin, [1938] 2013, pp. 262–265.

Adorno, T. W., "Late Capitalism or Industrial Society?", in V. Meja, D. Misgeld and N. Stehr (eds.), *Modern German Sociology*, Columbia University Press, New York, [1968] 1987, pp. 232–247.

Adorno, T. W., Letter 219 T. W. Adorno to M. Horkheimer, 8 June, 1941, in Th. Adorno-M. Horkheimer, *Briefwechsel*, Band II, 1938–1944, 2004.

Adorno, T. W., *Minima Moralia. Reflections on a Damaged Life*, Verso, London, [1951] 2005.

Adorno, T. W., *Negative Dialectics*, Routledge, London and New York, [1966] 1973.

Adorno, T. W., "On the Fetish-Character in Music and the Regression of Listening", in J. M. Bernstein (ed.), *The Culture Industry: Selected Essays on Mass Culture*, Routledge, London and New York, [1938] 2001, pp. 29–60.
Adorno, T. W., *Prisms*, The MIT Press, Cambridge, MA, [1967] 1983.
Adorno, T. W., *The Psychological Technique of Martin Luther Thomas's Radio Addresses*, Stanford University Press, Stanford, CA, [1975] 2000.
Adorno, T. W., "Reflections on Class Theory", in R. Tiedemann (ed.), *Can One Live After Auschwitz? A Philosophical Reader*, Stanford University Press, Stanford CA, [1942] 2003, pp. 93–110.
Adorno, T. W., "The Schema of Mass Culture", in J. Bernstein (ed.), *The Culture Industry. Selected Essays on Mass Culture*, Routledge, London and New York, [1942] 2001, pp. 61–97.
Adorno, T. W., *Versuch über Wagner*, Suhrkamp, Frankfurt am Main, 1952.
Adorno, T. W., "Was bedeutet: Aufarbeitung der Vergangenheit", in T. W. Adorno (ed.), *Gesammelte Schriften*, vol. 10.2, Suhrkamp, Frankfurt am Main, [1959] 1973, pp. 555–572, accessibile online at: http://aawe.blogsport.de/images/Theodor-20W20Adorno2020Was20heisst.pdf.
Adorno, T. W., M. Horkheimer, *Briefwechsel: 1927–1969*, C. Godde and H. Lonitz (eds.), Suhrkamp, Frankfurt am Main, 2003–4.
Allen, A., *Critique on the Couch. Why Critical Theory Needs Psychoanalysis*, Columbia University Press, Columbia, 2020.
Alvater, E., "Il capitalismo si organizza: il dibattito marxista dalla guerra mondiale alla crisi del '29", in E. J. Hobsbawm, Georges Haupt, Franz Marek, Ernesto Ragionieri, Vittorio Strada, and Corrado Vivanti (eds.), *Storia del marxismo. Il marxismo nel età della terza internazionale*, vol. 3, Torino, Einaudi, 1980, pp. 823–876.
Antonio, R. J., "Immanent Critique as the Core of Critical Theory: Its Origins and Developments in Hegel, Marx and Contemporary Thought", *The British Journal of Sociology*, 32(3), 1981, pp. 330–345.
Arendt, H., *The Origins of Totalitarianism*, A Harvest Book, New York, [1951] 1976.
Babich, B., "Adorno's Radio Phenomenology: Technical Reproduction, Physiognomy and Music", *Philosophy & Social Criticism*, 40(10), 2014, pp. 957–996.
Bauer, O., H. Marcuse, A. Rosenberg (eds.), *Faschismus und Kapitalismus. Theorien über die sozialen Ursprünge und die Funktion des Faschismus*, Europäische Verlagsanstalt, Frankfurt, 1967.
Benhabib, S., *Critique, Norm and Utopia. A Study of the Foundations of Critical Theory*, Columbia University Press, New York, 1986.
Benjamin, W., *Moscow Diary [1926–7]*, Harvard University Press, Cambridge, MA, 1986.
Benjamin, W., *On the Concept of History*, Verso, London, [1942/1950] 2005.
Benjamin, W., "Theories of German Fascism", in *Selected Writings*, vol. 2, part 1, Belknap Press, Harvard University, Cambridge, MA, [1930] 2005, pp. 312–321.
Benjamin, W., *The Work of Art in the Age of Mechanical Reproduction*, Belknap Press, Harvard University Press, Cambridge, MA, [1946] 2008.
Bernstein, E., *The Preconditions of Socialism*, H. Tudor (ed.), Cambridge University Press, Cambridge, [1899] 2012.
Bettelheim, A., *Les Problèmes Théoriques et Pratiques de la Planification*, Presses Universitaires de France, Paris, 1946.
Bettelheim, B., M. Janowitz, *Dynamics of Prejudice: A Psychological and Sociological Study of Veterans*, Harper & Brothers, New York, 1950.
Bondì, D., "Max Horkheimer in esilio. La sorveglianza politica e l'idea di Democrazia", *Studi germanici*, 15/16, 2019, pp. 347–374.
Borkenau, F., *The Totalitarian Enemy*, Faber & Faber, London, 1940.
Breuer, S., *Kritische Theorie*, Mohr Siebeck, Tübingen, 2016.

Breuer, S., "The Truth of Modern Society? Critical Theory and Fascism", *New German Critique*, 4(2), 131, 2017, pp. 75–103.
Broué, P., *The German Revolution 1917–1923*, Brill, Leiden and Boston, [1971] 2005.
Brunkhorst, H., *Solidarity: From Civic Friendship to a Global Legal Community*, The MIT Press, Cambridge, MA, [2002] 2005.
Brunner, J., "Looking in the Hearts of the Workers, or: How Eric Fromm Turned Critical Theory into Empirical Research", *Political Psychology*, 15(4), 1994, pp. 632–654.
Brzezinski, C. F., Z. K. Brzezinski, *Totalitarian Dictatorship and Autocracy*, Harvard University Press, Cambridge, MA, 1965.
Buchwalter, A., "Hegel, Marx, and the Concept of Immanent Critique", *Journal of the History of Philosophy*, 29(2), 1991, pp. 253–279.
Buhrnam, J., *The Managerial Revolution What Is Happening in the World*, The John Day Company, New York, 1941.
Caffé, F., "La crisi del liberismo", in M. Telò (ed.), *Crisi e piano. Le alternative degli anni Trenta*, De Donato, Bari, 1979, pp. 21–30.
Campani, C., *Pianificazione e teoria critica. L'opera di Friedrich Pollock dal 1923 al 1943*, Liguori editore, Napoli, 1992.
Carr, E. H., R. W. Davies, *A History of Soviet Russia: 4 Foundations of a Planned Economy, 1926–1929*, vol. 1, part 2, Palgrave MacMillan, London, 1969.
Ceppa, L., "Lo stato autoritario di Max Horkheimer", *Rivista di storia contemporanea*, Loescher editore, Torino, 3/IX, 1980, pp. 445–458.
Chambers, S., "The Politics of Critical Theory", in F. Rush (ed.), *The Cambridge Companion to Critical Theory*, Cambridge University Press, Cambridge, 2004, pp. 219–247.
Cooke, M., "Totalitarianism and the Welfare State", *Radical Philosophy*, May/June 89, 1998, pp. 16–26.
Corradini, E., *Il nazionalismo italiano*, Historica edizioni, Cesena, [1914] 2020.
Cortella, L. (ed.), *Teoria critica e metafisica*, Mimesis, Milano, 2009.
Croce, B., "Chi è 'fascista'?", in R. De Felice (ed.), *Il fascismo. Interpretazioni dei contemporanei e degli storici*, vol. 2, Laterza, Roma and Bari, [1944] 1970, pp. 397–401.
Croce, B., "Il fascismo come pericolo mondiale", in B. Croce (ed.), *Scritti e discorsi politici (1943–1947)*, vol. 1, Laterza, Roma and Bari, 1973, pp. 7–15.
Dahms, H. F., "Chapter 1 The Early Frankfurt School Critique of Capitalism: Critical Theory between Pollock's 'State Capitalism' and the Critique of Instrumental Reason", in H. F. Dahms (ed.), *The Vitality of Critical Theory*, Emerald Group Publishing Limited, Bradford, 2011, pp. 3–44.
Dahms, H. F., "The Early Frankfurt School Critique of Capitalism", in P. Koslowski (ed.), *The Theory of Capitalism in the German Economic Tradition*, Springer Verlag, Berlin and Heidelberg, 2000, pp. 309–361.
Demirović, A., *Der nonkonformistische Intellektuelle. Die Entwicklung der Kritischen Theorie zur Frankfurter Schule*, Suhrkamp, Frankfurt am Main, 1999.
Dessauer, F., *Streit um die Technik: Technik prägt Menschen*, Herder Verlag, Freiburg im Breisgau, 1959.
Dubiel, H., *Kritische Theorie der Gesellschaft*, Juventa Verlag, Weinheim und München, 1988.
Dubiel, H., *Wissenschaftsorganisation und politische Erfahrung. Studien zur frühen Kritischen Theorie*, Suhrkamp, Frankfurt am Main, 1978.
Dubiel, H., A. Söllner, *Wirtschaft, Recht und Staat im Nationalsozialismus. Analysen des Instituts für Sozialforschung 1939–1942*, Europäische Verlagsanstalt, Hamburg, 1992.
Eco, U., "Ur-Fascism", in *How to Spot a Fascist*, The New York Review of Books, [1995] 2020, pp. 1–11.
Emery, N., *For Nonconformism: Max Horkheimer and Friedrich Pollock. The Other Frankfurt School*, Brill, Leiden and Boston, 2023.

Eyck, E., *A History of the Weimar Republic*, vol. 2, Harvard University Press, Cambridge, MA, 1963.
Fischer, L., "The Frankfurt School and Fascism", in B. Best, W. Bonefeld, and C. O'Kane (eds.), *The Sage Handbook of Frankfurt School Critical Theory*, 2 vols., Sage, London, 2018, pp. 799–815.
Fisichella, D., *Totalitarismo. Un regime del nostro tempo*, Nuova Italia Scientifica, Roma, 1987.
Florinsky, M. T., *Fascism and National Socialism. A Study of the Economic and Social Policies of the Totalitarian State*, Macmillan, New York, 1936.
Forst, R., *The Right to Justification. Elements of a Constructivist Theory of Justice*, Columbia University Press, New York, 2014.
Fraenkel, E., *The Dual State. A Contribution to the Theory of Dictatorship*, Oxford University Press, Oxford, [1941] 2017.
Freud, S., *Civilization and Its Discontents*, W.W. Norton, New York, [1930] 1961.
Freud, S., *The Future of an Illusion*, Norton and Company Inc., New York, [1927] 1961.
Freud, S., *Group Psychology and the Analysis of the Ego*, The Hogarth Press, London, [1921] 1949.
Freud, S., *On Narcissism*, Routledge, London and New York, [1914] 2012.
Freud, S., *Totem and Taboo*, Routledge, London and New York, [1913] 2001.
Fried, F., *Das Ende des Kapitalismus*, Eugen Diederichs Verlag, Jena, 1931.
Fromm, E., *Beyond the Chains of Illusion: My Encounter with Marx and Freud*, Continuum Press, New York, [1962] 2009.
Fromm, E., *Der autoritär-masoschistische Charakter*, in E. Fromm, "Sozialpsychologischer Teil", in M. Horkheimer (ed.), *Studien über Autorität und Familie. Forschungsberichte aus dem Institut für Sozialforschung*, Klampen, Lüneburg, [1936] 1987, pp. 110–135.
Fromm, E., "Die gesellschaftliche Bedingtheit der psychoanalytischen Therapie", *Zeitschrift für Sozialforschung*, 4(3), 1935, pp. 365–397.
Fromm, E., *Escape from Freedom*, Avon Books, New York, [1941] 1965.
Fromm, E., "The Method and Function of an Analytic Social Psychology", in E. Fromm (ed.), *The Crisis of Psychoanalysis*, Holt, Rinehart and Winston, New York, [1932] 1970, pp. 135–162.
Fromm, E., "Psychoanalytic Characterology and Its Application to the Understanding of Culture", in S. S. Sargent and M. W. Smith (eds.), *Culture and Personality*, Viking Press, New York, [1932] 1949, pp. 207–214.
Fromm, E., "Sozialpsychologischer Teil", in M. Horkheimer (ed.), *Studien über Autorität und Familie. Forschungsberichte aus dem Institut für Sozialforschung*, Klampen, Lüneburg, [1936] 1987, pp. 77–135.
Fromm, E., *The Working Class in Weimar Germany: A Psychological and Sociological Study*, Leamington Spa, Warwickshire, Berg, [1929] 1980.
Fuchshuber, T., "The Controversy Over Friedrich Pollock's State Capitalism", *History of the Human Sciences*, 29(2), 2016, pp. 23–41.
Fuchshuber, T., *Rackets. Kritische Theorie der Bandenherrschaft*, ça ira, Freiburg-Wien, 2019.
Gaeta, F., *Democrazie e totalitarismi dalla prima alla seconda guerra mondiale. Profili di storia contemporanea 1918–1945*, Il Mulino, Bologna, 1989.
Galli, C., *Genealogia della politica. Carl Schmitt e la crisi del pensiero politico moderno*, Il Mulino, Bologna, 1996.
Galli, C., "Strategie della totalità, Stato autoritario, Stato totale, totalitarismo, nella Germania degli anni Trenta", *Filosofia Politica*, 1, 1997, pp. 27–62.
Gangl, M., G. Raulet (eds.), *Jenseits instrumenteller Vernunft-Kritische Studien zur "Dialektik der Aufklärung"*, Peter Lang, Frankfurt am Main und New York, 1998.
Gentile, E., *Fascismo. Storia e interpretazione*, Laterza, Roma and Bari, 2002.

Geuss, R., *The Idea of a Critical Theory. Habermas & the Frankfurt School*, Cambridge University Press, New York, 1981.
Griffin, R., *The Nature of Fascism*, Routledge, London and New York, [1991] 2006.
Grossman, H., *The Law of Accumulation and Breakdown of the Capitalist System*, Brill, Leiden, [1929] 2021.
Grossmann, H., J. Gumperz, M. Horkheimer, K. A. Wittfogel, "Diskussionen aus einem Seminar über Monopolkapitalismus", in M. Horkheimer (ed.), *Gesammelte Schriften. Band 12. Nachgelassene Schriften 1931–1949*, Fischer, Frankfurt am Main, 1985, pp. 417–430.
Grünberg, C., "Festrede gehalten zur Einweihung des IfSs für Sozialforschung an der Universität Frankfurt a. M. am 22 Juni 1924", in *Frankfurter Universitätsreden*, Druck u. Verlag: Univ. Druckerei Werner u. Winter, Frankfurt am Main, [1924], pp. 1–16.
Gurland, A. R. L., *The Collapse of German Democracy and the Expansion of National Socialism*, PhD Thesis, 1940, *Horkheimer Archiv*, Na 1, 694, accessible online at: https://sammlungen.ub.uni-frankfurt.de/horkheimer/content/titleinfo/5668712.
Gurland, A. R. L., "Fight against Antisemitism within the Framework of Germany's Education for Democracy. Draft Program", *Horkheimer Archiv*, 1947, pp. 1–62.
Gurland, A. R. L., "Technological Trends and Economic Structure Under National Socialism", *Zeitschrift für Sozialforschung*, 9(2), 1941, pp. 226–263.
Gurland, A. R. L., O. Kirchheimer, F. Neumann, *The Fate of Small Business in Nazi Germany*, Kessinger Publishing, Whitefish, MT, [1943] 2010.
Habermas, J., *Knowledge and Human Interests*, Beacon Press, Boston, [1968] 1971.
Habermas, J., "Questions and Counter-Questions", *Praxis International*, 4(3), 1984, pp. 229–249.
Habermas, J., *The Structural Transformation of the Public Sphere*, The MIT Press, Cambridge, MA, 1962.
Habermas, J., *The Theory of Communicative Action*, vols. 1 and 2, Beacon Press, Boston, 1981, 1984.
Harcourt, B., "Rethinking Capitalism with Friedrich Pollock, Frank Neumann, and the Frankfurt School", 2020, accessible online at: https://blogs.law.columbia.edu/abolition1313/bernard-e-harcourt-rethinking-capitalism-with-friedrich-pollock-franz-neumann-and-the-frankfurt-school/.
Heitmann, L., J. Blumenfeld, "Society as 'Totality': On the Negative-Dialectical Presentation of Capitalist Socialization", in B. Best, W. Bonefeld, and C. O'Kane (eds.), *The Sage Handbook of Frankfurt School/Critical Theory*, vol. 3, Sage, London, 2018, pp. 589–606.
Herf, J., *Reactionary Modernism. Technology, Culture and Politics in Weimar and the Third Reich*, Cambridge University Press, Cambridge, 1985.
Hilferding, R., "Die Aufgaben der Sozialdemokratie in der Republik", in C. Stephan (ed.), *Zwischen den Stühlen oder über die Unvereinbarkeit von Theorie und Praxis. Schriften Rudolf Hilferdings 1904–1940*, Dietz J. H. W. Nachf, Berlin, [1927] 1982, pp. 212–236.
Hilferding, R., *Finance Capital. A Study of the Latest Phase of Capitalist Development*, T. Bottomore (ed.), Routledge, London, [1910] 1981.
Hilferding, R., "State Capitalism or Totalitarian State Economy", in C. W. Mills (ed.), *The Marxists*, Dell, New York, [1940] 1962, pp. 334–339.
Hitler, A., *Mein Kampf*, Jaico Publishing House, Mumbai, [1925–6] 2006.
Hitler, A., *Vortrag Adolf Hitlers vor westdeutschen Wirtschaftlernim Industrie-Klubzu Düsseldorf am 27 Januar 1932*, Auflage Eher-Verlag, München, 1932.
Honneth, A., *Critique of Power: Reflective Stages in a Critical Social Theory*, The MIT Press, Cambridge, MA, [1985] 1991.

Honneth, A., *The Idea of Socialism: Towards a Renewal*, Polity Press, Cambridge, 2017.
Honneth, A., "A Social Pathology of Reason: On the Intellectual Legacy of Critical Theory", in F. Rush (ed.), *The Cambridge Companion to Critical Theory*, Cambridge University Press, New York, 2004, pp. 336–360.
Honneth, A., *The Struggle for Recognition: The Moral Grammar of Social Conflicts*, Polity Press, Cambridge, [1986] 1995.
Horkheimer, M., "Allgemeiner Teil", in M. Horkheimer (ed.), *Studien über Autorität und Familie*, Dietrich zu Klampen Verlag, Lüneburg, [1936] 1963, pp. 3–76.
Horkheimer, M., *Anfänge der bürgerlichen Geschichtsphilosophie*, Suhrkamp, Frankfurt am Main, [1930] 1971.
Horkheimer, M., "Art and Mass Culture", *Zeitschfrift für Sozialforsching*, 9(2), 1941, pp. 290–304.
Horkheimer, M., *The Authoritarian Personality*, T. W. Adorno, E. Frenkel-Brunswik, D. J. Levinson, R. Nevitt Sanford, Verso, London and New York, [1950] 2019.
Horkheimer, M., "The Authoritarian State", *Telos*, 15(3), [1942] 1973, pp. 3–20.
Horkheimer, M., "Authoritarianism and the Family", in R. Nanda Anshen (ed.), *The Family Its Function and Destiny*, Harper, New York, [1949] 1959, pp. 381–398.
Horkheimer, M., "Briefwechsel 1941–1948", in M. Horkheimer (ed.), *Gesammelte Schriften*, Band 17, Fischer, Frankfurt am Main, [1941–8] 1996.
Horkheimer, M., "Briefwechsel Horkheimer an Neumann", August 2, 1941, in "Briefwechsel 1941–1948", in *Gesammelte Schriften*, Band 17, S. Fischer, Frankfurt am Main, 1996.
Horkheimer, M., *Dawn & Decline. Notes 1926–1931 and 1950–1969*, The Seabury Press, New York, [1934] 1978.
Horkheimer, M., "Die Juden und Europa", *Zeitschrift für Sozialforschung*, 8(1/2), 1939, pp. 115–137.
Horkheimer, M., "Die Philosophie der absoluten Konzentration", *Zeitschrift für Sozialforschung*, 7(3), 1938, pp. 376–387.
Horkheimer, M., "Die Rackets und der Geist", in A. Schmidt and G. Schmid Noerr (eds.), *Gesammelte Schriften, Vol. XII: Nachgelassene Schriften 1931–1949*, S. Fischer, Frankfurt am Main, 1985, pp. 287–291.
Horkheimer, M., *Eclipse of Reason*, Continuum, London and New York, [1947] 2004.
Horkheimer, M., "Egoism and Freedom Movements: On the Anthropology of the Bourgeois Era", in M. Horkheimer (ed.), *Between Philosophy and Social Science*, The MIT Press, Cambridge, MA and London, [1936] 1993, pp. 49–110.
Horkheimer, M., "Eine besondere Art von Antisemitismus", in *Gesammelte Schriften. Dialektik derAufläbrung und Schriften 1940–1950*, Band 5, Fischer Verlag, Frankfurt am Main, [1949–50] 1987, pp. 344–346.
Horkheimer, M., "The End of Reason", *Walter Benjamin zum Gedächtnis, Zeitschrift für Sozialforschung/Study in Philosophy and Social Science*, 9(3), 1941, pp. 366–388.
Horkheimer, M., "Es geht um die Moral der Deutschen", [interview] in *Gesammelte Schriften* vol. 7, Fischer, Frankfurt, 1985, pp. 480–485.
Horkheimer, M., "Fortune Polls on Antisemitism", *Nachlass Max Horkheimer*, 1947, pp. 1–18.
Horkheimer, M., *Gesammelte Schriften. Nachgelassene Schriften 1931–1949*, Band 12, Fischer, Frankfurt am Main, 1985.
Horkheimer, M., "History and Psychology", in *Between Philosophy and Social Science*, The MIT Press, Cambridge, MA and London, [1932] 1993, pp. 111–128.
Horkheimer, M., "[Idee, Aktivität und Programm des Instituts für Sozialforschung]", in *Gesammelte Schriften*, Band 12, Fischer, Frankfurt am Main, [1938] 1985, pp. 131–222.
Horkheimer, M., "Ideologie und Wertgebung", in K. G. Specht (ed.), *Soziologische Forschung in Unserer Zeit*, VS Verlag für Sozialwissenschaften, Wiesbaden, 1951, pp. 220–227.

Horkheimer, M., "Kritische Theorie gestern und heute", in *Gesammelte Schriften*, Suhrkamp, Frankfurt am Main, VIII, [1969] 1970, pp. 336–353.
Horkheimer, M., "The Lessons of Fascism", in H. Cantril (ed.), *Tensions That Cause Wars: Common Statement and Individual Papers, UNESCO*, University of Illinois Press, Champaign, [1950], pp. 209–242.
Horkheimer, M., "Materialism and Metaphysics", in M. J. O'Connell and Others (trans.), *Critical Theory. Selected Essays. Max Horkheimer*, Continuum Publishing, New York, [1933] 2002, pp. 10–46.
Horkheimer, M., "Montaigne and the Function of Skepticism", in *Between Philosophy and Social Science*, The MIT Press, Cambridge, MA and London, [1938] 1993, pp. 265–312.
Horkheimer, M., "A New Concept of Ideology?", in *Between Philosophy and Social Science*, The MIT Press, Cambridge, MA and London, [1930] 1993, pp. 3–27.
Horkheimer, M., "On the Sociology of Class Relations", *Horkheimer Archiv [MHA]*, University Library Frankfurt, MHA: IX, 16, 4 [1943], available online at: https://nonsite.org/max-horkheimer-and-the-sociology-of-class-relations/.
Horkheimer, M., "Philosophie als Kulturkritik", in *Gesammelte Schriften, Bd. VII, Vorträge und Aufzeichnungen 1949–1973*, Fischer, Frankfurt am Main, 2014, pp. 81–103.
Horkheimer, M., "Plan des Forschungsprojekts über Antisemitismus", in M. Horkheimer (ed.), *Gesammelte Schriften. Band 12. Nachgelassene Schriften 1931–1949*, Fischer, Frankfurt am Main, 1985, pp. 165–171.
Horkheimer, M., "The Present Situation of Social Philosophy and the Tasks of an Institute for Social Research", in *Between Philosophy and Social Science*, The MIT Press, Cambridge MA and London, [1931] 1993, pp. 1–15.
Horkheimer, M., "The Rationalism Debate in Contemporary Philosophy", in *Between Philosophy and Social Science: Selected Early Writings*, The MIT Press, Cambridge, MA and London, [1934] 1993, pp. 217–264.
Horkheimer, M., "Sociological Background of the Psychoanalytic Approach", in E. Simmel (ed.), *Anti-semitism. A Social Disease*, International Universities Press, New York, 1946, pp. 1–10.
Horkheimer, M., "Traditional and Critical Theory", in M. J. O'Connell and Others (trans.), *Critical Theory. Selected Essays. Max Horkheimer*, Continuum Publishing, New York, [1937] 2002, pp. 188–243.
Horkheimer, M., *Vernunft und Selbsterhaltung*, S. Fischer, Frankfurt am Main, [1942] 1970.
Horkheimer, M., "Vorbemerkung des Herausgebers (Kurt Mandelbaum und Gerhard Meyer, 'Zur Theorie der Planwirtschaft')", *Zeitschrift für Sozialforschung*, 3(1), 1934, pp. 228–230.
Horkheimer, M., "Vorwort zu den Studies in Prejudice", in *Gesammelte Schriften. Dialektik der Aufklärung und Schriften 1940–1950*, Band 5, Fischer Verlag, Frankfurt am Main, [1949–50] 1987, pp. 406–411.
Horkheimer, M., "Zum Begriff der Vernunft", in *Max Horkheimer, Gesammelte Schriften Band 7: Vorträge und Aufzeichnungen 1949–1973*, Fischer Verlag, Frankfurt am Main, [1952] 1985, pp. 22–35.
Horkheimer, M., "Zum Problem der Voraussage in den Sozialwissenschaften", *Zeitschrift für Sozialforschung*, 2, 1933, pp. 407–412.
Horkheimer, M., "Zur Psychologie des Antisemitismus", in M. Horkheimer (ed.), *Gesammelte Schriften. Band 12. Nachgelassene Schriften 1931–1949*, Fischer, Frankfurt am Main, 1985, pp. 172–183.
Horkheimer, M., "Zur Psychologie des Totalitären", in M. Horkheimer (ed.), *Gesammelte Schriften, Vorträge und Aufzeichnungen, 1949–73*, Band 8, S. Fischer Verlag, Frankfurt am Main, [1954] 1985, pp. 77–83.
Horkheimer, M., T. W. Adorno, *Dialectic of Enlightenment*, Stanford University Press, Stanford, CA, [1947] 2002.

Horkheimer, M., T. W. Adorno (eds.), "Institut für Sozialforschung", in *Soziologische Exkurse*, Europäische Verlagsanstalt, Hamburg, [1956] 2013.
Horkheimer, M., T. W. Adorno, "Research Project on Anti-Semitism", *Studies in Philosophy and Social Science*, 9(1), 1941, pp. 124–143.
Horkheimer, M., S. H. Flowerman (eds.), *Studies in Prejudice*, Harper & Brothers, New York, 1949.
Horkheimer, M., E. Fromm, H. Marcuse (eds.), *Studien über Autorität und Familie*, Forschungsberichte aus dem Institut für Sozialforschung, [1936] 1987.
Iakovou, V., "Totalitarianism as Non-State. On Hannah Arendt's Debt to Franz Neumann", *European Journal of Political Theory*, 8(4), 2009, pp. 429–447.
Ingram, D., *Critical Theory and Philosophy*, Paragon House, St. Paul, MN, 1990.
Institut für Sozialforschung (IfS), "Cultural Aspects of National Socialism. A Research Project", *Horkheimer Archiv*, 1941, pp. 1–117.
Institut für Sozialforschung (IfS), *International Institute of Social Research. A Report on Its History, Aims and Activities 1933–1938*, Sonderdruck, New York, 1939, pp. 1–36, accessible online in *Horkheimer Archiv*, at: https://sammlungen.ub.uni-frankfurt.de/horkheimer/content/pageview/6623269.
Institut für Sozialforschung (IfS), *International Institute of Social Research: A Short Description of Its History and Aims*, Sonderdruck, New York, 1935, pp. 1–15, accessible online *Horkheimer Archiv*, at: https://sammlungen.ub.uni frankfurt.de/horkheimer/content/pageview/6623269.
Institut für Sozialforschung (IfS), *Studies in Antisemitism. A Report*, *Horkheimer Archiv*, 1944, pp. 1–144.
Institut für Sozialforschung (IfS), "Ten Years on Morningside Heights: A Report on the Institute's History, 1934 to 1944", online, L. Löwenthal and F. Pollock collection.
Jackobs, J., *The Frankfurt School. Jewish Lives and Antisemitism*, Cambridge University Press, Cambridge, 2015.
James Gregor, A., *The Faces of Janus. Marxism and Fascism in the Twentieth Century*, Yale University Press, New Haven, CT and London, 2000.
James Gregor, A., *Mussolini's Intellectuals. Fascist Social and Political Thought*, Princeton University Press, Princeton, NJ, and Oxford, 2005.
Jameson, F., *Late Marxism. Adorno or the Persistence of the Dialectic*, Verso, London, 1990.
Jay, M., *The Dialectical Imagination. A History of the Frankfurt School and the Institute of Social Research 1923–1950*, Heineman, London, 1973.
Jay, M., "The Frankfurt School's Critique of Karl Mannheim and the Sociology of Knowledge", *Telos*, 20, 1974, pp. 72–89.
Jay, M., "'In Psychoanalysis Nothing Is True But the Exaggerations': Freud and the Frankfurt School", in M. Jay (ed.), *Splinters in Your Eye*, Verso, London and New York, 2020, pp. 41–52.
Jay, M., "The Jews and the Frankfurt School: Critical Theory's Analysis of Anti-semitism", *New German Critique*, 19(1), 1980, pp. 137–149.
Jay, M., *Marxism and Totality. The Adventures of a Concept from Lukács to Habermas*, University of California Press, Berkeley, 1984.
Jay, M., *Permanent Exiles. Essays on the Intellectual Migration from Germany to America*, Columbia University Press, New York, 1985.
Jay, M., *Trump, Scorsese, and the Frankfurt School's Theory of Racket Society*, accessible online at: https://lareviewofbooks.org/article/trump-scorsese-and-the-frankfurt-schools-theory-of-racket-society/ 5 April, 2020.
Kalecki, M., "The Fascism of Our Times (1964)", in V. S. Conttren (ed.), *Selected Works of Michał Kalecki. Great War, Inflation and Fascism*, Huebunkers, 2021, accessible online at: https://huebunkers.wordpress.com/2020/03/21/selected-works-of-michal-kalecki-great-war-inflation-and-hitlerism/.
Keynes, J. M., *The End of Laissez-Faire*, Hogarth Press, London, 1926.

Keynes, J. M., *The General Theory of Employment, Interest and Money*, Macmillan & Co, London, 1936.
Kirchheimer, O., "Changes in the Structure of Political Compromise", *Zeitschrift für Sozialforschung*, 9(2), 1941, pp. 264–289.
Kirchheimer, O., "Criminal Law in National Socialist Germany", *Zeitschrift für Sozialforschung*, 8(3), 1939, pp. 444–463.
Kirchheimer, O., "In Quest of Sovereignty", *Journal of Politics*, 6(2), 1944, pp. 139–176.
Kirchheimer, O., "Legality and Legitimacy", in W. E. Scheuerman (ed.), *The Rule of Law under Siege: Selected Essays of Franz L. Neumann and Otto Kirchheimer*, University of California Press, Berkeley, [1932] 2019, pp. 44–63.
Kirchheimer, O., "The Legal Order of National Socialism", *Zeitschrift für Sozialforschung*, 9(3), 1941, pp. 456–475.
Kirchheimer, O., "Recent Trends in German Treatment of Juvenile Delinquency", *Journal of Criminal Law and Criminology*, 29(3), 1938, pp. 362–370.
Kirchheimer, O., "State Structure and Law in the Third Reich", in W. Scheuemann (ed.), *The Rule of Law under Siege. Selected Essays on Franz L. Neumann and Otto Kirchheimer*, University of California Press, Berkeley, [1935] 1996, pp. 142–171.
Kirchheimer, O., J. Herz, "Leadership Principle and Criminal Responsibility (July 18, 1945)", in R. Laudani (ed.), *Secret Reports on Nazi Germany. The Frankfurt School Contribution to the War Effort. Franz Neumann, Herbert Marcuse, Otto Kirchheimer*, Princeton University Press, Princeton, NJ and Oxford, 2013, pp. 464–474.
Kirchheimer, O., N. Leites, "Remarks on Carl Schmitt's Legalität und Legitimität", in W. E. Scheuerman (ed.), *The Rule of Law under Siege: Selected Essays of Franz L. Neumann and Otto Kirchheimer*, University of California Press, Berkeley, [1932] 1996, pp. 64–100.
Korsch, K., *Marxism and Philosophy*, Verso, London, [1923] 2013.
Kouvélakis, S., *La critique défaite. Émergence et domestication de la Théorie critique. Horkheimer-Habermas-Honneth*, Éditions Amsterdam, Paris, 2019.
Kracauer, S., "Soziologie als Wissenschaft. Der Detektiv-Roman. Die Angestellten", in I. Mülder-Bach e I. Belke (eds.), *Siegfried Kracauer Werke*, vol. 1, Suhrkamp Verlag, Berlin, [1930] 2004–2012.
Kracauer, S., *Totalitäre Propaganda*, Suhrkamp, Berlin, [1936–38] 2013.
Kühnl, R., *Fascismus Theorien. Ein Leitfaden. Aktualisierte Neuauflage*, Diestel Verlag, Heilbronn, 1990.
Lange, O., F. M. Taylor, *Economic Theory of Socialism*, McGraw-Hill Inc, [1938] 1956.
Le Bon, G., *The Crowd. A Study of the Popular Mind*, Dover Publications, Mineola, NY, [1895] 2002.
Lenhard, P., "Capitalismo di Stato e automazione", in N. Emery (ed.), *Automazione e teoria critica a partire da Friedrich Pollock*, Mimesis, Milano and Udine, 2018, pp. 73–102.
Lenhard, P., "Friedrick Pollock und der 'westliche Marxismus'. Einleitung zum ersten Band der Gesammelten Schriften", in F. Pollock (ed.), *Marxistische Schriften. Gesammelte Schriften*, Band I, ça ira-Verlag, Freiburg-Wien, 2018, pp. 7–22.
Lenin, V., "Imperialism, the Highest Stage of Capitalism", in *Lenin's Selected Works*, vol. 1, Progress Publishers, Moscow, [1917] 1963, pp. 667–766.
Lenin, V., *State and Revolution*, Penguin, London, [1917] 1993.
Löwenthal, L., "The Crisis of the Individual: II. Terror's Atomization of Man" [1946], accessible online at: https://www.commentary.org/articles/leo-lowenthal/the-crisis-of-the-individual-ii-terrors-atomization-of-man/.
Löwenthal, L., N. Guterman, *Prophets of Deceits*, Harper & Brothers, New York, [1949] 2021.
Löwith, K., *My Life in Germany Before and After 1933: A Report*, University of Illinois Press, London, [1940] 1994.

Luini, A., "Autorität und Familie in der italienischen Soziologie", in M. Horkheimer, E. Fromm, and H. Marcuse (eds.), *Studien über Autorität und Familie*, Forschungsberichte aus dem Institut für Sozialforschung, [1936] 1987, pp. 808–823.

Lukács, G., "Grand Hotel 'Abgrund'", *Világosság*, 8/9, [1933] 1977, pp. 572–579.

Lukács, G., *History and Class Consciousness*, The MIT Press, Cambridge, MA, [1923] 1971.

Lukács, G., *The Theory of the Novel. A Historico-Philosophical Essay on the Forms of Great Epic Literature*, The Merlin Press, London, [1916] 1971.

Luxemburg, R., *The Accumulation of Capital*, Routledge, London and New York, [1913] 2003.

Mandelbaum, K., G. Meyer, "Zur Theorie der Planwirtschaft", *Zeitschrift für Sozialforschung*, 3(2), 1934, pp. 228–262.

Mann, M., *Fascists*, Cambridge University Press, Cambridge, 2004.

Mannheim, K., *Ideology and Utopia*, Routledge, London, [1929] 1991.

Marcuse, H., "33 Theses", in D. Kellner (ed.), *H. Marcuse. Technology, War and Fascism. Collected Papers of Herbert Marcuse*, vol. 1, Routledge, London and New York, [1947] 1998, pp. 215–229.

Marcuse, H., "The Affirmative Character of Culture", in D. Kellner (ed.), *Art and Liberation*, Routledge, London and New York, [1937] 2007, pp. 82–112.

Marcuse, H., *Counterrevolution and Revolt*, Beacon Press, Boston, 1972.

Marcuse, H., "Critical Philosophy: A Personal Perspective with Dr. Herbert Marcuse", in D. Kellner and C. Pierce (eds.), *Philosophy, Psychoanalysis and Emancipation*, Routledge, London and New York, [1979] 2011, pp. 226–233.

Marcuse, H., "Dissolution of the Nazi Party and Its Affiliated Organizations (July 22, 1944)", in R. Laudani (ed.), *Secret Reports on Nazi Germany. The Frankfurt School Contribution to the War Effort. Franz Neumann, Herbert Marcuse, Otto Kirchheimer*, Princeton University Press, Princeton, NJ and Oxford, [1943] 2013, pp. 253–263.

Marcuse, H., *Eros and Civilization*, Routledge, London and New York, [1955] 2023.

Marcuse, H., *An Essay on Liberation*, Beacon Press, Boston, 1969.

Marcuse, H., "Freedom and Freud's Theory of Instincts", in *Five Lectures: Psychoanalysis, Politics, and Utopia*, Beacon Press, Boston, [1956] 1970, pp. 1–27.

Marcuse, H., "From Ontology to Technology: Fundamental Tendencies of Industrial Society", in D. Kellner and C. Pierce (eds.), *Philosophy, Psychoanalysis and Emancipation*, Routledge, London and New York, [1960] 2011, pp. 132–140.

Marcuse, H., "The German Communist Party (July 10, 1944)", in R. Laudani (ed.), *Secret Reports on Nazi Germany. The Frankfurt School Contribution to the War Effort. Franz Neumann, Herbert Marcuse, Otto Kirchheimer*, Princeton University Press, Princeton, NJ and Oxford, 2013, pp. 67–98.

Marcuse, H., "German Social Stratification (November 26, 1943)", in R. Laudani (ed.), *Secret Reports on Nazi Germany. The Frankfurt School Contribution to the War Effort. Franz Neumann, Herbert Marcuse, Otto Kirchheimer*, Princeton University Press, Princeton, NJ and Oxford, 2013, pp. 74–94.

Marcuse, H., "Ideengeschichtlicher Teil", in M. Horkheimer, E. Fromm, and H. Marcuse (eds.), *Studien über Autorität und Familie*, Forschungsberichte aus dem Institut für Sozialforschung, [1936] 1987, pp. 136–228.

Marcuse, H., "The New German Mentality", in D. Kellner (ed.), *H. Marcuse. Technology, War and Fascism. Collected Papers of Herbert Marcuse*, vol. 1, Routledge, London and New York, [1942] 1998, pp. 139–190.

Marcuse, H., "On the New Left", in D. Kellner (ed.), *The New Left and the 1960s*, Routledge, London and New York, [1967] 2005, pp. 122–127.

Marcuse, H., *One-Dimensional Man*, Routledge, London and New York, [1964] 2002.

Marcuse, H., "Philosophy and Critical Theory", in Horkheimer and Marcuse, "Philosophy and Critical Theory", in *Critical Theory and Society*, Routledge, London, [1937] 1990, pp. 58–77.

Marcuse, H., "The Potentials of World Communism (August 1, 1949)", in R. Laudani (ed.), *Secret Reports on Nazi Germany. The Frankfurt School Contribution to the War Effort. Franz Neumann, Herbert Marcuse, Otto Kirchheimer*, Princeton University Press, Princeton, NJ and Oxford, 2013, pp. 591–610.

Marcuse, H., "Progress and Freud Theory of Instincts", in *Five Lectures: Psychoanalysis, Politics, and Utopia*, Beacon Press, Boston, 1970, pp. 28–43.

Marcuse, H., "Protosocialism and Late Capitalism: Toward a Theoretical Synthesis Based on Bahro's Analysis", *International Journal of Politics*, 10(2/3), "Rudolf Bahro: Critical Responses", 1980, pp. 25–48.

Marcuse, H., *Reason and Revolution: Hegel and the Rise of Social Theory, [1941/1954]*, Routledge, London, 1955.

Marcuse, H., "Re-examination of the Concept of Revolution", *Diogenes*, 16(64), 1968, pp. 17–26.

Marcuse, H., "Repressive Tolerance", in R. P Wolff, B. Moore Jr., and H. Marcuse (eds.), *A Critique of Pure Tolerance*, Beacon Press, Boston, [1965] 1969, pp. 81–123.

Marcuse, H., "Some Social Implications of Modern Technology", in D. Kellner (ed.), *H. Marcuse. Technology, War and Fascism. Collected Papers of Herbert Marcuse*, vol. 1, Routledge, London and New York, [1941] 1998, pp. 39–66.

Marcuse, H., *Soviet Marxism. A Critical Analysis*, Columbia University Press, New York, [1958] 1969.

Marcuse, H., "State and Individual under National Socialism", in D. Kellner (ed.), *H. Marcuse. Technology, War and Fascism. Collected Papers of Herbert Marcuse*, vol. 1, Routledge, London and New York, [1942] 1998, pp. 67–93.

Marcuse, H., "Status and Prospects of German Trade-Unions and Works Councils (May 27, 1946)", in R. Laudani (ed.), *Secret Reports on Nazi Germany. The Frankfurt School Contribution to the War Effort. Franz Neumann, Herbert Marcuse, Otto Kirchheimer*, Princeton University Press, Princeton, NJ and Oxford, 2013, pp. 557–590.

Marcuse, H., "The Struggle Against Liberalism in the Totalitarian View of the State", *Zeitschrift für Sozialforschung*, [1934] 1968, pp. 3–42.

Marcuse, H., "USA: Questions of Organization and the Revolutionary Subject. A Conversation with Hans Magnus Enzenberg", in D. Kellner (ed.), *The New Left and the 1960s*, Routledge, London and New York, [1970] 2005, pp. 137–141.

Marcuse, H., F. Gilbert, "The Significance of Prussian Militarism for Nazi Imperialism: Potential Tensions in United Nations Psychological Warfare (October 20, 1943)", in R. Laudani (ed.), *Secret Reports on Nazi Germany. The Frankfurt School Contribution to the War Effort. Franz Neumann, Herbert Marcuse, Otto Kirchheimer*, Princeton University Press, Princeton, NJ and Oxford, 2013, pp. 61–73.

Marramao, G., "Ripensando gli anni Trenta", in AAVV, *Stato e Capitalismo negli anni Trenta*, Atti del seminario organizzato dall'Istituto Gramsci, Editori Riuniti/Istituto Gramsci, Roma, 1979, pp. 13–36.

Marx, K., *Capital. A Critique of Political Economy*, F. Engels (ed.), vol. 3, International Publishers, New York, [1894] 1996.

Marx, K., *The Civil War in France*, Martino Fine Books, Eastford, CT, [1871] 2014.

Marx, K., *A Contribution to the Critique of Political Economy*, C. H. Kerr, Chicago, IL, [1859] 1904.

Marx, K., *Theses on Feuerbach*, [1845], accessible online at: https://www.marxists.org/archive/marx/works/1845/theses/index.htm.

Massing, P. W., *Rehearsal for Destruction: A Study of Political Anti-semitism in Imperial Germany*, Harper & Brothers, New York, 1949.

McLaughlin, N., "Origin Myths in the Social Sciences: Fromm, the Frankfurt School and the Emergence of Critical Theory", *The Canadian Journal of Sociology*, 24(1), 1999, pp. 109–139.

Meinecke, F., *The German Catastrophe. Reflections and Recollections*, Beacon Press, Boston, 1963.

Micaloni, L., *Inconscio e critica. Psicoanalisi, società e politica nella Scuola di Francoforte*, Mimesis, Milano, 2023.

Mosse, G., *The Crisis of German Ideology. Intellectual Origins of the Third Reich*, Schocken Books, New York, 1981.

Mosse, G., *The Fascist Revolution. Towards a General Theory of Fascism*, The University of Wisconsin Press, Madison, 1999.

Mouffe, C., *The Democratic Paradox*, Verso, London, 2005.

Mussolini, B., E. D. Susmel, "Dottrina del Fascismo", *Istituto dell'Enciclopedia Italiana*, Roma, [1932] 1934.

Mussolini, B., E. D. Susmel (eds.), *Opera Omnia*, vol. 17 (22 giugno 2021–13 gennaio 1922), La Fenice editore, Firenze, 1951–1980.

Mustè, M., C. Scognamiglio, *Il giudizio sul nazismo. Le interpretazioni dal 1933 ad oggi*, 2005, edizioni di www.filosofia.it.

Neumann, F., *Behemoth. The Structure and Practice of National Socialism 1933–1944*, Ivan R. Dee, Chicago, [1942] 2009.

Neumann, F., "Der Funktionswandel des Gesetzes im Recht der bürgerlichen Gesellschaft", *Zeitschrift für Sozialforschung*, 6(3), 1937, pp. 542–596.

Neumann, F., "The Free Germany Manifesto and the German People (August 6, 1943)", in R. Laudani (ed.), *Secret Reports on Nazi Germany. The Frankfurt School Contribution to the War Effort. Franz Neumann, Herbert Marcuse, Otto Kirchheimer*, Princeton University Press, Princeton, NJ and Oxford, [1943] 2013, pp. 149–166.

Neumann, F., H. Marcuse, F. Gilbert, "Anxiety and Politics", *tripleC*, 15(2), [1957] 2017, pp. 612–636.

Neumann, F., H. Marcuse, F. Gilbert, *The Democratic and the Authoritarian State*, The Free Press of Glencoe, Collier Macmillan, London, [1957] 1964.

Neumann, F., H. Marcuse, F. Gilbert, "Possible Patterns of German Collapse (September 21, 1943)", in R. Laudani (ed.), *Secret Reports on Nazi Germany. The Frankfurt School Contribution to the War Effort. Franz Neumann, Herbert Marcuse, Otto Kirchheimer*, Princeton University Press, Princeton, NJ and Oxford, [1943] 2013, pp. 106–117.

Neumann, F., H. Marcuse, F. Gilbert, "Problems Concerning the Treatment of War Criminals (September 25, 1944)", in R. Laudani (ed.), *Secret Reports on Nazi Germany. The Frankfurt School Contribution to the War Effort. Franz Neumann, Herbert Marcuse, Otto Kirchheimer*, Princeton University Press, Princeton, NJ and Oxford, 2013, pp. 457–463.

Nolte, E., "Economics and Politics in the Twentieth Century", in F. Neumann (ed.), *The Democratic and the Authoritarian State: Essays in Political and Legal Theory*, The Free Press of Glencoe-Collier-Macmillan, London, [1951] 1957.

Nolte, E., *Three Faces of Fascism*, Holt, Rinehart and Winston, New York, [1963] 1965.

Nolte, E., "Vergangenheit, die nicht vergehen will", *Frankfurter Allgemeine Zeitung*, June 6, 1986.

Payne, S., *Fascism: Comparison and Definition*, University of Wisconsin Press, Madison, 1980.

Petrucciani, S., *La Scuola di Francoforte. Storia e attualità*, Carocci Editore, Roma, 2023.

Pohrt, W., *Brothers in Crime*, Fuego, Bremen, 2015.

Polanyi, K., *The Great Transformation*, Beacon Press, Boston, [1944] 2001.

Pollock, F. "Zur Marxschen Geldtheorie", in P. Lenhard (ed.), *Marxistische Schriften. Gesammelte Schriften*, Band 1, Freiburg, ça ira-Verlag, [1928] 2018, pp. 129–152.

Pollock, F., "Die planwirtschaftlichen Versuche in der Sowjetunion 1917–1927", in J. Gleixner and P. Lenhard (eds.), *Friedrich Pollock Schriften zu Planwirtschaft und Krise*. Gesammelte Schriften II, ça ira-Verlag, Freiburg-Wien, [1929] 2021, pp. 23–468.

Pollock, F., "Die gegenwärtige Lage des Kapitalismus und die Aussichten einer planwirtschaftlichen Neuordnung", *Zeitschrift für Sozialforschung*, 1(1–2), 1932, pp. 8–27.
Pollock, F., "Bemerkungen zur Wirtschaftskrise", *Zeitschrift für Sozialforschung*, 3(2), 1933, pp. 321–354.
Pollock, F., "Economics of War. Influences on Preparedness on Western European Economic Life", *American Economic Association*, 30(1), 1940, pp. 317–325.
Pollock, F., "Is National Socialism a New Order?", *Zeitschrift für Sozialforschung*, 9(3), 1941, pp. 440–455.
Pollock, F., "State Capitalism: Its Possibilities and Limitations", *Zeitschrift für Sozialforschung*, 9(2), 1941, pp. 200–225.
Pollock, F., *Automation. A Study of Its Economic and Social Consequences*, Praeger, New York, [1956] 1957.
Postone, M., "Critique, State and Economy", in F. Rush (ed.), *The Cambridge Companion to Critical Theory*, Cambridge University Press, Cambridge, 2004, pp. 165–193.
Poulantzas, N., *Fascism and Dictatorship. The Third International and the Problem of Fascism*, Verso, London, [1970] 2018.
Rabinow, P. (ed.), "Politics and Ethics: An Interview", in P. Rabinow (ed.), *The Foucault Reader*, Pantheon, New York, 1984, pp. 373–380.
Rauchway, E., *The Money Makers: How Roosevelt and Keynes Ended the Depression, Defeated Fascism, and Secured a Prosperous Peace*, Basic Books, New York, 2015.
Rauschning, H., *The Revolution of Nihilism. Warning to the West*, Alliance Book Corporations Longman Green & Co., New York, [1939] 1940.
Reich, W., "Der Masochistische Charakter", *Internationale Zeitschrift für Psychoanalyse*, XVIII, 3, 1932, pp. 303-351.
Reich, W., *Character Analysis [1933]*, Farrar Strauss & Giroux, New York, [1945] 1972.
Reich, W., "Dialectical Materialism and Psychoanalysis", [1929], *Studies on the Left*, 6(4), 1966, pp. 5–45.
Reich, W., *The Mass Psychology of Fascism*, Farrar, Straus and Giroux, New York, [1933] 1980.
Rensmann, L., *The Politics of Unreason. The Frankfurt School and the Origins of Modern Antisemitism*, SUNY Press, Albany, 2017.
Robinson, P. A., *Freudian Left: Wilhelm Reich, Geza Roheim, Herbert Marcuse,* Joanna Cotler Books, New York, 1990.
Rossi, E., *Padroni del vapore e fascismo*, Laterza, Roma and Bari, 1966.
Rusconi, G. E., "La parabola della socialdemocrazia tedesca durante la repubblica di Weimar", in M. Telò (ed.), *Crisi e piano. Le alternative degli anni Trenta*, De Donato, Bari, 1979, pp. 193–208.
Schecter, D., *The Critique of Instrumental Reason from Weber to Habermas*, Continuum International Publishing, London, 2010.
Scheit, G., "Rackets", in B. Best, W. Bonefeld, and C. O'Kane (eds.), *The Sage Handbook of Frankfurt School Critical Theory*, vol. 3, Sage, London, 2018, pp. 1551–1566.
Scheuermann, W., *Between the Norm and the Exception. The Frankfurt School and the Rule of Law*, The MIT Press, Cambridge, MA and London, 1994.
Schiller, H.-E., "The Administered World", in B. Best, W. Bonefeld, and C. O'Kane (eds.), *The Sage Handbook of Frankfurt School Critical Theory*, vol. 2, Sage, London, 2018, pp. 834–851.
Schmidt, A., *Die Kritische Theorie als Geschichtsphilosophie*, Carl Hanser Verlag, München and Wien, 1978.
Schmidt, A., 'Praxis' [Practice], in Hans-Georg Backhaus (ed.), *Gesellschaft: Beiträge zur Marxschen Theorie*, vol. 2, Suhrkamp, Frankfurt am Main, 1974, pp. 264–306.
Schmitt, C., *Der Hüter der Verfassung*, Duncker & Humblot, Berlin, [1931] 2016.
Schmitt, C., *Legality and Legitimacy*, Duke University Press, Durham, NC, [1932] 2004.

Schumpeter, J., "The Instability of Capitalism", *The Economic Journal*, 38(151), 1928, pp. 361–386.
Scuccimarra, L., "Assoggettamento, repressione, emancipazione. Alle origini della psico-politica francofortese", *Filosofia Politica*, 1, 2022, pp. 49–68.
Searle, J., *Speech Acts: An Essay in the Philosophy of Language*, Cambridge University Press, Cambridge, 1969.
Sharpe, M., "Capitalism and the Far Right: Revisiting the Pollock-Neumann Debate in the Era of Trumpism", *Philosophy & Public Issues (New Series)*, 11(2), 2021, pp. 173–212.
Söllner, A., *Geschichte und Herrschaft. Studien zur materialistischen Sozialwissenschaft 1929–1942*, Suhrkamp, Frankfurt am Main, 1979.
Sombart, W., *Modern Capitalism*, vol. 1–2, K a Nitz, Albany, New Zealand, [1902–27] 2019–23.
Stackelberg, R., "Cultural Aspects of National Socialism: An Unfinished Project of the Frankfurt School", *Dialectical Anthropology*, 12, 1988, pp. 253–260.
Stahl, T., "What Is Immanent Critique?", in *SSRN Working Papers*, 2013, accessible online at: http://ssrn.com/abstract=2357957, https://doi.org/10.2139/ssrn.2357957.
Stephan, A., *Im Visier des FBI. Deutsche Exilschriftsteller in den Akten amerikanischer Geheimdienste*, J.B. Metzler Verlag, Stuttgart and Weimar, 1995.
Sternberg, F., *Der Imperialismus*, Verlag Neue Kritik, Frankfurt am Main, [1926] 1971.
Sternhell, Z., *The Birth of Fascist Ideology. From Cultural Rebellion to Political Revolution*, Princeton University Press, Princeton, NJ, [1989] 1994.
Sweezy, M. Y., *The Structure of the Nazi Economy*, Harvard University Press, Cambridge, MA, 1941.
ten Brink, T., "Economic Analysis in Critical Theory: The Impact of Friedrich Pollock's State Capitalism Concept", *Constellations*, 22(3), 2015, pp. 333–340.
Thompson, M., "The Base-Superstructure Hypothesis and the Foundations of Critical Theory", in H. Dahms (ed.), *Mediations of Social Life in in the 21st Century* (Current Perspectives in Social Theory), vol. 32, Emerald Publishing, UK, 2014, pp. 161–194.
Thomspon, M., *The Domestication of Critical Theory*, Rowman and Littlefield, London and New York, 2016.
Tillich, P., "The Totalitarian State and the Claims of the Church", *Social Research*, 1, 1934, pp. 405–433.
Togliatti, P., "Alcuni problemi dell'Internazionale Comunista", in P. Togliatti (ed.), *Problemi del movimento operaio internazionale*, Editori Riuniti, Roma, 1962, pp. 299–333.
Traverso, E., *Il totalitarismo. Storia di un dibattito*, Mondadori, Milano, 2002.
Traverso, E., *The Origins of Nazi Violence*, The New York Press, New York and London, 2003.
Trotsky, L., *Die verratene Revolution*, Editions de Lee—Dynamo Verlag Zürich-Antwerpen-Prague, 1936.
Tugan-Baranowsky, M. I., *Theoretische Grundlagen des Marxismus*, Duncker & Humblot, Leipzig, 1905.
Villari, L., "Processi di razionalizzazione nei sistemi fascisti", in M. Telò (ed.), *Crisi e piano. Le alternative degli anni Trenta*, De Donato, Bari, 1979, pp. 135–152.
Voegelin, E., *Rasse und Staat*, J.C.B. Mohr, Tübingen, 1933.
Weber, M., *Economy and Society*, K. Tribe (ed.), Harvard University Press, Cambridge, MA, [1921] 2019.
Weber, M., *The Protestant Ethic and the Spirit of Capitalism*, Routledge, London, [1904] 2005.
Weil, F., *Argentine Riddle* (Issued in cooperation with the Latin American Economic Institute), John Day Company, New York, 1944.

Weil, F., "Neuere Literatur zum 'New Deal'", *Zeitschrift für Sozialforschung*, 5(1), 1936, pp. 404–410.
Weil, F., "Neuere Literatur zur deutschen Wehrwirtschaft", *Zeitschrift für Sozialforschung*, VII(1), 1938, pp. 200–218.
Wheatland, T., *The Frankfurt School in Exile*, University of Minnesota Press, Minneapolis and London, 2009.
Wiggershaus, R., *The Frankfurt School: Its History, Theories, and Political Significance*, MIT Press, Cambridge, MA, [1986] 2007.
Wilson, M., *Das Institut für Sozialforschung und seine Faschismusanalysen*, Campus Verlag, Frankfurt am Main and New York, 1982.
Wittfogel, K. A., "Die Theorie der orientalischen Gesellschaft", *Zeitschrift für Sozialforschung*, 7(1–2), 1938, pp. 90–122.
Wittfogel, K. A., "The Foundations and Stages of Chinese Economic History", *Zeitschrift für Sozialforschung*, 4(1), 1935, pp. 26–60.
Wittgenstein, L., *Philosophical Investigations*, Wiley-Blackwell, Oxford, [1953] 2009.
Wittgenstein, L., *Tractatus Logico-Philosophicus*, Routledge, London, [1922] 1994.
Wood, A., *Karl Marx*, Routledge, London, 2004.
Zoninsein, J., "Rudolf Hilferding's Theory of Finance Capitalism", in P. Koslowski (ed.), *The Theory of Capitalism in the German Economic Tradition*, Springer, Berlin and Heidelberg, 2000, pp. 275–304.

Index